LABOR RISING

LABOR RISING

The Past and Future of Working People in America

Edited by

Daniel Katz and Richard A. Greenwald

Requests for permission to reproduce selections from this book should be mailed to: Permissions Department, The New Press, 38 Greene Street, New York, NY 10013.

Published in the United States by The New Press, New York, 2012
Distributed by Perseus Distribution

LIBRARY OF CONGRESS CATALOGING-IN-PUBLICATION DATA

Labor rising : the past and future of working people in America / edited by Richard A. Greenwald, Daniel Katz.
     p.   cm.
ISBN 978-1-59558-518-9 (pbk.)
1. Labor movement—United States—History.   2. Working class—United States—History.   I. Greenwald, Richard A.   II. Katz, Daniel, 1962–
HD8066.L327   2012
331.880973—dc23   2012001464

Now in its twentieth year, The New Press publishes books that promote and enrich public discussion and understanding of the issues vital to our democracy and to a more equitable world. These books are made possible by the enthusiasm of our readers; the support of a committed group of donors, large and small; the collaboration of our many partners in the independent media and the not-for-profit sector; booksellers, who often hand-sell New Press books; librarians; and above all by our authors.

www.thenewpress.com

Composition by dix!
This book was set in Scala

Printed in the United States of America

10 9 8 7 6 5 4 3 2 1

CONTENTS

DISCARD

Acknowledgments   vii

Foreword   *Alice Kessler-Harris*   ix

Introduction   *Daniel Katz and Richard A. Greenwald*   I

Part One: Community and Coalitions   II

Building a New Working-Class Politics from Below
Shelton Stromquist   14

Learning from the Right: A New Operation Dixie?
Bethany Moreton and Pamela Voekel   26

Reimagining a Multicultural Labor Movement
Through Education   *Daniel Katz*   37

What Labor Looks Like: From Wisconsin to Cairo,
Youth Hold a Mirror to History of Workers' Struggles
Michelle Chen   53

Bringing the Organizing Tradition Home: Campus-
Labor-Community Partnerships for Regional Power
Nancy MacLean   65

Part Two: Place Matters   81

Placing Labor   *Andrew Herod*   83

Home as Work   *Eileen Boris*   100

Contingent, Transient, and At-Risk: Modern Workers
in a Gig Economy   *Richard A. Greenwald*   III

Part Three: State and Policy   123

Postmortem: Yellow Dogs and Company-Dominated
Elections   *David Brody*   126

Solidarity, Citizenship, and the Opportunities of
Disasters   *Jacob A.C. Remes*   143

The Hour When the Ship Comes In   *Leon Fink*   154

Getting Over the New Deal   *Jefferson Cowie*   164

Your American Dream, My American Nightmare
Kimberley L. Phillips   174

Part Four: Political Economy   189

Organized Labor: Declining Source of Hope?
Bill Fletcher Jr.   191

Eco-Keynesianism, Green Jobs, and Labor's Need
to Embrace Climate Justice   *Andrew Ross*   201

On Economics and Labor Solidarity
Marcellus Andrews   214

Ghost Marks and Rising Spirits in an Industrial
Landscape: Communication and Imagination in
the Rebirth of Labor   *Elizabeth Faue*   227

Part Five: Beyond Borders   237

Immigrant Workers and Labor's Future   *Ruth Milkman*   240

The Foundations of Modern Farm Worker Unionism:
From UFW to PCUN   *Matthew Garcia and
Mario Sifuentez*   253

Supply-Chain Tourist: Or How Wal-Mart Has
Transformed the Contemporary Labor Question
Nelson Lichtenstein   267

Forgetting and Remembering: Workers, the U.S. Empire,
and the Post-9/11 Era   *Dorothy Fujita-Rony*   278

Bananas, Elephants, and a Coup: Learning International
Solidarity the Hard Way   *Dana Frank*   289

Afterword: Labor Rising?   *Frances Fox Piven*   303

About the Contributors   313

ACKNOWLEDGMENTS

The genesis of this volume occurred a few years ago in the boisterous environs of a hotel bar during the annual meeting of the Organization of American Historians. After a meeting of the Labor and Working-Class History Association, the conversation turned, as it often does for labor scholars, to the relevance of our work as historians to the wider labor and social justice movements. As we debated the relative merits of doing high theoretical analyses or sometimes engaging in the study of obscure historical moments, one thing became clear to us: every single one of our friends and colleagues entered into scholarly study because of a drive to contribute to movements that fight on behalf of ordinary people—workers, immigrants, women, and racial-ethnic minorities.

That evening, as the conversation turned to the state of labor today, what the movement needs, and how it needs to change or expand, our friends became even more animated. They argued, sometimes at high decibel levels, about how lessons from labor's past struggles and victories could be applied today. It was during one particularly good-natured brawl that the co-editors turned to one another grinning and said almost at the same time, "What a book this would make!" Among those gleeful belligerents, many of whom ended up contributing to this book, and all of whom have supported us throughout the process, were Jennifer Klein, Nancy MacLean, Bethany Moreton, Kim Phillips, Jacob Remes, Jarod Roll, Shel Stromquist, and Heather Thompson.

Soon after that OAH meeting, we approached Alice Kessler-Harris about the idea. She responded immediately, helping us to think about how to develop a wish list of contributors balanced by themes, perspectives, and demographics. For that and the advice she gave us throughout the planning of this book project, we are very grateful to her. We then took the idea to Marc Favreau, who followed up his enthusiasm (fueled by the intoxicating ambience of a Brooklyn biergarten) with a contract, which we needed to pull the volume together. He championed this project unwaveringly and never failed to nip at our heels when we appeared to be dragging our feet. We are also grateful for those frequent Friday afternoons during which Lara Vapnek, Brendan O'Malley, Jonathan Soffer, Daniel Levinson Wilk, and Ted Hamm offered us their encouragement and insights, along with their conviviality. And we would like to thank the many scholars who have helped shape our thinking on labor over the past few years, first and foremost the contributors to this volume.

In addition, Dan would like to thank Barry Eisenberg, Carolyn Helmke, Tara Maldonado, Laura McEnaney, Dave Staiger, Peggy Tally, Diane Ramdeholl, and Christopher Whann for their unflagging support. Jeffrey Trask and Jacob Remes offered valuable suggestions for improving my essay in this volume. As I write this, I am transitioning from Empire State College, where I spent the last seven years happily in the company of wonderful students and colleagues, to the National Labor College, where I'd been appointed the dean of labor studies. Rich is to blame. He made joining "the dark side" seem like a really fun idea, not to mention important and fulfilling. That can be said about this volume as well. I have utterly enjoyed working with Rich and thank him for his friendship and mentorship. And, as always, I thank Patricia Jerido, Christina Jerido, and Amanda Jerido-Katz for their faith and pride in me.

Richard would like to thank the following for pushing him to become an engaged scholar: Liz Faue, George Sanchez, Robin D.G. Kelley, Bob Weisbuch, Eileen Boris, Ryan Harbage, Howard Stanger, Dewar MacLeod, Danny Walkowitz, Liz Cohen, Andrew Ross, and Jonathan Lethem. Drew University and St. Joseph's College, my current academic home, encouraged my scholarly activity even with the demands of being a dean. It is rare that institutions provide this level of freedom for scholarship to administrators, so I am very thankful. I also need to thank Dan Katz, who is a first-rate scholar, an activist, and now a good friend. My wife, Debbie, and my two kids, Daniel and Annie, have provided the love and forgiveness an academic needs to write.

FOREWORD

Alice Kessler-Harris

What is the future of working-class America? Does it lie within the labor movement or outside it? In an age of rapid and flexible global production and distribution, how can a working-class movement stretch beyond national borders to gather strength and power? When capital flows govern the world of human relations, how is working-class community to be imagined? And how to reach out beyond the present dismal outlook for workers all over the world, to imagine a world in which social justice prevails for poor people everywhere? The essays in this book address this formidable set of questions and more. In general and specific ways, they provide ways of thinking about what we mean when we use words like "class" and "worker." Above all, they provide a sense of possibility, even of optimism, that there might be constructive ways of restoring power and influence to working people everywhere.

Within the United States, and worldwide, questions about the future of workers flow from a dramatic transformation in the economic structure that began with the end of World War II, escalated in the 1970s, and has now reshaped the world within which we live. At the end of the war and into the 1950s, economists and the public imagined that industrial production would be the engine of prosperity. In Western industrial societies, workers and their employers saw themselves as participants in an unspoken compact. With the aid of machinery, and prodded by new managerial techniques, workers would produce the goods and services that would provide comfortable lives for a rapidly expanding middle class. In return, workers would receive wages sufficient to enable them to provide comfortable lifestyles for families, and enough leisure to enjoy them. The state, in turn, would provide the education, transportation, and infrastructure necessary to provide hardworking individuals a boost into the labor force; for those lost by the wayside, and for the elderly and unfit, it would offer a safety net of health care, old age pensions, and welfare.

The plan worked fairly well in the 1950s, but by the 1960s it was already creating demands for racial and gender equality, which the system could not accommodate. It was upset in part by a major commitment to policing the globe, which produced a war in Vietnam that channeled resistant young people into tasks they did not want to fulfill. As capital discovered it could make more money by leveraging and investing in financial instruments, economic energy turned to making money out of money, rather than out of the sale of goods. Goods production shifted overseas, where labor demanded no social compact, and American corporations walked away from their commitments to workers, claiming the expense as too great. By the 1970s, the economy had embarked on its bifurcated course. Manufacturing turned from industrial nations to the developing world, where labor could be obtained more cheaply and capital could be used more profitably; industrial labor unions, which had successfully defended the jobs and living standards of their members (and arguably raised the standards of the population at large), became helpless to preserve jobs and membership. The search for wealth, no longer rooted in manufacturing and trading commodities, turned to buying, selling, and betting on instruments of finance.

In these arenas, government regulation and intervention quickly lost purchase. A new economic mantra—one of free market capitalism—replaced old standards of social responsibility and a careful balance of interests. Milton Friedman's notion of "free to choose" proved to be only the tip of an iceberg that harbored rigid ideas of free markets, notions of a predatory poor, and insistence on government as too big. With astonishing speed, the old social compact vanished. Corporations abandoned towns, communities dispersed, the quality of public services diminished; the safety net, never very strong, developed holes. In this context even the idea of a working class found itself under threat. Commentators had earlier spoken about a "new working class" made up of service providers rather than of goods producers. But that working class had little common identity; many in it had bought their own homes, owned more than one automobile, benefited from two adult income earners, and lived lifestyles commonly associated with the middle class. Workers identified less with their jobs than they did with ethnic or racial groups and religion. The media participated by reinforcing the notion that satisfaction lay in rising levels of consumption, rather than in human relations.

As working class cohesion diminished, so too has labor union power and political clout eroded. Several essays in this collection touch on the ways in which government regulation has increasingly stifled the capacity of unions to organize, none more powerfully than David Brody's poignant description of what he calls the clogged pipeline to unionization. Rules and regulations adopted in the 1930s to enable workers to organize and exercise collective power have now been turned to the advantage of employers, who have successfully used the courts to assert their right to influence their employees. The price of "free speech" for employers has been paid by employees, whose right to free association has slowly been strangled. In the private sector, the sense that collective action might be an effective weapon has vanished; public unions, even those of teachers, police, and firemen, find themselves under attack for "feeding at the public trough." Intellectuals and academics, faced now with rethinking the role of labor, must imagine a new world where capital and labor no longer share an interest in production for prosperity.

In this new world, a "free market" in both capital and labor creates a free-for-all where government hands are tied and unrestrained capital is falsely said to engender prosperity. Labor historians commonly trace the shift in power from labor into the hands of the wealthy to the 1970s. For the labor movement, the symbolic moment of defeat came during the unsuccessful strike of air traffic controllers in 1981, which presaged a long period of declining labor militance. Since then, the annual number of major strikes has diminished to near zero, and despite significant victories in organizing janitors, health care workers, and home-help aides, the proportion of trade union members among workers sinks daily. New union initiatives such as worker centers and services to families have done little to stem the tide or to restore the public sense that labor unions function as more than representatives of "special interests." The difficult position in which unions now find themselves raises questions of where power now resides, and what might be done to wrest it from the hands of those who believe it is, and should be, a function of the market.

Perhaps the strongest, and most discouraging, indication of the increasing power of free market capitalism has been the spread of new political mantras that suggest a changing consciousness among workers. No longer susceptible to New Deal slogans of economic security and shared responsibility, the new politics advocates slogans such as "free to choose" and demonizes government regulation by declaring "big government" the enemy of ordinary people. In a society where everyone worthy identifies as "middle class," benefits for the poor and working people are described as "sucking at the government teat." Health care for all is described as "socialism"; competition has replaced cooperation as the way to prosperity.

Under the aegis of this new consciousness, the free market has run amok and the unprotected have been left to fight as best they can. The banking industry provides the quintessential example of the absence of government constraints. Left to their own devices when the Glass-Steagall Act was repealed in 1999, bankers created a series of financial instruments based on poorly supervised home mortgage loans so complicated that even they did not fully understand them. Trades in these instruments created a layer of risk and profits that encouraged banks to lend more and more, and to push house prices upward. When the market collapsed, it took down with it the relatively poor and young who had invested in homes they thought they would live in all their lives. Declining house prices and home foreclosures pushed many into homelessness and poverty. Yet bankers have not been held accountable, and their institutions were salvaged by government subsidies offered without restrictions on their future activities.

A distorted economy continues to flourish under the free market banner. While corporations find endless ways to evade declining tax rates, and real income taxes levied on the highest income earners have dropped to the lowest levels in history, the safety net frays and one in every five children lives in poverty. As the numbers of workers searching for jobs hovers close to 10 percent, and including discouraged workers brings the rate closer to 18 percent of the potential workforce, newly created jobs tend to be poorly paid and lacking in benefits of any kind. Labor unions, which in the past successfully asserted the power of an organized working class to redress this situation, now find themselves stymied and lacking in the power to influence change; politicians insist that jobs can be created only by giving tax benefits to the wealthy. The gap between the incomes of the rich and the poor is wider than at any time since the age of robber barons in the 1890s, and yet the idea of eliminating a tax cut on the very rich finds its way into the press as a tax increase that would stifle the economy. Public attention to the widening wage gap has done little to provoke outrage. Instead of seeking redress from the wealthy and insisting on punishment for the bankers who had violated its trust, the public elects legislators who promise to shrink government further, to reduce government regulation, and to save money not by taxing the rich but by imposing greater austerity on the poor.

For observers, these trends raise questions of where power is now located and why it is so difficult to influence. Implicit in the pieces included here are questions about the origins of an ideological conviction that government is the problem, not the solution, and about trust in a free market to get us out of a mess that it has created. We are only now beginning to understand how the powerful free market ideology, the insistence on the negative aspects of regulation, emerged from the conscious efforts of conservative economists and think tanks funded in the 1970s. Not a few commentators have noted that in the face of a widespread economic decline that began in 2008, sometimes called the Great Recession, few workers took to the streets in protest. How do we understand why young people gave up their dreams and a stricken public seemed apathetic and unmoved?

Surely some of the answers to these questions lie in the absence of visible and available alternatives. Ideas of social democracy or of some form of socialism no longer provide, for most people, the alternative possibility they once offered. To many, the absence of a "left" worthy of the name closes off a path they once could have followed. We grapple with ways of understanding the current crisis that will enable us to move forward. We wonder if there is a way for ordinary people to grasp current economic reality, much less to think about regulating it. But others among us focus on the question of power. We wonder if our intellectual horizons—our capacity to imagine alternatives—has been limited by our failure to interrogate questions of power. Where is it harbored; how is it wielded and deployed? How do workers now imagine it? How can organized labor confront and influence it? The essays in this collection may not provide answers to these questions, but they offer a rich and provocative array of thoughts, suggestions, and ideas about how to move forward in challenging times.

LABOR RISING

INTRODUCTION

Daniel Katz and Richard A. Greenwald

Last winter, when the nation's eyes were on Wisconsin, many of the writers in this volume could not help but think about the past. Newly elected governor Scott Walker, together with a new majority of Republicans in the legislature, sought to strip public sector unions and workers of their legal rights to bargain collectively. Many of the nation's labor leaders sat on the sidelines, while local union members and some unexpected allies began to rally, then march, then occupy the halls of state power. Thousands around the state, then around the country, poured into Madison as the national and world media finally took notice.

It has been a long time since there was that kind of attention paid to unions, let alone the daily coverage of workers spontaneously rising up. And what coverage there had been was dedicated to defeat, decline, and division. Thirty years ago, Ronald Reagan broke the air traffic controllers union. And for at least a generation now, it has been a bumpy downward spiral. What made Wisconsin so remarkable was that it seemed, at least for a moment, that tectonic plates were shifting. Labor, organized labor, was fighting back. Images of public employees occupying the statehouse brought back memories of the sitdown strikes of the early Congress of Industrial Organizations, the great CIO that ushered in a new day for American workers during the Great Depression. Students, farmers, community activists, and average citizens demanding accountability joined Wisconsin union members. One hundred thousand people chanted a refrain from the Seattle protests against the World Trade Organization a decade earlier, "This is what democracy looks like!" Many of us thought that maybe Wisconsin was the start of another new day.

What the Seattle WTO demonstrations highlighted and we hope too for Wisconsin, though it is still too soon to tell, is a long tradition in American history where workers mobilized at the forefront of some the most important, transformative social reforms in our history. Indeed, workers' rights and their rights to organize have been critical for the health and growth of American democracy. When members of the Missouri Volunteers' Turner Brigade marched to stop the plundering of the arsenal at Camp Jackson by secessionists on the eve of the Civil War, they carried a banner depicting a workman's hammer smashing the shackles of slavery. When Mother Jones organized the Children's Crusade in 1903, a march to abolish child labor, from Philadelphia to President Roosevelt's home in Oyster Bay, New York, she struck a blow for the rights of all children, universal education, and workers' health and safety. Garment workers traumatized by the 1911 Triangle Shirtwaist Factory fire won precedent-setting demands for statewide fire safety laws, protecting people of all classes. The rise of the CIO in the 1930s resulted in the largest union surge in American history and a slew of New Deal reforms, including Social Security, that helped set the stage for a vastly expanded American middle class who understood these "entitlements" as rights. And when Sleeping Car Porters president A. Philip Randolph organized the March on Washington Movement in 1941, he forced FDR to sign Executive Order 8802. That action barred employment discrimination in all government agencies and military contractors, opening up opportunities for generations of workers and professionals of every race to rise in wealth and power.

Now, organized labor as a whole did not always support these efforts. And sometimes, frankly, they were dragged kicking and screaming into the fray. But when unions did get behind an issue, they helped move the national agenda in important ways. They provided institutional, organizational, and monetary support, not to mention political heft, which helped these movements make history. One just has to remember that the 1963 March on Washington, where Reverend Dr. Martin Luther King Jr. gave his famous "I have a dream" speech, was co-sponsored, supported and funded by the United Auto Workers, among other unions. In short, labor helped make America a better place to live and work for most Americans.

Social transformations in America have always moved forward in fits and starts, and unevenly. But efforts at reform have succeeded when working people gathered their resources and fought back during economic, political, and social crises. We believe that we are now living through one of these transformational moments.

More workers find themselves in a desperate place. They haven't had a raise, a real raise, since 1979. They are working, according to economist Juliet Schor, longer hours than ever before, in a constant struggle just to preserve what they might once have had. They have it harder in many ways than their parents' and grandparents' generations. The effective unemployment rate in the United States hovers near 18 percent. The income disparity between rich and poor is now larger than it was during the Gilded Age. And in a postindustrial America, there are simply too few good jobs left in the blue-collar world. Women still make only 69 cents for every dollar a man makes. The income gap between black and white is at a twenty-five-year high and, as many urban centers gentrify, the poor are further marginalized and often hidden—out of sight and out of mind of the wealthy and privileged.

Meanwhile, both Republican and Democratic politicians continue to erode the social safety nets of the New Deal and Great Society programs that unions helped to create. Workers today do not have nationally recognizable advocates. Politicians have given up on them, preferring to talk about middle-class issues, never about the working class, or at most referring sometimes to working families. And their unions, *our* unions, are in decline, weak and fractured, with few leaders willing or able to rally the troops, to fight the good fight. While there never was a golden age for labor, times were certainly better than today. In the 1950s and 1960s, few governors would have openly attacked unions; that would have been the realm of fringe groups. But now the media consider attacks on workers mainstream, when they consider them at all. At a time when class seems to matter most, the language for discussing it has dropped from the vocabulary of public discourse. When certain pundits and politicians bring class into the conversation, they are accused of promoting class warfare. We have lost our ability to put issues of class, and also equality, back on the table. Our culture is silent on matters of class, spending more time discussing reality TV.

As we write this, the recession rages on and the stock market is a roller coaster. There are still 11 million undocumented workers and their families working and living in the shadows and the margins of the American economy. Estimates are that nearly 30 percent of the workforce is now contingent, including day laborers, contract workers, freelancers, and consultants. As political scientist Jacob Hacker has put it, we are living through "The Great Risk Shift." Economic risk, which used to be borne by corporations and governments, now has been shifted to individuals. Gone are retirement and health care plans. So too are concerns for safety and health. Today's workers hope they stay healthy and know they will work till they drop, as there is little alternative. As Jefferson Cowie and Nick Salvatore have stated, we are reverting back to an earlier age of history, when workers were independent actors and had little protection.

What is at the root of this shift? Well, clearly one element is globalization. While we have lived in a global economy for hundreds of years, its lived effects have not been felt on this scale. Starting in the late 1970s, the world either flattened or sped up (you choose your metaphor). In either case, as the federal government loosened regulations, American corporations jumped borders looking for cheaper labor and soaring profits. The United States hemorrhaged millions of jobs. And not just any jobs; these were too often unionized jobs, high-wage jobs that offered security and what we might call an American standard of living. In the wake of this industrial exodus, what was left was the Rust Belt. Cities like Flint and Detroit in Michigan, Akron and Cleveland in Ohio, and hundreds of other communities abandoned and wounded as jobs left. Many of these cities and towns never recovered, leaving scars that have never faded.

Another root cause is the intensifying neoliberalism that has dominated domestic economic and international trade policies for the last few dozen years. More attention is paid to the stock market, to interest rates, than actual work. Politicians pace nervously when the market falls as unemployment dips below 5 percent, and the corporate media cheer when company prices soar after layoffs are announced. The stock scroll has become the nation's collective heart rate, measuring the health of the nation. The Federal Reserve's meetings and pronouncements on interest rates, and Standard and Poor's credit rating for the United States, overshadow the lived economy of average Americans. The market-driven political system forgets people in favor of economic efficiencies. And privatization of public resources further siphons wealth and services from working people, and lays waste to public unions, the last significant organized sector left.

Politically, workers are simply unrepresented. In 2008, in the wake of the worst economic collapse since the Great Depression, the media's gaze turned to, and stayed on, banks (commercial and investment), not in anger but in worry. Major companies like GM and AIG were bailed out and banks were bolstered, but workers were virtually ignored. Sure, unemployment was extended, but only for a time. And nothing else of serious consequence was done for working people during the crisis. Where was Barack Obama's Works Progress Administration or his Wagner Act? The president who came into office with such "hope" became just another consensus politician right before our eyes. His most powerful economic policy makers— Geithner, Summers, and Goolsbee—are all Wall Street stalwarts and neoliberal champions. Workers have watched as high-profile mine and oil rig disasters unfolded, realizing that if only proper enforcement of existing regulations occurred workers would not have died or been injured. We have watched as Obama failed to push for card check.

American workers know that the current system is broken, at least for them. Politically they have little voice. Culturally they are isolated. And economically they are suffering. Workers also know that the current model of labor organization doesn't serve them. We are living within the shadow of what was once a great social movement. Many of the names (UAW, Teamsters, AFSME, IBEW, etc.) are the same, but the fire is out of the beast's belly. Instead, many unions have spent the last decade embroiled in what can only be seen as a personality disorder, as mergers and splits, especially in the AFL-CIO, have destabilized what is left of the movement. And, more importantly, it has distracted unions from the real work that needs to be done: organizing and protecting workers.

The good news is that we have been here before and the rumor of labor's demise has often been exaggerated. The thrilling moments of labor's rise have just as often succeeded long periods of despair. As scholars of labor's past, we are well aware that small, perhaps even seemingly isolated, moments of resistance during those times can turn out to be the foundations on which future organizations are built. There have been sporadic bursts of energy from labor unions in recent years to give us glimmers of hope. During the 1999 Seattle World Trade Organization meeting, unions and environmental groups, the so-called Teamsters and turtles moment, suggested a new momentum and a new partnership. There are new models of workers' organizations happening in our midst. Alternatives to traditional unions have emerged. Worker centers throughout the country that organize workers not in the shop or workplace, but rather in the community, have begun to grow among immigrant workers. In New York State, Domestic Workers United, also a grassroots organization of immigrants—nannies and household and home care workers—succeeded in passage of the Domestic Workers Bill of Rights law. In 2006, we witnessed the largest strike and labor protest in our history, the May Day immigrant rights demonstrations. Millions of workers came out to make their plight visible and to forge bonds in their communities. This protest was designed to send a political signal to state capitals and Washington. But these developments received far too little support from traditional labor unions. In fact, most unions failed to recognize them as labor organizations and missed opportunities to rekindle a broad-based labor movement.

As scholars interested in labor's past and hoping for labor's future, we know that history does not repeat itself. Every epoch has its unique circumstances. But the study of familiar patterns and forgotten responses can inform and inspire creative new collective action, or just as likely help activists and leaders recognize moments of opportunity when they emerge. On close inspection, virtually every community of workers and their allies that has acted offers insights that are useful as workers, activists, and labor leaders strive to rebuild and reimagine a new labor movement. *Labor Rising* accesses forgotten victories of the distant, not so distant, and recent past. But through these essays we are also reminded that labor's failures and frustrations were not always complete or inevitable and can obscure winning strategies that could, perhaps should, be revisited.

There are certainly overlapping and complementary themes across these essays, but each author brings a unique vision and interpretation to this volume, sometimes at odds with one another. That is as it should be. We invited authors to be opinionated, to use their particular understanding of labor's past to inform their best prescription for how working people in America need to move forward and not to worry about whether their ideas mesh with one another. Each author identified the problems he or she thought were most critical. For some, the central question for labor was how to reposition movements for American workers' rights within a global labor movement. For others, the question was how to redefine the scope of American labor to include undocumented and casual workers and employees of sectors traditionally ignored by unions. And yet others concentrated on relationships between unions and communities of allies, organizing strategies, or labor's relationship to the state. All authors here are concerned with seeking collective solutions to the problems of working people's declining fortunes and power. And most agree that the complexity of problems requires a multiplicity of responses on many fronts.

The intended audiences for this collection of essays differ, sometimes subtly, as each author has imagined who might show up for his or her particular soapbox oratory. Some of the essays are directed to the leadership of established unions and their respective federations. Others are aimed at local communities of union activists or their allies. But the volume as a whole casts the widest possible net to include those concerned with all kinds of working-class organizations as well as traditional labor unions, national leaders and local activists, scholars and ordinary people with a deep curiosity about labor's future.

We are at a crossroads and this must be a moment of pushback in a postindustrial America and an age of global assembly lines. Any reinvented labor movement will have to have a different structure and philosophy from what exists now, just as the CIO differed from the AFL in the 1930s. Taken as a whole, then, the essays in *Labor Rising* argue for a new labor movement that is simultaneously transnational and community-based, that is fully inclusive and supports a broad social agenda, and that will lead toward greater democracy. In a global society, worker organizations need to find common cause with similar groups all over the world. They need to understand and respond to global challenges, but do so in ways that make sense locally and sustainably. They must also build a movement of workers who may not be linked by a common mass workplace.

Labor Rising brings together twenty-four profound thinkers who point at signals, directions, or moments of hope or action. Collectively, they believe the labor movement is not beaten, not a relic of history, but rather a central feature in a democratic society. It needs to rise again for democracy to have meaning in America. But, as these authors demonstrate, it will not and should not look like your father's union.

We have structured the book into five broad themes, as suggested by the authors. Part I, titled "Community and Coalitions," addresses the need for working-class organizations to build a labor movement by cultivating community-based partnerships that create lasting coalitions. The authors identify communities that offer potential for working-class power, support local and transnational struggles, and grapple with how best to nurture and sustain those relationships. The authors in Part Two, "Place Matters," focus their attention on how working-class power must also be understood by the physical and geographical place where workers toil. They suggest reconsidering strategies that are especially important to an increasingly contingent and isolated workforce. In Part Three, "State and Policy," the essays discuss the ways in which workers and unions can assert their power to affect the distribution of local resources and global trade. The authors propose demands that labor needs to make on the state regarding labor law, equal opportunity, and fair labor standards. In Part

Four, "Political Economy," the authors suggest that the complexity of the current global crises, including the financial system meltdown and climate change, requires equally complex responses. They argue in different ways that labor needs to publicly challenge assumptions about neoliberalism and reimagine the state as a vehicle through which workers can achieve a measure of social justice. Finally, Part Five, "Beyond Borders," speaks to the need for labor to reimagine itself as part of a global movement that supports the organization of workers across political boundaries and embraces all workers in the United States regardless of citizenship status.

The events of 2011 have indelibly linked the cities of Cairo, Madison, Madrid, London, and New York as flashpoints of a broad popular pushback against the global neoliberal economy. As we conclude the production of this volume, the Occupy Wall Street demonstrations are heating up. Within days of this writing, labor unions in New York City have begun to declare solidarity with the protesters and are planning mass rallies. The corporate media, unable to ignore any longer what began as a handful of protesters sleeping in Zuccotti Park, are still "confused" that there does not seem to be any one leader or specific set of demands. Yet in late September, thousands who did understand the links—between the privatization of public resources, corporate greed, home foreclosures, union busting, and tax breaks for the rich—found common purpose and demonstrated at One Police Plaza the day after the Transport Workers Union officially voted to join the protests. On October 1, seven hundred demonstrators were arrested as they marched across the Brooklyn Bridge.

And as we walked through the park, listened to the speeches, and marched with union members, unemployed workers, indebted students, and worried middle-class professionals, we noticed that the themes of this book were reverberating throughout. Activists, more pouring in each day, are connecting with protesters across the country and around the globe, continuing to construct a global movement. Through the "occupation" of the park, they consciously build a democratic space open to all, dominated by no one person or group. They are building coalitions among all groups with common grievances.

The demands for government and corporate accountability to the "99 percent" of the people who are disenfranchised from the political system in the United States and around the world are being articulated clearly. And as unions help to swell the crowds and grow the movement, we see concrete hope for labor's rise in the twenty-first century.

Part One

Community and Coalitions

After the Civil War, as American industry grew and wealth became more concentrated, workers suffered dangerous work and living conditions, debilitating disease, starvation, humiliation, and brutal crackdowns on strikes and union organizing. Union activity was often made illegal or extralegal. But workers continued to build unions, almost always by drawing on the power of the institutions and leaders of the communities in which they lived, and by supporting sometimes far-flung efforts by other workers around the country and around the world. The national labor laws passed in the 1930s legitimized unions and spurred the labor movement's unprecedented growth through the 1940s. As unions became more powerful, more complex, and more accepted in the political fabric of the United States, their reliance on communities and coalition partners diminished.

Now the labor laws that once allowed unions to thrive are used as weapons to choke the life out of them. Labor has been waking slowly over the last decade or so to the need to rebuild a movement from a foundation of community-based partnerships and coalition building. But in this era of an American postindustrial society, in which people work electronically from long distances, or survive with multiple jobs, and live outside tight-knit or extended family neighborhoods, what do we mean by "community"? Where do unions and other working-class organizations go to find community? How do we build trust and grow coalitions of mutual support among activists and community-based organizations? And how do we link our aspirations for a transnational movement to local struggles in a way that acknowledges and strengthens both? The essays in this section begin to answer those questions.

Drawing upon scholarly history and history of which he was a part, Shelton Stromquist begins this section and the book arguing for what he calls a "translocal" vocabulary through which local unions and working-class organizations foster organic movements that are connected internationally. Workers over time and across continents, he observes, create communities of resistance that respond to real day-to-day grievances without the urging of large hierarchical national or international organizations. Direct action and participatory democracy need to be supported by cross-fertilized local movements.

Bethany Moreton and Pamela Voekel remind us that communities which may conflict with our worldviews nevertheless have much to offer unions and other groups trying to build coalitions with workers who are steeped in both Christian and capitalist values. The evangelical right and the closely associated business culture of Wal-Mart have worked for decades to appeal to poor working women by taking seriously their senses of morality, self-image, and self-worth as service workers. Moreton and Voekel argue that the labor left needs to engage in a battle with right-wing ideology on college campuses, sites of education and employment, and other workplaces by reframing labor rights as a moral issue.

Daniel Katz suggests that right-wing ideology regarding citizenship status and ethnic identity has also dominated the national conversation in ways that drive wedges between working-class allies. Establishing parallels between anti-immigration and American nationalist sentiments prevalent today and the anti-immigration, racist, and antiunion period of the 1920s, he argues that the case of the International Ladies' Garment Workers' Union can be instructive in building a multicultural union movement today. The ILGWU, with the support of a network of sister organizations in the Jewish labor and socialist movements, built a powerful union in the 1930s by appealing to the racial and ethnic identities of its members through educational and cultural mechanisms.

For Michelle Chen, labor's rise will require an attention to young workers who have the potential to fill the ranks of a militant movement but are also primed to take leadership. Recent events from Cairo to Madison to the Kingsbridge section of the Bronx suggest that youth both understand their vulnerabilities in the new economic order and intuitively understand that powerful unions are the way forward. Though youth rarely have direct experience with unions, many, though not all, have the advantage of being open to gender and racial differences that divided earlier generations.

Nancy MacLean sees opportunities for building coalitions of youth, labor, community, academic, and religious activists around the campuses on which most of the contributors of this volume work. She implores her colleagues to learn the skills of grassroots organization. Recalling success that she and other activists in Chicago enjoyed, she argues that academics can work as activists in partnership with unions, clergy, and other working-class organizations to support local labor struggles, promote careers in social justice work among students, and launch living wage campaigns on campus.

BUILDING A NEW WORKING-CLASS POLITICS FROM BELOW

Shelton Stromquist

The old labor film *The Inheritance* has a simple refrain that I've always found powerfully instructive: "Every generation's got to do it again." It's a useful reminder. Despite all the changes in the world of labor, the economic ups and downs, the global restructuring of manufacturing, the job losses in Rust Belt communities, the attacks on the very right of collective bargaining, the crisis in social democracy and rightward drift of national politics, the new transmigrations that defy heavily policed borders, the decline in union density, we still face some of the same challenges that working people have always faced. How do we build and sustain a vital movement for social justice and equality capable of contesting for power and remodeling our workplaces, our communities, and our countries into the humane and just world to which we aspire? The challenge is clearly transnational to a degree it has never been before. Our organizing, our political engagement, and the history we write must ultimately rise to that challenge. But it all starts locally.

In 1950, a young African American teamster from Waterloo, Iowa, Edwin Hollins—a refugee from the debilitating foundry in the local John Deere plant—joined a caravan of several fellow teamsters, all white, as they hauled their cargo from Waterloo to Peoria. They stopped for lunch at a diner in Savanna, Illinois. The restaurant's manager pulled Hollins aside and told him that he'd have to eat his lunch in the truck. Not wanting to make a fuss, he started to take his food outside. Bobby Rose, another teamster, asked why he wasn't eating with the rest. When Hollins said he'd been told it was against local custom for him to eat in the restaurant, Rose stood up and said, "You eat in here or won't no goddamned body ever eat in here again." And, addressing the manager, Rose said, "How'd you like it to have these six sons-a-bitches drive into this place with you in it?" The restaurateur conceded that he wouldn't like that and put Hollins's food on a plate for him to eat with his union brothers. On subsequent stops at the restaurant there was never any question raised about Hollins's right to eat with his union brothers.

This was no organized act of desegregation. It happened nearly a decade before the lunch counter sit-ins in Greensboro, North Carolina. It was a spontaneous act of solidarity by union brothers, an expression of their mutualistic culture at a moment of robust postwar union strength. It was local and organic. With hundreds of such unsung acts, workers gave meaning to a slogan, adopted by the CIO and the left, "Black and White, Unite and Fight." Through their actions, they made it their own.

My own scholarship and my political experience have been in perpetual dialogue with the "local" as the primary arena in which the networks of solidarity—which give fiber and strength to any meaningful social movement—must be built. As my academic work gravitated to the study of the Knights of Labor and the American Railway Union, I was struck by the vitality of local mixed assemblies as entry points for workers irrespective of skill or trade or industry. These local chains of solidarity built on workers' organic community ties and became the basis for collective action in strikes, boycotts, and ultimately politics in places like Hornellsville, New York; Creston, Iowa; and Two Harbors, Minnesota.

EXPERIENCE: LOCAL MOVEMENT BUILDING

I had witnessed and participated in such movement building from below during 1964 and 1965 in Vicksburg, Mississippi, and Selma, Alabama. Members of the local black community in Vicksburg welcomed the Student Nonviolent Coordinating Committee (SNCC) and its white college-student summer recruits into their homes and community, sensing a moment had arrived that carried real possibilities for social change after decades, indeed centuries, of violent intimidation. With courage and deepest conviction, people like Eddie Thomas (a barber), Pink Taylor (a retired sleeping car porter), and Bessie Brown (the mother of six young children) risked everything to claim

the right to vote, to hold meetings in churches in the face of Klan beat-
ings and intimidation, and to build from the grassroots a new political party—the Mississippi Freedom Democratic Party (MFDP). They
would be the local architects of a new, powerful social movement. In
Selma, the audacity of young kids by the hundreds, such as Ola Mae
Waller and her friends, built their own youthful ties of social solidarity, dancing and singing, "Oh Wallace, you never can jail us all. Oh
Wallace, segregation's bound to fall," directly in the face of the brutal
Sheriff Jim Clark and George Wallace's state troopers. They inspired
a movement that enabled their elders to claim voting rights and to
walk to Montgomery to register those claims if they so chose. They
made passage of the 1965 Voting Rights Act possible.

My work with the Council of Federated Organizations (COFO)
and SNCC helped inoculate me against the anticommunism that
some erstwhile supporters of the movement, like Al Lowenstein,
were actively purveying and against the corporate liberal model of
social change reflected in the social programs of Kennedy and Johnson. That "liberal" orientation revealed itself most graphically in the
Democratic Party's affront to Fannie Lou Hamer and the MFDP at
the 1964 national convention. But, by 1966, I also recognized that
whatever useful limited role whites had played in the movement to
that point had now largely passed. I welcomed and applauded the
turn to "black power" and moved on to other localities and their quest
to build a new society.

In Tanzania, East Africa, I encountered a remarkable social transformation under way in 1966. Inspired by President Julius Nyerere's
"Arusha Declaration" that laid out a national commitment to building
an African socialism, rooted in the nation's agrarian economy and
its remembered precolonial culture of communal interdependence,
farmers in different parts of the country undertook to construct this
new society from below. Working with poor, proud farmers in two
different communal experiments over two years, I witnessed men
and women committing their energies and their social vision to the
arduous work of clearing new land, planting and harvesting jointly
owned crops, constructing improved dwellings with local materials, and meeting to consider their next steps in this grassroots social

experiment. An older generation of farmers, like Hasani Kombo and Mzee Saidi, keepers of the oral tradition of communalism in a Handeni village, joined members of a younger, politically inspired generation, such as Mwinjuma Thabiti, to give tangible meaning to a national campaign for Ujamaa (familiness/socialism). The politics of implementing African socialism in postcolonial Africa proved challenging. The lingering debris of colonialism and the intrusive Cold War and neocolonial policies of former and would-be colonizers created profound barriers to social experimentation and successful development, limiting or even undermining the spread of locally based socialism.

Back in the United States in 1968, I reencountered now at high tide a broad-based and inspiring social movement against the war in Vietnam. Settling in Milwaukee, my wife, Ann, and I gravitated to a unique urban Catholic Worker community that combined militant action against the war and the draft with community-based organizing for fair housing, community-controlled schools, and the direct action of poor communities and the homeless to force local power structures to address their needs and priorities. Such "communities of resistance" had appeared across the country and, despite the turn to violence by some segments of the movement, they carried forward the legacy of the early civil rights movement by using nonviolent action to build community, provide direct human services, and "speak truth to power," whether manifested in draft boards, city councils, school boards, or powerful corporations. Working at different points as a machinist's helper and occasional baker, I saw a need for union representation more responsive to the rank and file than I found. To my delight, I also discovered that an emerging field of "new labor history" was beginning to address the very questions that were arising from my own experience on the shop floor and from oral histories that a group of high school students and I collected from surviving militants from the Allis-Chalmers strike of 1946–47. How had working people built networks of solidarity to challenge the entrenched power that governed their lives—in their workplaces and their communities? How did they understand their identities as workers—as women and men, as immigrants and native-born, as people of color, both white and black—in a society that bore the scars of slavery and its aftermath? How can we account for the ebb and flow of social mobilization by the "powerless"? (Having witnessed in the previous decade, in Mississippi, in Tanzania, and now in Milwaukee, such cycles in local movement building and collective action, I sought a deeper historical context.) On what storehouses of ideas and tradition did workers and their allies draw for inspiration? How did collective memory, informal learning, and political organization generate and renew a social vision that might inspire people to act?

EDUCATION: CLASS AND COMMUNITY

Coming back to formal education after some years of community work, I found in the "new labor history," and in the emerging networks of labor historians, people who took up precisely the intellectual (and political) challenges these questions raised. In Pittsburgh, a cadre of graduate students working with David Montgomery carried their academic work into the community through strike support activity, oral history, and community living. We examined the social conflicts and solidarities of the shop floor, the structures of power and cross-class alliances that working-class community bred, the forms of collective action that working men and women devised, and the new kinds of politics they practiced. We saw that history brought to life in our own work and that of others by excavating the fabric of workers' daily lives historically in places like Pittsburgh's iron and glass communities (John Bennett), in coal mining villages of West Virginia (Fred Barkey and David Corbin), antebellum artisan communities (Bruce Laurie), Midwestern railroad towns (Stromquist), among turn-of-the-century Chicago teamsters (Steve Sapolsky), in the fragile cross-race alliances in Richmond (Peter Rachleff), the ethnic ties in Chicago's immigrant Packingtown (Jim Barrett), in auto parts local unions in Detroit (Peter Friedlander), among militant electrical workers (Ron Schatz), Knights of Labor cooperatives in countless local communities (Clare Dahlberg), in the rules by which skilled iron workers fought to maintain their control of production

(David Montgomery), or the community alliances that workers built to challenge outside monopoly (Herbert Gutman).

What this new work suggested, among other things, was a more diverse working class and a wider spectrum of working-class collective action. Even as some of this new work exposed the deep cultural roots of racism and patriarchy, so did it also find spaces in which workers constructed from the organic solidarities of the workplace and neighborhood new forms of resistance. The Knights used the boycott and sympathy strike as powerful tools. They built alliances that crossed racial and gender boundaries that had hobbled and would in the future constrain workers' ability to organize effectively. But it was in the realm of politics that workers tested the limits of the class-based social order that governed their lives and built strategies to address the issues of concrete and immediate concern—housing, sanitation, urban transit, standards of employment, clean water, cheap fuel, disease control, and leisure facilities.

SCHOLARSHIP: TRANSLOCAL WORKING-CLASS POLITICS

In my own recent studies, I have become intrigued by the local, simultaneous political initiatives workers around the world undertook at the turn of the century. The crises of urban life and the hardships imposed by the ongoing Industrial Revolution led workers in many and diverse settings to invent a new politics that directly addressed those hardships, bypassing existing liberal and conservative parties. The depression of the 1890s and the mass strike waves that swept through transportation, mining, and manufacturing sectors of the world's industrializing countries provided the catalyst for political experimentation at the grassroots that soon produced independent electoral challenges by laborites and socialists to city councils, school boards, and poor-relief agencies. Although frequently marginalized at national party congresses and hamstrung by franchise restrictions, municipal activists nonetheless crafted platforms, established communication with comrades in other cities across national boundaries, and mounted campaigns for local office. In the early years

(1894–1905) they won scattered victories but rarely governing control. Nonetheless, the tenor of municipal politics took a laborist and more democratic turn with the disruption of traditional elite forms of local governance.

In subtle but often significant ways, improvements came to workers' lives through their own self-activity. The scope of the local state expanded through municipalization of water, gas, and electricity. Cities undertook municipally financed public housing and instituted public baths and municipally owned markets. City employment expanded at the expense of private contract labor with wages and working conditions that set new standards locally. Activists engaged the battle for municipal control of streetcars. And workers won access to public space for their celebrations and public protests.

This grassroots activism focused on the city as an arena of struggle and political mobilization. It also posed a challenge to the future course of social democratic politics, even as parliamentary-oriented party elites asserted their claims to leadership. The twentieth century is littered with national social democratic movements that may have shared or even won power, at least temporarily, but in the long run abandoned their social democratic agendas. The renewal, periodically, of grassroots municipal politics has been an impressive countercurrent. Never entirely secure and frequently operating from a minority position, those political initiatives, because they connected with real, day-to-day grievances of working-class people, provided a wellspring for political renewal.

Recent scholarship documenting the transatlantic and transglobal flow of social reform ideas and programs in the late nineteenth and early twentieth centuries reminds us how interconnected these histories were. Nowhere was this flow more evident than in the realm of urban politics. The political ideas and the transnational experience of political organizers cross-fertilized local movements. Edward Bellamy's *Looking Backward* was sold throughout the Western world in cheap agitational editions to finance organizing campaigns. Henry George's single tax idea found a receptive audience in Australia, New Zealand, Britain, and Sweden, shaping the thinking of working-class activists and middle-class reformers. The Knights of Labor and the Industrial Workers of the World exerted a powerful influence in Australia and New Zealand, as they did in parts of Europe and Latin America. At key points in this period, Americans such as Milwaukee social democrat Walter Thomas Mills or New Zealand revolutionary activist Patrick Hickey moved easily between their respective countries. After returning to New Zealand from several years organizing for the Western Federation of Miners in Colorado, Hickey led the Blackball miners' strike in 1908 and the "Red Feds." He eventually ran for and held municipal office in both New Zealand and Australia. Mills helped to reconstruct a New Zealand Labour Party at a crucial juncture in its development in the early 1910s. Visits by Sidney and Beatrice Webb to survey local government just before the turn of the century in the United States, Australia, and New Zealand were preceded in Australia by the legendary British docker Ben Tillett and followed soon thereafter by Labour Party activist Tom Mann, who would return several years later to be arrested in support of strikers and political activists in Broken Hill, New South Wales. Bradford's Labour city councillor E.R. Hartley sojourned for nearly a year among municipal socialists in Australia and New Zealand. The traffic moved in other directions as well. A young Christchurch, New Zealand, organizer, "Jimmy" Thorn, went off for four years to organize for the Independent Labour Party in Britain; Australian railway union leader Claude Thompson traveled in the industrial union and labor party circles of Europe and America, acquiring along the way honorary memberships in the American Labor Union and the Western Federation of Miners; evolutionary socialist Eduard Bernstein spent a decade exiled in London, observing directly the experience of independent labor activists and sharing his own evolving socialist ideas with sympathizers in London. Irish socialist and republican leader James Connolly organized in the United States before returning to Dublin to lead the Easter uprising in 1916; Axel Danielsson in Malmö, Sweden, participated in the Scandinavian Workers Congresses of the early 1890s and meetings of the Second International, reporting on these internationalist currents to the Swedish readers of his newspaper, *Arbetet*.

What made such circulation feasible was that these political itin-erants entered worlds that were undergoing remarkably similar so-cial and political changes; they spoke a common *political* language, read each other's tracts, and understood the common problems they confronted. The observant labor and socialist press in each country reported developments in the others. The global dimensions of this movement have been at times neglected or underestimated by histo-rians and contemporary activists. Not only did such politics appear in widely dispersed local settings across the industrializing world circa 1890–1920, the movements were also tightly and self-consciously linked through transnational contacts, exchanges of information, and traveling activist-organizers. Delegates to international socialist gatherings brought back colorful reports of the successes comrades had achieved elsewhere. Common threads defined these local strug-gles across national boundaries.

WHAT IS TO BE DONE? REAFFIRM LOCAL POLITICAL STRUGGLE

Workers today face a grim world in which capital mobility, media con-centration, and the complicity of governments have circumscribed the ability of workers and communities to assert their control over the conditions they face. The prospects for national legislation that might level the playing field seem more remote than ever, as the effective abandonment of the struggle for the Employee Free Choice Act re-vealed. Immigration reform legislation seems hamstrung with little prospect of an opening for undocumented workers to claim their rights as workers or citizens. In the short term, Tea Party governors in Wisconsin, Ohio, New Jersey, and other states have succeeded in dismantling the right of public workers to collective bargaining, even in the face of mass mobilization. The capacity of big corporations and the U.S. Chamber of Commerce to reshape political debate by dump-ing millions of dollars into political campaigns, enabled now by the Supreme Court's *Citizens United* decision, has so skewed national and state politics to the right, at least for the time being, that little prospect of building an effective national challenge seems in the cards. The

Obama administration, elected on a wave of hopefulness, is belea-guered and hampered by its own halfhearted and ill-conceived efforts to build a shaky bipartisanism with a newly energized, corporate-financed right-wing Republicanism.

But, as some might say, we have them right where we want them! Below the radar, local community activism, already well under way, again points the direction for the rebirth of a new popular politics capable of challenging for power, before the power structure realizes the scope of what's happening. At least that's where our new "hope" lies.

The new local politics takes many forms—living wage campaigns, stricter enforcement of environmental regulations, expansion of municipally owned enterprises, support for local union organizing, building and strengthening co-ops, and defending the rights of un-documented workers. Like earlier generations of activists, we must "think globally and act locally." We need to campaign for representa-tion on city councils, schools boards, local zoning and housing com-missions, and police review panels. We need to bypass the existing channels of national power and influence in which our demands and interests get redirected, diluted, and diminished, and build new structures of power and solidarity from below. The disappointments of the Obama presidency provide a powerful object lesson for those who seek a genuine progressive, democratic alternative.

New local progressive alliances, with labor at their core, need to set clear priorities. First, we need to reopen the struggle for home rule by revising city charters to enable cities to better control their destinies economically. Second, we need to mount new campaigns to extend the public sector through municipalization of city services that now rest in private hands and to defeat privatization at every turn by winning, for instance, municipal franchises for cable television, recycling, and other basic services; to declare cities as sanctuaries for undocumented immigrants who seek to build a life for themselves as good citizens and effective workers; to strengthen co-ops as the base for an alternative economy; to establish a "living wage" environment for local businesses and college campuses; to create green municipal energy parks with cheap energy for small business development; and to develop a host of other initiatives, many of which are already under way in different localities.

Such local initiatives can from the outset establish transnational linkages with cities and community organizations internationally that share ideas and resources, build support networks, and even mount parallel campaigns, much in the manner of municipal activists of a century ago. Living wage campaigns in U.S. cities and some states find their counterparts in the UK and Australia. Labor solidarity efforts link workers in the United States, Mexico, and other parts of Latin America. The fight to limit child labor has taken on transnational action in India, Southeast Asia, Brazil, and elsewhere. In the United States, grassroots progressive politics acquired a new lease on life in the last decade, with vigorous local movements such as Progressive Maryland and living wage campaigns in Baltimore, its surrounding counties, and at the University of Georgia, the College of William and Mary, and other universities. A coalition of cities, calling itself "Cities for Progress," passed strong resolutions against the war in Iraq and has moved on to living wage campaigns and struggles against Wal-Mart. In Madison, Wisconsin, "Progressive Dane" has crafted a local platform and run candidates for local office with some success, and in Iowa City, Iowa, FAIR! has worked on fair and open housing, municipalization of the electric utilities, and endorsement of local progressive candidates. Iowa Citizens for Community Improvement (ICCI) has won important victories for migrant workers and prevented the gutting of state clean air and water laws.

We need a new "translocal" political vocabulary that affirms the common struggle to make grassroots democracy a living reality in communities and workplaces around the globe, not filtered through the leadership of national or international figureheads. We lack good historical models for how the integrity of such local mobilization can be sustained and nurtured. What is clear is that social movements must remain linked to their own grassroots, must practice "participatory democracy" (to use an old SDS term), and must actively and self-consciously resist the "oligarchical" tendencies that Robert Michels more than a century ago identified as a virus to which popular movements are themselves susceptible. New national and international structures of solidarity may emerge from local activism. World and regional social forums are an important point of contact and means to build translocal ties and coordinate international actions. New forms of struggle are being invented, or redeployed in new ways, through the direct sharing translocally of organizing experience among workers, as recently occurred between Chinatown (NYC) and Shanghai garment workers; international boycotts of abusive firms like Koch Industries' subsidiaries, BP, and Hyatt Hotels; and anti-corporate sit-ins across Britain directed at tax-cheating businesses, such as cell phone giant Vodafone, facilitated through social media contacts that mobilized activists in London, Leeds, and some of the country's smallest and most conservative hamlets.

Across the United States and around the globe, local trade unionists and community activists are reinvesting their political energies locally, building workers' centers and inter-union alliances, creating new methods of struggle, and renewing their communities from below. In doing so, they are taking a page from previous generations of local activists and union builders, and in the bargain affirming the old adage that "every generation's got to do it again."

LEARNING FROM THE RIGHT: A NEW OPERATION DIXIE?

Bethany Moreton and Pamela Voekel

In the generation after 1968, as the left's industrial frame of reference rusted away, a vibrant, creative, and highly effective social movement was nurtured on college campuses. It mobilized the idealism and energies of a new generation of students, many of whom were the first in their families to acquire white-collar credentials. In the South and West particularly, it helped ease the transition from farms to offices, from small towns to Sun Belt cities. It brought political engagement to the schools and their host communities and allowed young people to experience their activism in a world historical context. Drawing insight and personnel from the postmodern religious revival and the post-Fordist workplace, this movement helped shift the national terms of debate decisively—to the right. If labor is looking for fresh ideas, they are hidden in plain sight down at the sorority house, the business school, and the Campus Crusade for Christ.

"Sit down and buckle your seatbelts! What I am about to tell you will shock and disgust you," wrote Georgia legislator Calvin Hill in a 2009 e-mail to his supporters. While the state faced a staggering $2.2 billion budget shortfall, the Republican state representative raised the alarm that "your tax dollars are being used at our state universities to pay professors to teach your children classes like 'Male Prostitution' and 'Queer Theory.'" As CNN reported support from the Christian Coalition, Hill and fellow Republican Charlice Byrd demanded that the state fire the faculty members and cease this "major misuse of the state university system's budget." When it became clear that the legislators had mistaken a list of faculty areas of expertise for an actual course catalogue, Hill retreated to the less inflammatory position that, in a time of economic crisis, state universities should confine themselves to marketable disciplines like science, business, and math.

On the surface, this tawdry dustup repeats a familiar story line: with free-market orthodoxy in disarray, the conservative movement of the last thirty years might be expected to fall back on its most reliable hot-button issues rather than address the shortcomings of casualization, privatization, and financial speculation. In Georgia, decades of ideological contempt for state services meant the newly homeless and jobless swamped the meager resources available to them, while the parallel disdain for public oversight had encouraged a frantic level of financial speculation and predatory lending. As Representative Hill went postal on queer theory, Georgia was leading the nation in the number of troubled banks, and one out of every eight mortgage holders in the state was either behind on payments or in foreclosure. Tellingly, the Republicans' target wasn't even male prostitutes themselves—the entrepreneurial class, who, it could be argued, was making queer theory pay. Rather, the object of ire was the parasitical class of public employees with their relative job security and their guaranteed pensions, the people you love to hate when free-market policies have stripped these assets from private sector employment.

According to a standard left analysis, then, the brief flurry over "steamy sex classes" could be just a pathetic footnote to the endless culture wars. Wasn't this another case of the cynical manipulating the irrational, of the oligarchs fanning religious prejudice over fringe issues to distract the citizenry from the real culprit: the free market, antigovernment, antilabor ideology that they support even while losing out under its precepts? For more than a generation, after all, the conservative counterrevolution in America blurred the distinction between the invisible hand of the market and the all-powerful hand of God. In the dominant narrative of the Republican ascendancy, this slippage represents the greatest con in recent history: while you defend marriage or protect the unborn, please pay no attention to the financial wizard behind the curtain. He can shift the tax burden ever further down the food chain, offshore jobs, shred the social safety net, punish rising productivity with stagnant wages, and construct an international economy on the pattern of Caesars Palace, just so long as he periodically hollers "Abortion!" or "Gay agenda!" What's the matter with Kansas, asked the left in frustration; why do those people in the pews keep enabling a political order that eats them for lunch? Couldn't they figure out that "family values" were just a fig leaf for an economic vision that would make Darwin blush? Weren't Jerry Falwell and Milton Friedman really rather strange bedfellows at the end of the day?

But Christian hostility to abortion and homosexuality was not a soft distraction from hard issues; it was itself part of an economic vision, one that gave reproduction its due. The rise of "family values"—of intense religious concern with physical and social reproduction—corresponded to the rise of the service economy in America, or the replacement of productive industries with reproductive ones. As Wal-Mart surpassed Exxon-Mobil and General Motors to become the largest corporation on earth and factories fled for the border, work came increasingly to look like home. The feminization of work—that is, the demand for traditionally female "people skills" like patience, communicativeness, and nurturance—threw the old heroic narrative of masculine productivity into a crisis. A new Christian emphasis on service offered both a pattern for organizing the service workplace and an ethos for valuing that work, now performed by men as well as women. The weekly Bible study groups, Christian colleges, megachurches, and Promise Keepers of the Sun Belt offered a new way to find meaning and morality in the market. Simultaneously, the public disinvestment from education turned even nondenominational colleges and universities into the ideological apparatus of free market fundamentalism.

Several strains of innovation on the right have successfully tied the changed nature of work to a full-fledged economic vision. The same retail workers that progressive unions sought to organize report that they are more likely to turn to God for help on the job than to a union, a feminist organization, or a government agency. During the 1970s and 1980s, as evangelical, fundamentalist, and Pentecostal Christians demonized nonreproductive sex, some service companies learned from their female employees how to value motherly service and transformed that knowledge into managerial gospel. Drawing in a new workforce—white rural mothers, accustomed to the family as an economic unit—the Arkansas-based Wal-Mart, for example, took advantage of the broad national consensus that the work of serving others was not really work, that women were not really workers.

The second stage in transferring this Sun Belt business culture to the international economic order involved blending Christian service ideals with free market theories, and taking this novel alloy into college business classrooms. With vocational degrees in business now the country's leading undergraduate major by far, fundamental debates over the distribution of resources in human society are effectively off the table in the most populated classrooms. Business as a discipline assumes rather than argues its fundamentals. By asking how rather than why or whether, the business curriculum can represent management's interests as the common good or even as a law of nature.

Yet while this tax-free ideological apparatus passes as an apolitical bystander in the canon wars, its architects have not been content to rest on their laurels. Though the right keeps up a steady drumbeat of alarm about the overrepresentation of card-carrying Democrats among adjunct lecturers in comp lit, the long green goes to unabashed free market advocacy projects. The current wave of on-campus proselytizing claims an ancestor in the pro-corporate mobilization of the 1970s. A handy crib sheet to this strategy is the notorious Powell Memo, a vitriolic private missive that the Tobacco Institute's corporate lawyer Lewis Powell wrote to the U.S. Chamber of Commerce in 1971, just a few months before his elevation to the U.S. Supreme Court. Why, he demanded of the venerable business lobbying organization, would the Chamber's members tolerate student radicalism when the graduates would go on to institutionalize their countercultural values as the next generation of lawmakers and regulators, teachers and writers? Weren't American corporations tired of being thrashed by the civil rights lawyers and the tree huggers and the consumer protection crowd?

Singling out the campus as the key terrain of struggle, Powell urged his colleagues at the Chamber to exercise the prerogatives of ownership: given that corporate taxes and donations helped fund American higher education, given that advertising underwrote the media, surely business should be getting more ideological bang for its buck in the marketplace of ideas. The Chamber and its allies, Powell counseled, must promote deregulation as an intellectual position by monitoring the faculties of history departments and the content of textbooks, flying its speakers to podiums around the country, and indeed buying a full-fledged private intellectual apparatus to crowd out the long-haired devotees of scholarship and public service. The most spectacular fruit of this vision has been America's corporate-funded knowledge factories, the think tanks that turn the scholarly commons into a duty-free shop. But Powell and his comrades also urged players like the Chamber to demand that business schools— who knew their master's voice when they heard it—provide courses aggressively defending deregulated capitalism. The charge of American "economic illiteracy" joined a growing chorus from businessmen convinced that the only position from which they could be criticized was a position of ignorance: to know the market was to love it, so the challenge was simply to get the word out.

One result was a river of corporate-funded advocacy materials pouring into American primary and secondary schools. State legislatures enthusiastically passed graduation requirements in "economics," but declined to fund them, opening the door for antilabor, anti-regulation propaganda penned by the Chamber itself or by the right-wing Foundation for Economic Education and paid for by the likes of DuPont and General Motors. As the public funding for higher education dried up, struggling smaller colleges courted donors with blueprints for "private enterprise centers" with explicit advocacy goals, and dozens of endowed professorships in "free enterprise" cropped up at colleges and universities from coast to coast. Corporations bankrolled the cynical co-optation of student idealists—often animated by Christian commitment—through organizations like Students in Free Enterprise that presented capitalism as an embattled cause and sent nineteen-year-olds to parrot Milton Friedman in front of third-graders for college credit. Business faculties successfully lobbied to

turn the Small Business Administration into a vehicle of federal sub-
sidy for their services, renting out their undergraduates' consulting
acumen to struggling mom-and-pops on the government's nickel. No
one could find much evidence that the young people's advice could
undo the devastation of small business by corporate welfare, deregulation, and international free-trade agreements, but it enhanced the
B-school's standing within the university and the community and
gave the students a cause greater than profit.

In one spectacular example of managerial ideology masquer-
ading as education, the philanthropic arm of the commercial bank
BB&T has bought a place on curricula for free-enterprise cult figure
Ayn Rand on campuses around the South. The BB&T Charitable
Foundation has created sixty programs dedicated to the laudable goal
of "teaching and research on the moral foundations of capitalism"—
surely a goal to gladden the heart of even the pinkest historian of
slavery or satanic mills. But the titles give away the agenda: the College of Charleston's Initiative for Public Choice and Market Process,
Marshall University's BB&T Center for the Advancement of American Capitalism. The foundation spent $2 million to create a chair in
Randian precepts at the University of Texas, which announces the
gift under its perceptive slogan "What starts here changes the world."
Indeed: the University of North Carolina at Charlotte saw no threat to
its intellectual reputation when it agreed to teach Rand's free-market
potboiler *Atlas Shrugged* as a required text in order to seal the deal
with the donor. The University of Georgia's Terry College of Business announced its intention to use part of its similar grant to hand
out free copies of this "best defense of capitalism ever written" to in-
coming business students. For its part, regional powerhouse Duke
University huffily rejected the suggestion that it would allow such
meddling in its curriculum even while failing to identify the head
of its Values and Ethics in the Marketplace Program as a representative of the Ayn Rand Institute. "The ARI," explains its website, "seeks
to spearhead a cultural renaissance that will reverse the anti-reason,
anti-individualism, anti-freedom, anti-capitalist trends in today's culture. The major battleground in this fight for reason and capitalism

is the educational institutions—high schools and, above all, the universities, where students learn the ideas that shape their lives." Lewis Powell couldn't have said it better himself.

Seen against this backdrop, Southern campuses in particular ought to be of intense interest to the left. Rather than "whistling past Dixie" on the road to national influence, the labor movement could learn a lot both from the right's collegiate takeover and from the resistance it has spawned. The human resources of these Southern schools were available for wholesale co-optation a generation ago in part because they were so undervalued by a labor left still deeply invested in its brawny identity politics. The movements and unions that have grown out of the service sector have since begun to transform the institutional structure of America's official labor movement. But as long as free-market fundamentalism functions as common sense for most of the country, the very concept of rights at work could become as quaint as the Little Red Songbook.

Obviously, the progressives will not easily tap support like the financial backing of a Dow Chemical, a Wal-Mart, or a BB&T. This is no small obstacle in a landscape where corporate citizenship grants the largest agglomerations of capital the loudest voice, from elections to curricula. But the answer to right-wing indoctrination posing as education is not left-wing indoctrination. It is rather genuine education, in class and behind the scenes at the neoliberal university.

The student activists we have seen at the University of Georgia easily make connections, for example, among administrators who regard the university as a business, a curriculum that Taylorizes learning, and a campus workforce segmented by race, sex, and immigration status. When the university's laudable Initiative on Poverty and the Economy identified its own home county as consistently one of the poorest in the nation, it pointed to classic patterns of college towns around the country: not only does the university, as the largest employer by far, effectively set a ceiling on area wages, it also creates a secondary tier of low-wage service establishments in its wake—bars, restaurants, and music venues. Like many such towns, ours even before the crash of 2008 was marked by high employment coupled with high poverty, as many residents worked two and three jobs. An ad hoc committee of the University Council studied the university's role in area poverty and produced a report recommending concrete steps to be taken immediately. When the university's president declined to implement the proposal, he unwittingly created a generation of first responders in the defense of the commonweal.

The student activists, clear about their own role in the university's service economy, have educated the entire community on living wages with op-eds, public rallies, petitions signed by thousands, and a student-made documentary that played on campus and in area churches. Visiting speakers from Jesse Jackson to the late Manning Marable to Elayne Brown endorsed the cause from their podiums. In public appearances, administrators met tough questions from students in the audience. Staff members often waited until the administrators left, then thanked students for being willing to say out loud what employees felt too vulnerable to voice.

From the political economy of the campus, the students followed the trail to the statehouse, where legislators robbed Peter and Pedro to send Paul off to college in a Lexus. With the state's lottery-funded full scholarship program a victim of its own success, the legislature voted to raise the eligibility standards and lower the benefits rather than cap income of recipients' families at $140,000. "$140,000 isn't what it used to be," retorted the Republican chairman of the Senate Higher Education Committee. "Welcome to the real world. Government can't fix everything." Lottery players are now even less likely to be subsidizing their own children's education, but rather those of Atlanta suburbanites. At the same time, the University Board of Regents undertook to root out the undocumented students allegedly free-riding through Georgia's public campuses and crowding out the natives. After investigating over three hundred thousand students—at an undisclosed cost—the regents found five hundred undocumented students, all of whom were subsidizing their native-born peers by paying out-of-state tuition. Undaunted by this encounter with reality, the regents rushed to bar the undocumented from enrolling in any of the state's five most competitive campuses, no matter how much they are willing to pay for the privilege. Student activists responded by publicly linking the issues in organizations like Georgia Students for Public

Higher Education and the Georgia Undocumented Youth Alliance. Some signed on to help create Freedom University, a weekend class taught by UGA faculty, advised by some of the country's most distinguished scholars, and open to any qualified Georgian regardless of immigration status (www.freedomuniversitygeorgia.org).

These students thus make direct connections among the financial crisis, the conservative fiscal remedies proposed in statehouses around the country, the funding structure of higher education, the casualization of academic labor, the scapegoating of undocumented immigrants, and the administrative elephantiasis that has raised the price of higher education so sharply while undermining many of its core functions. The chants become interchangeable to those who see the connections: "Up, up with education, down, down with _____"—deportation, segregation, incarceration.

And while students and employees of color seldom have trouble seeing the shadow of the plantation across the quad, whites can be catapulted to new levels of commitment by the outsized reactions their activism calls forth. When the sweetheart of Sigma Chi is tailed by campus security, a radical is born. She's a formidable addition to our ranks, proving that the service economy's enclosure of "people skills" can be imitated for less commercial purposes. The university is, among other things, a massive and concentrated site of reproductive labor. In service industries, management appropriated as corporate cant the noble idea of "servant leadership," using it to reinterpret their position over employees as a personal virtue, not a difference in power. But the notion itself is still useful, and still needed where the New Left heritage of radical posturing and one-off confrontations still overshadows the patient work of setting up the folding chairs and hauling the pizza boxes out to the dumpster.

After UGA's largest rally in recent memory, for example, students and allies spontaneously marched to a dining hall, where hundreds chanted "Thank you! Thank you!" to cheering employees. Here the left embraced the right's fundamental organizing tenet, celebrating reproductive labor—but adding the critical caveat that it merits full remuneration and secure working conditions. Likewise, a campaign for a sliding-scale day care center at UGA collected thousands of petition signatures, and brought upwards of hundreds of staff, faculty, and students out for a rally. The group finally won the campus child care center from an all-male upper administration that had remained oblivious to its benefits for decades.

All these unlikely successes suggest there is no need to create a labor movement by building coalitions with feminists, queers, or immigrants on campuses. The real challenge is to the trailing edge of the labor left that still pines for the glory days of the burly steel-puddler or the aggrieved hard hat, that true knight of labor who got his feelings hurt when the blacks and the broads and the gays all started whining. It's time to kiss good-bye this shirtless icon of pale male identity politics and instead recognize that those insurgent liberation movements *are themselves the labor movement.*

And they are already on campus. The recent economic crisis and a generation of cuts to financial aid have narrowed the artificial distinction between "students" and "workers." If they're lucky, the students are already working—and experiencing wage theft; surveillance; labor segmentation by race, sex, and citizenship status; on-the-job harassment; and all the routine insults to dignity that come with low-wage, high-stress, insecure employment. Moreover, they are less certain that their diplomas are a sure ticket out of their McJobs, especially given the debt burden many carry upon graduation. These recession-era students worry more about the conditions of service work than did their upwardly mobile predecessors. Furthermore, as has long been true, many of the students called to living wage campaigns and anti-sweatshop movements come from working-class or religious backgrounds, or both. UGA's activists have included the children of carpet factory operatives, janitors, out-of-work underwriters, and undocumented immigrants. They have worked alongside feminist Christians, sorority sisters, the reigning Miss Thomasville, and the queer exodus from the ranks of pro-life activists and megachurches. Their various forms of bicultural dexterity render them stunningly effective in multiple settings, and they know that Robin Kelley and Lisa Duggan can kick Ayn Rand's ass.

When black, brown, and white women control resources and set the agenda, the groundwork for change gets built even in the stony soil of the Old Confederacy. Meeting, greeting, eating, listening, and forging collectivities precede confrontations with powerful elites. And the transformed culture elevates everyone. Even a classic "boys-of-the-left" action like taking over the administration building follows a new script: the occupiers hand out apologies and homemade muffins to the hourly employees whose work they are disrupting, and male activists pick up after the marchers, because they understand that the tool of labor heroism is not a bullhorn but a broom.

When the labor left embraces the right's glorification of service, when it fights back against the neoliberal university, and when it speaks of economic justice as a moral imperative, miracles can happen even in the land of Jim, Jane, and Juan Crow. Labor's dynamism today comes from sectors like janitorial work, health care, and public employment, service arenas in which men and women of color, immigrants, and white women predominate. The campus—simultaneously a public service workplace, a repository of student talent, and the right's own favored training ground—is full of lessons for America's labor future. The movement is not just *about* reproductive labor; the movement *is* reproductive labor.

REIMAGINING A MULTICULTURAL LABOR MOVEMENT THROUGH EDUCATION

Daniel Katz

"¡Sí se puede!" ("Yes we can!") thousands of immigrants and their supporters roared as they marched down Broadway and crossed Canal Street on May 1, 2006. Flags of every Latin American country, including Puerto Rico, waved in the wind interspersed with American flags and signs proclaiming "We are America." It was perhaps the largest workers' demonstration in American history. Watching from the sidewalk were the electrical union apprentices in my undergraduate U.S. history class, whom I insisted attend with me. They didn't have to participate, I told them, but they had to observe, and try to understand what these images and proclamations meant. Indeed, only a few joined me to wade into the crowds and strike up conversations.

For six years, I taught construction worker apprentices in a program at Empire State College in New York City. Most attended as a requirement of their apprenticeship and, for good reasons, most were pessimistic about their long-term prospects. Over the last decade or so, there has been a steady decline in construction industry union-density even in New York, the most union-populated city in the highest union density state in the country. The International Brotherhood of Electrical Workers (IBEW), one of the most powerful and politically influential unions in the state, now represents around 50 percent of workers in the city's industry, down from 90 percent in the 1990s. Most journeymen (including a handful of women) work only half the year if they work at all. Residential construction, mostly in the outer boroughs, is now dominated by nonunion contractors often employing undocumented workers or even union members moonlighting in nonunion jobs. Union members are frustrated by economic and political developments that are beyond their control: a stagnant construction industry that can provide only periodic work; changing technologies like computerization and prefabrication that take more work off the job site or offshore; and challenges to long-established firms—where union members once could count on spending a career working—from small fly-by-night companies hiring transient workers. Many of my students felt greater affinity and affection toward their employers than their union, which an increasing number regarded as a bureaucratic layer of management. In any case, they saw the union as impotent and its decline inevitable.

When I asked my students whom they blamed, their overwhelming answer was "They are taking our jobs." I pressed them with more questions: Who are they and who are we? Why do you believe this? What are your main sources of information? My students, their answers revealed, lived in an information landscape dominated by conservatively charged sources like the *New York Post*, Howard Stern, and Fox News, reinforced informally by family members and the culture on the job. Many of my students argued that illegal immigrants— often "Mexicans"—were coming to take their jobs away. "We" were deserving American citizens. "They" were foreigners who did not belong and perhaps should even have been imprisoned and deported.

In response to this anti-immigrant attitude, I offered an immigration history elective, which I designed to give a historical context to the perceived conflict in the construction industry between legal and illegal workers. I tried to show that politicians and employers used the issue of immigration to distract workers from demanding structural changes in the political economy. I also began to revise my curriculum in American and labor history courses to further emphasize the enormous contributions of immigrants to the American labor movement and how anti-immigrant, antiunion, and racist ideologies were often intertwined. This was a delicate dance as my students' anti-immigrant expressions were not strictly or obviously racist. A growing number of apprentices are legal immigrants from the Caribbean, Latin America, and East Asia, and many white and nonwhite apprentices alike insisted (and I believed them) that they did not think about illegal immigration in racial terms.

I tried to teach my building trades worker-students that a study of historical and contemporary immigration policies reveals how restriction has been an instrument of the modern state to determine which racial and ethnic groups are more deserving as citizens. Anti-immigration politics have been used to divide workers, first in the 1880s restricting Chinese immigration, and in the 1920s restricting Jewish and Italian immigration, among others. In recent decades it has been used to create an underclass of vulnerable Latin Americans and, increasingly, Africans and Asians. For many employers, there is good reason to keep their undocumented workers underpaid, scared, and in conflict with workers who are legally working in the country. So while the Obama administration has deported as many as one million undocumented immigrants, there is neither political will nor economic incentive for politicians and employers to actually deport all of the 11 million undocumented aliens living in the United States. Ubiquitous, terrorizing, but incomplete deportation raids are all the better to keep the labor movement divided and weak.

In the end, I have no evidence that more than a handful of my students were swayed by my historical argument. Among the students I took to the historic "Day Without an Immigrant" May Day march in 2006, only a handful admitted to being inspired by witnessing a group of workers fighting back against terrible odds. What they heard—from the popular media they consume to complaints from coworkers—and what they did not hear from their unions confirmed the beliefs that the fragility of the economy, the frailty of their unions, and the fecklessness of the politicians their unions support were constants. The only variable they imagined could or should be changed was the presence of illegal immigrants. And most doubted anything would be done. This fatalism is not unique to construction workers, which makes them as good a group as any to keep in mind when asking: What is the answer to their despair? How can we rebuild a labor movement that will combat the debilitating and divisive anti-immigrant and xenophobic messages that seemed to hold sway over my students?

AN EARLIER PERIOD OF DESPAIR

For answers to these questions, I look to models of success during a similar period of xenophobia, racism, and union decline. In the

1920s and 1930s, the Jewish-led International Ladies' Garment Workers' Union (ILGWU) successfully built one of the most powerful and
influential unions of the mid-twentieth century by promoting multiculturalism through labor education. It did not act alone. The union
joined in a mutually supporting network of autonomous institutions
sharing like-minded aims as well as memberships, listenerships, and
readerships. The ILGWU and its sister organizations promoted education as a means to build social relationships and transmitted their
messages about social justice and multiculturalism through every
media and in every available venue. Even as mainstream unions, popular culture, and mass media dismissed, derided, or vilified blacks,
Italians, and other immigrants, these union activists reached out to
black leaders and institutions, and even to workers originally hired to
cross their picket lines. In doing so, the movement reinforced its commitments to racial-ethnic inclusion and built a loyal corps of rank-
and-file union leaders.

The entire American labor movement was in rapid retreat
throughout the 1920s. After a decade of dramatic labor gains in the
1910s, American manufacturers and politicians laid siege to the most
militant and radical elements of the labor and socialist movements.
The Red Scare that followed the Russian Revolution and the postwar strike wave of 1919 forced socialist politicians out of office, communists underground, and thousands of suspected radical activists
out of the country in mass deportations. During the retrenchment of
the 1920s, American nationalism was underpinned by, and in turn
supported, linked concepts of anti-immigration, antiunionism, and
white supremacy. Congress passed immigration restriction legislation. Employers adopted the American Plan to keep out or crush the
union presence in major industries. The Ku Klux Klan rose again as
part of a racist backlash against immigrants and blacks who migrated
into Southern cities and out of the South into Northern and Western cities. Sacco and Vanzetti stood as a symbol of politically radical
immigrant contagions to be controlled and, if necessary, eliminated.
Most unions, especially those dominated by skilled white men, refused to acknowledge the rights of black workers especially to join

their union. Some allowed for separate Negro locals and accepted a caste system in which blacks earned less. At the end of the decade, the Great Depression left millions of people jobless, exacerbating the fear and hatred that divided workers and weakened the labor movement.

Against these social, political, and economic forces, the Jewish labor and socialist movements survived the 1920s and enjoyed brilliant success in the 1930s. When workers responded in unprecedented numbers to strike calls in the 1930s, the ranks of radical and militant unions swelled. Leftists were situated to seize on opportunities to stabilize their unions and retain newly joined members because of several factors. First, Jewish leftists shared a worldview that understood anti-Semitism, nativism, American nationalism, and racism as interdependent, and they opposed all four. Second, throughout the 1920s, even as union membership declined and the left was in general retreat, socialists, like Communists and other smaller left groups, founded and reinforced a plethora of sustaining organizations. These unions, summer camps, theaters, benevolent societies, and schools offered alternative visions for the future. Third, they also invested in newspapers and radio stations that amplified the voices of labor and socialist leaders, providing a counter-narrative to mainstream education and media.

These three factors also affected the way Jewish socialists treated black workers especially. Unlike most AFL unions that excluded black workers, Jewish unions affiliated with Communist and socialist parties competed with one another for the attentions and loyalties of black and other minority workers. This was especially remarkable because manufacturers often hired blacks as strikebreakers or simply to divide the workforce in the hopes of breaking the union. Drawing from a common tradition of Yiddish socialism and a revolutionary worldview among Jews in the Russian Empire and world diaspora, Communists and socialists appealed to workers' racial-ethnic cultures through a broad strategy of educational programs. Perhaps the most successful union to do so, the ILGWU was one of the largest and most important institutions on the Jewish left before World War II.

A MULTICULTURAL WORLDVIEW

Key ILGWU leaders from the 1910s to the 1930s developed their political and cultural consciousness in the multiethnic revolutionary
movements of the Russian Empire. The Russian Empire supported
a brutal system of capitalism in which starving workers labored endless hours in filthy and dangerous conditions for little money. The
czarist state suppressed unions and other democratic institutions as
it subordinated all ethnic minority cultures to the dominant Russian
language and Orthodox Christianity. Gymnasium and university
education, the singular path to the professions and middle classes,
strictly enforced the Russian cultural domination. So the fight to establish unions and confront the ravages of unregulated capitalism
was linked to the celebration of ethnic identity and education.

At the end of the nineteenth century, Jews constructed an ideology of Yiddish socialism that rooted their revolutionary politics
in their ethnic culture and encouraged comrades from other ethnic
groups to do the same. Fannia Cohn, to take one example, had been
a member of the Socialist Revolutionary Party in Russia from 1901
until she emigrated to the United States in 1904. In New York, she
developed broad educational, cultural, and social programs that reinforced the multicultural and social justice messages at the heart
of her worldview. Cohn was the leading architect of education in the
ILGWU and began designing programs to integrate Jewish and Italian members in the 1910s.

During the 1920s, as the ILGWU declined precipitously, she
and others nevertheless continued to reach out in creative ways to
all workers, especially black workers. In 1927, she produced a musi-
cal pageant based on Walt Whitman's poem "The Mystic Trumpeter"
at Unity House, the union's retreat. The show included 150 actors,
dancers, and chorus members and was meant to convey "a social message to suffering humanity." The cast members were mainly ILGWU
members but also members of the Workmen's Circle fraternal society, the Brookwood Labor College (led by the Dutch Reform minister
A.J. Muste), and several other unions—including the Brotherhood
of Sleeping Car Porters (BSCP). The latter's inclusion meant 2,500

spectators witnessed black porters perform on stage alongside white ILGWU members. As at many union educational events, a social dance followed the program, including all members and guests. The interracial dance violated some of the most virulent taboos of white supremacy, underscoring the union's bold dedication to building a multicultural movement.

In both Jewish and mainstream labor journals, Cohn explained the importance of the whole range of educational programs, including theater, social, and recreational programs. "It is our aim to cultivate in our members an appreciation of beauty and art which tends so much to increase the enjoyment of life, and, at the same time, to awaken the will to despise the dirty tenements, oppose unsanitary conditions in their shops and abolish slums," she wrote. Formal classes, she argued, taught workers not only methods of organizing in their industry but also economic principles, politics, and the impact of major social forces. She emphasized that these classes addressed the history of struggles by workers from diverse backgrounds. "They heard how other workers, members of other races, speaking other languages, also struggled for many years . . . [and] succeeded finally in winning the improved conditions which prevail today, and in raising society to a higher level."

ILGWU officers like Cohn became important ambassadors from the ILGWU to other unions and organizations trying to organize black workers. In late 1927, together with local and international union leaders, Cohn founded the Trade Union Committee to Aid the Pullman Porters Union to raise money for the BSCP and lobby the American Federation of Labor to accept affiliation of the black union. Cohn also represented the ILGWU at conferences of the BSCP and joined the Urban League as a representative of the ILGWU in 1928. In return, A. Philip Randolph and other BSCP union dignitaries frequently spoke at ILGWU meetings and conventions. Randolph sat on the boards of a number of important institutions dominated by Jewish socialists, including WEVD, the radio station launched in October 1927 in honor of Eugene V. Debs. Radio, the new media of its day, was a powerful vehicle to communicate with existing and potential union members. Alongside newspapers like the Yiddish-language, socialist *Jewish Daily Forward*, WEVD allowed unions to broadcast a wide range of programs, from organizing and strike appeals in a variety of languages to music and other cultural shows aimed at specific ethnic constituencies.

BUILDING A MULTICULTURAL UNION

The Depression hit the ILGWU hard. The union, which had over one hundred thousand members in the beginning of the 1920s, was on the verge of bankruptcy by 1933, with only a portion of the forty thousand remaining members employed and paying dues. For those lucky enough to find employment, long hours, low pay, and dangerous conditions had returned to the garment industry. On August 16, 1933, the dressmakers in New York's garment industry went out on strike despite, or perhaps because of, the dire condition of the ILGWU. Sixty thousand dressmakers walked off their jobs and flooded union halls throughout the city, far beyond the most optimistic expectations of union leaders. By September, the ILGWU had grown fivefold to over two hundred thousand members—nearly twice the number of members at the height of the union's power in the early 1920s. The union membership, roughly 75 percent women, encompassed a greater diversity of cultures than ever before. In addition to the Jewish and Italian workers who made up the majority of the membership, the Jewish-led union organized over four thousand black and over three thousand Spanish-speaking workers, many of whom had never before been union members.

The extraordinary victory in New York was fragile, and union officials at all levels recognized the immediate concerns presented by the abrupt expansion of the ILGWU. Leaders confronted the challenges of rebuilding the union's infrastructure and inculcating union principles before the newcomers drifted away from the organization. First-time union members had to learn how unions organized and then to formulate and articulate their demands. They had to learn how to exercise the power of an organized workforce to win everything from pay raises and shorter hours to safer work conditions and a more reasonable work pace, then they had to establish systems to enforce concessions won from employers. Hundreds of union members had to be trained as shop-floor leaders who could represent coworkers in grievances, monitor contracts, and lead workers out on strike when necessary. Some had to learn English, and many needed to become public speakers. As leaders, they would have to rally coworkers to action, even though some of them had never taken such actions before. Most important, workers from many different racial-ethnic cultures had to learn to trust one another.

Within weeks of the dressmakers' unprecedented victory, Cohn urged leaders to meet the union's challenges by embracing an expanded program of educational activities that she had pioneered and nurtured over the previous twenty years. Cohn defined education expansively to envelop the many complex facets of workers' lives. She predicated the design of union education on the assumption that workers and their families needed structured programs and the space to explore and develop new ideas about class, race, and society. This view trusted that workers, if given enough opportunities, would naturally create lasting bonds among themselves, treating racial and ethnic diversity as a strength rather than a divisive barrier. Cohn and the union leaders and activists who embraced this assumption developed programs for political, social, and multicultural education.

In the most ambitious local education program in the ILGWU, the New York Dressmakers Local 22 established eight education centers in neighborhoods around the city and gave special attention to programs aimed at the thousands of black and Spanish-speaking workers who had recently joined the ILGWU. In Harlem, blacks could gather in a local union branch to make political decisions and to explore their identity as African American trade unionists through courses such as "The Negro in American History." In East Harlem, Local 22 established a parallel branch for Spanish speakers. All branches sponsored classes, choirs, orchestras, and lectures as local union leaders encouraged each major ethnic and racial group to host elaborate balls and festivals that provided opportunities to demonstrate group identity and leadership. At the same time, black and Spanish-speaking members also participated in most of the programs offered by the locals and the international union in their main centers in the midtown-Manhattan garment district.

Throughout 1934 and 1935, the union celebrated multiculturalism at social events such as dances. The ILGWU newspaper *Justice* reported that six thousand dressmakers and friends attended the Dressmakers' International Ball sponsored by the Harlem section of Local 22 on January 19, 1935. The union highlighted the parallels between the vigorous, coordinated movements of dancing and those of pickets and marches. "Over the stage hung a huge banner showing dressmakers of various races, colors and nationalities parading through the garment district with arms upraised and fists clenched, marching on to victory under the flag of the union." Just as it had in the 1920s, interracial dancing and socializing illustrated a remarkable level of intimacy and dedication to inclusion. In 1930s New York City, many dance halls, restaurants, and hotels still refused admission to black patrons. But under the auspices of the union, workers of all ethnic and racial groups mixed in union dances.

For Fannia Cohn and local union leaders who embraced these ideas, education also meant developing a class consciousness that imagined a socialist society eclipsing the misery and exploitation inherent in the capitalist system. They believed that workers needed both practical and theoretical education in militant unionism, particularly regarding shop-floor struggle. Beginning in 1934, Local 22 education director Will Herberg attracted some of the leading radical theorists of the socialist and labor movements from the Rand School of Social Science, the New School, and Columbia University, who taught economics, trade-union theory, Marxist analysis, and history to thousands of ILGWU members.

Local 22 established a central Dressmakers Educational Center at Washington Irving High School, offering advanced classes on economic, social, and trade-union subjects to those students considering whether to run for shop- and local-level offices. Because the classes were voluntary and had an open enrollment, candidates for leadership in the local were largely self-selected, though union officials urged those members whom they hoped to groom for leadership to attend classes. Local 22 manager Charles "Sasha" Zimmerman used the leadership courses to recruit minority members into the union's leadership, and black women students soon assumed higher-profile roles in the local, including several elected to the Local 22 executive board in 1934. Eldica Riley and Edith Ransom, who was elected to the paid position of business agent in 1935, both chaired important committees in the union and helped form the Negro Labor Committee, a national coalition drawn from AFL unions. Local 22 classes attracted young women interested in expanding their political roles by offering them practical skills for shop-floor leadership and local union activism. Many of the mostly women students in the Local 22 public speaking class, for example, joined the Union Defenders Committees (UDCs) that were organized to patrol shops to enforce contract provisions, especially maximum hours and restricted workdays, and to report violations by employers and complicit members. The UDCs also mobilized members for mass action.

Local unions formed athletic teams and the International organized leagues that included teams from various socialist institutions, such as the Workmen's Circle, to cultivate identification with the union and the labor movement. During periods of mobilization, Local 22 used sites of recreational activities to educate and recruit members for organizing and strike-related responsibilities. The participation of workers' families in the union's cultural activities facilitated activism and strengthened the union's bonds with members' relatives who were not employed in the garment shops. Social and recreational activities also built interracial camaraderie in the shops that opened opportunities for black and Hispanic women to be elected to office from shops in which they were minorities.

Physical activity and social bonding helped build a militant union. Members developed confidence in their own bodies through dancing and playing sports. They became strong in the company of one another and learned to cooperate. Physical athleticism helped prepare workers to join a picket and to defend the line against strikebreakers or to risk arrest. Photographic essays in educational literature consistently included physical-educational activities with images of picketing and arrests, reinforcing the integrated purposes of social, physical, and political education and underscoring Fannia Cohn's linking education with militant action.

EXERCISING MULTICULTURAL UNION POWER

The power of union education to mobilize the multicultural membership of the dressmakers' locals came into sharp relief during the contract negotiations in the winter of 1935–36. The contracts negotiated during the great upsurge in membership two years earlier were set to expire on January 1, 1936. The dress manufacturers association tried to undermine the gains won in the 1933 strike, demanding mandatory overtime, the elimination of a minimum wage, and the freedom to fire workers at will. In response, the union mobilized members and their families wherever they were involved with the union. In December 1935, the Local 22 Education Committee established a council representing twenty-seven sports, social, and cultural groups with thirty-three delegates "to meet periodically to coordinate the work and exchange experiences," bringing the classes, athletic teams, and social clubs into the political structure of the local.

Throughout January and into the middle of February 1936, *Justice* reported on the mass mobilization of the 110,000 union members employed in the New York City–area dress industry, demonstrating the integrated strategy of social and cultural programming, multiculturalism, and militant unionism. The union publicized interracial and interethnic basketball games attended by hundreds of members. The newspaper also featured a concert at Town Hall of the combined Negro, Spanish, Jewish, and Italian choruses and orchestras in the union to which hundreds more came. The Italian Dressmakers' Local 89 had already mobilized six hundred members of the Italian Union Defender's Committee. Local 22's UDC numbered one thousand members, formed at eleven neighborhood section meetings in December. Julius Hochman, as chairman of the ILGWU Joint Dress Board, called a mass meeting at the Manhattan Opera House of building chairmen and Union Defender Committee members in early January to coordinate the work of all local unions in preparation for a general strike. Five thousand members "stormed the doors" of the Opera House. Three subsequent meetings at Madison Square Garden with tens of thousands in attendance led to the settlement of contracts in February 1936, without having to strike, providing for unprecedented guarantees.

Garment workers built their union in the interwar years by reinforcing their commitment to transformative visions of society and challenging dominant values about race, immigrant cultures, and internationalism. In this respect, it was not important which of the major and minor radical parties held influence in or controlled specific institutions of the Jewish left, but that there was a common underlying sensibility shared by allies and rivals alike. Rather than isolate issues and narrowly interpret the function of the union as limited to workers at work when they were working, union visionaries saw the linkages among social, political, and economic forces in general. Specifically, they understood the critical strategy of appealing to an underclass of marginalized and unprotected black workers, and appealing to the racial-ethnic cultures of black and immigrant members and their communities.

REIMAGINING A MULTICULTURAL AND TRANSFORMATIVE LABOR MOVEMENT

Returning to my earlier questions, how could the multicultural case of the ILGWU inform a revived labor movement that would inspire my students in the building trades, give them hope, and combat the currents of xenophobia and anti-immigration? Such a movement is critical today. For one thing, there are good reasons to be optimistic about a Latino-influenced revival in American labor. Like Russian Jews a century ago, many Latino immigrants come to the United States from revolutionary and radical labor and socialist movements and a prophetic religious tradition. The Justice for Janitors campaigns in Los Angeles in the 1990s and the May Day 2006 "Day Without an Immigrant" march are two examples of the potential for Latinos to organize on a mass scale. But despite their growing numbers in U.S. unions, Latinos, especially undocumented immigrants, have been vilified and their cultures disparaged, much as other immigrants and blacks were disparaged in the 1920s. The top levels of the AFL-CIO reversed its long-standing anti-immigration policy in recent years, but continued xenophobia in the labor movement demonstrates that to embrace Latin American workers regardless of immigration status is not simply a matter of policy change. A revived union movement, like that of the early twentieth century, will require workers of different racial-ethnic groups to learn to trust one another.

The ILGWU and other Jewish unions, parties, and institutions of the left built that trust through political, social, and multicultural education. The International Brotherhood of Electrical Workers Local 3, the union to which most of my students belonged, already supports a number of ethnic clubs that members are encouraged to join. It is important to celebrate cultural diversity among union members; just as unfamiliarity breeds fear, an intimate introduction to multiple cultures breeds trust. But for that exploration to be a powerful tool to advance labor's goals, the labor movement needs to be engaged in a deeper discussion about race and ethnic cultural identity as it relates to social divisions, immigration, and global capitalism, comparable to the level of discourse in the ILGWU and throughout the left in the 1920s and 1930s.

Like those movements, a reimagined labor movement requires a broad new conversation that critically analyzes the circumstances of American and global labor in the context of the privatization of public resources, the global supply chain, free trade, American nationalism, anti-immigration, racism, and antiunionism. One union or one union's college program cannot be effective in isolation. The conversation must take place in the same kind of multiple venues that the ILGWU and other Yiddish socialists engaged: in the union offices and on the job; through the pages of their newspapers, over the radio, and in the theater and through their music; at vacation retreats and ethnic social gatherings; and among many like-minded unions.

That new movement must offer a transformative vision, support grassroots and community-based organizing, celebrate racial-ethnic cultural difference, and cultivate an ideal of democratic debate and intellectual and academic freedom within the movement. Perhaps ideas that resonated with socialism, anarchism, communism, social democracy, or liberalism of the early twentieth century will inspire new ideas today, but the new vision or visions will be twenty-first-century constructions. Like the Occupy Wall Street movement that is developing rapidly as we complete this volume, it is impossible to predict what new forms of self-government, participatory democracy, and vision of the future will emerge as the guiding principles of a new working-class movement. But emerge they must.

To be viable, that vision must also be reinforced by mutually supporting institutions, including schools, museums, summer camps, international study, community centers, theaters, old and new media outlets, and producer and consumer cooperatives. To construct such a movement requires the conscious and collaborative efforts of progressive unions, intellectuals and activists, artists and teachers, people of faith, immigration reform organizations, and international solidarity movements that are mentioned throughout the essays in this volume.

Especially, we need to rebuild an independent movement-focused media that follow the example of the ILGWU, the *Jewish Daily Forward*, and WEVD. Unions and working-class organizations need to form closer connections with and emulate shows like *Democracy Now!*, which has grown into a global network of small and local media outlets that others had dismissed. By offering her show to everyone from college radio stations and community access cable television to satellite stations, host Amy Goodman expanded her reach to nearly one thousand outlets in several countries. Eventually, mainstream PBS and NPR stations took notice and signed on, without Goodman having to moderate her content. *Democracy Now!*'s coverage of otherwise-ignored events has, in turn, forced mainstream organs to acknowledge them. The labor movement needs to draw on existing programs and encourage many, many such shows from multiple viewpoints.

Rebuilding a system of labor education that supports the architecture of a reimagined and integrated labor and working-class movement is critical. Like the ILGWU programs of the 1920s and 1930s, labor education needs to expand far beyond the narrow confines of steward training, or even workplace safety and health, to embrace a holistic inquiry into society. We need to invite an intellectual exploration throughout the liberal arts, encourage artistic expression, and promote political debate within the movement. Through labor education, activists in unions, worker centers, and community organizations should be able to forge global collaborations across national boundaries. Labor education needs also to sponsor social and recreational programming that involves family and other community members and celebrates workers' ethnic cultures. Specifically, we need to explore and rediscover the various and specific ways people have resisted oppressions and imagined a more just future. In short, we need to reimagine a labor movement in which workers and their families are enfranchised as active participants in a democratic movement through political, social, and multicultural education, open to all regardless of citizenship status.

WHAT LABOR LOOKS LIKE: FROM WISCONSIN TO CAIRO, YOUTH HOLD A MIRROR TO HISTORY OF WORKERS' STRUGGLES

Michelle Chen

Every revolution needs two essential ingredients: young people, who are willing to dream, and poor people, who have nothing to lose. Yet the social forces that make movements strong also incline them toward self-destruction. Hence, over the past few decades, uneasy intergenerational alliances have melted away as impatient young radicals bridle against the old guard of incumbent left movements. At the same time, when it comes to organizing, without patronizing, poor folks, activists continually struggle just to find the right language to talk about systemic poverty in a sanitized political arena that has largely been wrung dry of real class consciousness.

Today, of course, activists tend to speak eagerly about reaching out to "the youth," or of overcoming cultural rifts between middle-class professional organizers and the workers they seek to transform into the next vanguard. But the activism stemming from the recent economic crisis proves not only that the left could use some serious tactical upgrading and fresh blood, but also that movements cannot overturn entrenched social fault lines by sheer force of will. Like any embattled community that needs to rebuild, shepherding activism into the next generation requires that established organizers learn how to retire gracefully, that those moving onto the front lines learn how to temper urgency with patience—and that all sides recognize that there are things they don't know.

In Wisconsin in February 2011, no one knew what would happen as they gathered at the state capitol. A few picket signs, a megaphone or two, maybe a well-orchestrated sit-in until getting politely marched off by cops. But soon, the optics defied just about everyone's expectations. Middle-aged school teachers might have done a double take when they saw teenagers detour from their weekly mall trips to join the picket lines; sanitation workers who traveled to the statehouse with their union colleagues probably didn't anticipate marching alongside young Hmong community activists. The biggest surprise about turnout was the very absence of a defining image: there was no single movement or ideological agenda, no figurehead at the helm of the crowd. The only message emanating from the masses during those days was simply "No." No to a draconian piece of legislation that threatened a basic labor right that many workers had either forgotten or taken for granted, until it had been threatened with extinction.

So the slogan "This is what democracy looks like" had a ring of both pride and puzzlement: what could we divine about the "look" of democracy from this pastiche of contrasting faces, political orientations, and socioeconomic backgrounds?

After a parliamentary trick allowed the antiunion measure to slip through the legislature, the movement faced a moment of compunction: was it really about killing the bill? Or protecting unions? Or was it about the fight for the soul of the labor movement, and the question of whether Wisconsin had inaugurated a nostalgic revival or narrative of rebirth.

Technically, the protests sought to preserve the collectivebargaining rights of certain public sector unions. But many of the protesters may never have benefited from the collective-bargaining process, in large part because they were too poor, too new to the country, or above all too young to have been of a generation when unions were strong in America. They nonetheless intuitively grasped that collective bargaining represented the sovereignty of working people, principles that organized labor has historically embodied and championed.

So what does democracy look like? The answer will be defined by the young activists who are connecting with, rediscovering, and ultimately redefining labor with a capital L. Perhaps many of the youth who protested in solidarity with the Wisconsin demonstrations never grew up with any labor tradition in their families. Their parents may instead have worked low-paying service jobs or migrated from other countries without independent unions. But their introduction to the movement was through labor's historical link to broader struggles for social justice—a link that is often overlooked even by unions themselves. In Wisconsin, the idea of labor rights was presented as a counterpoint to a pattern of systematic exploitation of people and public resources: from the corporate underwriting of elections, to the distortion of school curricula by rigid testing regimes, to mounting frustration with chronic unemployment in an unmoored global economy. The new wave of labor activism had a youthful glow: rage polished by cynicism, but also galvanized by an idealism relatively unfettered by the left's historical baggage of ideological rifts, turf battles, and race and gender chauvinism. So now a reborn movement needs to cross a generation gap, which is also in many cases a culture gap, education gap, and racial gap.

Older progressive activists today stem from New Left movements that underwent a similar break with their antecedents. Many young radicals in the 1960s and 1970s repudiated the chauvinistic and parochial elements of their parents' labor movement. In his blue-collar revisionist memoir, *Striking Steel*, Jack Metzgar, who grew up as the son of a steelworker before going on to teach college, interrogated the white unionist heritage that appeared shamefully regressive in the face of the escalating antiwar and civil rights movements. Radical youth, who later became educated liberals, saw in the old-school factory workers of his father's generation an image of stiff-lipped industrial union men as "the principal perpetrators of racism, sexism and narrow-mindedness in American society. Who could remember that unions had once been more than a white male plot to keep blacks in their place? Who could remember that the Labor movement, as a social movement that made a difference, laid some of the ground work for the Civil Rights, community organizing, and women's movements?"

Fast forward to Madison, where tradition is entering a new day of reckoning: if the radical legacy of leftist unionism in the early twentieth century has waned, the public memory loss hasn't just been on the part of youth. Labor itself has suffered from collective amnesia, forsaking militancy for the softer politics of Beltway lobbying, burrowing in the tradition of "business unionism" while burying faded embers of feminist, antiracist, or anti-capitalist critiques. But there's a bolder, more vital strand of that tradition that must be rekindled in light of current struggles for social justice and human rights.

So the protests in Wisconsin (and solidarity rallies in Ohio, New York, and many other communities) blew some of the dust off of labor's "usable past" by showing young people how economic security dovetails with social justice and human rights. It's at the intersection of these struggles that a college student graduates with a lifetime of debt. Or a young single mother has to drop out of high school to work at the local big box retailer—the only place hiring in her neighborhood. Or a twelve-year-old Mixtec girl aches with longing when she sees her friends leave every morning on the school bus while she goes back to work the fields with her parents, who don't get paid until the season, and the semester, ends. Different voices harmonizing into one cry for justice, one that's often silenced by a socially tone-deaf political system.

LABOR'S FACE-LIFT

The labor movement may already belong to youth, but they don't know it yet. More than two-thirds of young people aged sixteen to thirty-four are in the workforce, but only about one in twelve belong to a union, according to the Labor Project for Working Families, a research initiative of Cornell University and UC Berkeley.

At the same time, youth unemployment edged up to a historical high of about 19 percent in mid-2010. Among black and Latino youth, the rate exceeded 30 and 20 percent, respectively. And while working young women had lower official jobless rates, unemployment among black and Latina women in their twenties more than doubled from 2007 to 2009, faring even worse than their male counterparts. Many months into our so-called recovery, countless young people in communities across the country—and many more in the impoverished Global South—are stuck on the sidelines of an economy they should be running.

Declining unionization rates are a symptom and a cause of this declining quality of life. Youth aren't naturally apathetic; there's no shortage of awareness or even anger at everyday labor issues like income inequality, lack of health care, or underemployment of highly educated workers. What's missing is brand recognition.

On a material level, it's easy to see why unions might hold limited appeal for younger workers who have no access to or desire for the kind of lifetime job security that strongly unionized sectors have traditionally enjoyed. On the other hand, a recent study by Jonathan Booth of the London School of Economics and Political Science noted that a big factor in unionization is simply the time when a worker has a chance to join a union. Enrollment generally happens when people first enter the workforce, and after a certain point opportunities for unionization tend to fall off. In the sample, older workers (aged twenty-one to forty-one) were tracked into union jobs at just about a third of the rate of their younger counterparts (aged sixteen to twenty-five), so *potential* for unionization is actually skewed toward the young end of the age spectrum. The study concludes, "younger workers are not less receptive to unions than older workers," but initial exposure to unionism, positive or negative, will shape attitudes toward the movement for years to come. From an organizer's standpoint, the takeaway is that you never get a second chance to make a first impression.

Even if they haven't been impressed by the labor movement, in an age of twenty-four-hour news and social media, young workers should be more aware than ever of the value of their contribution to the economy and their collective experience everyday in the cubicle, training center, or unemployment office. Their lives, grievances, and anxieties are constantly "shared"—in the metaphysical sense and the digital sense—by legions of peers. So they know that they're not the only ones dealing with unfair wages, tumbling from one part-time or temp gig to another, watching the value of their hard-earned degree erode as they e-mail job applications in their parents' basement. Then there is the psychological tax of having to live on credit, deprived of the chief source of wealth in the postwar era, real estate. Meanwhile, their parents' generation, once buoyed by the promise of intergenerational mobility, is entering retirement unable to chart either their children's economic destiny or their own as they age out of the workforce.

Some commentators have questioned whether the new normal is a shift in the time frame of life, as young people delay financial planning, marriage, and other major life decisions. Don Peck predicted in a seminal 2010 *Atlantic* article, "this era of high joblessness will likely change the life course and character of a generation of young adults—and quite possibly those of the children behind them as well. . . . It may already be plunging many inner cities into a kind of despair and dysfunction not seen for decades. Ultimately, it is likely to warp our politics, our culture, and the character of our society for years."

But such apocalyptic forecasts suggest the younger generation is somehow doomed. But in reality, boomers were slapped with the same dire predictions, and they generally survived, even achieved middle-class respectability. There are also indications that kids today are a *positive* exception to the generational boom-bust cycles. If globalization is potent enough to disrupt traditional pathways to upward mobility, doesn't it also have the potential to blaze new social systems—horizontal rather than hierarchical, dynamic rather than bureaucratic—that can guide us toward different kinds of wealth and fulfillment?

It may be true that younger Americans—historically lacking the class consciousness that is more ingrained in popular culture in Europe—tend to define themselves outside of class paradigms. But this isn't so much a reflection of a "loss of class consciousness" as it is a displacement of class politics by other movements and forms of identity. While "identity politics" has become a pejorative shorthand for "frivolity" among older liberals and conservatives alike, the very fact that there are still relatively few arenas for serious discussion on race, sexual and gender identity, immigration status, and other cultural fault lines shows how little space young people today have for grappling with these tensions. The way people frame problems of young versus old, rich versus poor, religious versus secular might in fact obscure more complex divisions in society for which "mainstream" political discourse has yet to develop a vocabulary. Today's haves and have-nots don't conceive of assets and power only in socioeconomic terms—not in a world where culture, sexuality, taste, language, and immigration status all mediate one's social standing.

If mainstream commercial culture militates against "class" as a common identifier, this is not simply a matter of materialism; it has much to do with the fact that many are entering the workforce from wildly different places in life, diverse in cultural background, tastes, and political consciousness. This is the cultural arena in which the labor movement must compete for shortened attention spans. On the other hand, many organizers tend to exploit young people as tokens to score hipness points for middle-aged organizations or they ignore them as inexperienced and uncommitted. Youth respond with corresponding enthusiasm or disengagement, for it's easy to tell when one's role in a movement is being taken for granted.

The events of September 11, 2001, were for many a catalyst that rejiggered our worldviews; suddenly we were situated in a much bigger world, full of people on whose misery our relative prosperity was fundamentally contingent. Ten years on, young people are still rising to the challenge, and occasionally slipping back into apathy or disillusionment. While the labor movement could easily let the zeitgeist slip away, public opinion suggests that 2011 could mark a paradigm shift in labor if it can articulate a message that resonates with young people's aspirations as individuals and as members of a broader social mobilization, one that is hungry for new blood in the ranks of nonprofit organizations, fresh ideas for campaigns, ingenuity in media production and network building, and a wholesale rethinking of what it means to organize in an increasingly messy political landscape.

But rethinking involves revisiting the past, too. The movements of the civil rights and Vietnam War eras handed down templates for organizing and direct action. They established a language for debating power, challenging traditional intellectual and economic hierarchies, and linking "third world" issues with U.S. economic imperialism and militarism. That's a usable past that can cast today's hardships in a global as well as historical light.

And the conflicts among activists today echo the social and economic divisions that drove past meltdowns within leftist movements. There is a broad underclass of youth who don't tweet, won't ever go to college, and might drop out of the workforce altogether because they see their job prospects as hopeless. If the labor movement lacks mass appeal among youth with enough time and energy to devote to a movement, it lacks currency among the truly destitute youth who have trouble even envisioning a future: kids who've grown up in high-poverty neighborhoods where opportunities for economic advancement are scarce, the school system devalues young minds, and children are afraid to hope. Racially charged criminal justice policies push many to cycle in and out of courts and prisons before they ever have a chance to land a steady job.

These kids are alienated from the unions that have fixated on saving "mainstream" workers and keeping the blue-collar "middle class" from slipping down the income ladder. These communities may have advocacy groups, churches, and other organizations that will stand up for their interests, but labor, as both a movement and a civic institution, is losing a generation of youth who desperately need a platform of economic enfranchisement outside of the school and economic and government agencies that have failed them.

FROM WISCONSIN TO KINGSBRIDGE

The showdown in Wisconsin offered a glimpse of what youth-labor solidarity could look like. But it's not always easy to mesh old-school labor sensibilities with the pluralism of a more freewheeling activist scene that stresses spontaneity and regeneration.

In the North Bronx, a campaign for economic equity brought together labor struggles and youth issues in unprecedented ways, but also exposed uncomfortable fault lines. In 2009 and 2010, the working-class community surrounding the Kingsbridge Armory was divided over a development plan for the site—a massive landmark structure that real estate developers, city officials, and neighborhood groups had all hoped to turn into a commercial and recreational hub. Eventually, a plan to transform the citadel-like space into a shopping mall emerged, backed with promises of new jobs for the neighborhood. Grassroots activists wanted more than just jobs, though; they seized on the armory as a battleground for a living wage campaign, pressing council members and developers to move forward with development on the condition that it would enable local people to earn enough to support families and provide resources for enriching local youth.

The Kingsbridge Armory Redevelopment Alliance, under the guidance of progressive local leaders, the Retail Workers Union, and the watchdog group Good Jobs New York, gave voice to community groups who envisioned a space where labor rights and youth rights were mutually respected. Early on in the planning process, community advocates called for a development plan that incorporated spaces and facilities for local schools. This campaign then evolved under the leadership of community groups such as the Northwest Bronx Community and Clergy Coalition into a broader agenda of an inclusive, democratic planning process. At the crux of their campaign was a call for decent wages and working conditions, rather than the dead-end retail jobs that many low-income young people have to take to scrape by.

But the grassroots coalition was at odds with the local building trades union, which supported developers' interests in rushing forward with the construction, hoping to generate short-term union jobs. The tension between these interests elucidated some of the fundamental rifts that thread through many low-income urban communities. The community's long-term interest in the project was apparently not a priority for the leadership of the building trades, who could wield their union clout to bargain over working conditions outside of the community arena, and could rely on union-supported jobs as long as the ground was being broken.

The battle over the armory continues. Although the initial plans fell through—prompting some criticism that the untenable demands of activists had left the community with no development at all—the neighborhood won a more enduring victory: the architecture of a new community alliance that drew from a broad cross section of the impacted area, from clergy to teachers, and even some progressive labor groups who pursued a more holistic, inclusive vision of economic development.

KINGSBRIDGE TO CAIRO

When fresh pizzas arrived at the Wisconsin statehouse courtesy of Egypt, there was more than culinary diplomacy at work. On the other side of the planet, a parallel convergence of labor and youth had inspired the overthrow of a dictator. Providing a hot meal to kindred spirits in Madison was just another way of nourishing the solidarity that the Arab Spring had seeded.

The protests in Wisconsin are not comparable to the Egyptian and Tunisian revolutions in scope or political valence. Still, the parallel images—protesters camped out in Tahrir Square and occupying the lobby of Midwest statehouse—are more than a cute diptych for your tumblr. They reflect a global youth crisis, as millions come of age in an unsustainable labor market.

Activists will argue for generations to come on whether or when capitalism is due for a complete collapse. But the fact is that the demographics of the global unemployment line are more troubling than ever today. Around the world, the International Labor Organization reported in 2010 that some 80 million youth were officially jobless— and the global youth unemployment rate the International Trade Union Confederation calls a "social time-bomb." That statistic also obscures the rates of employment in marginal and "underground" industries such as domestic and agricultural labor or work in the sex industries. The trend has prompted labor organizations around the world—who typically push a more ambitious political agenda than U.S. unions dare to—to call on governments across the industrialized world to invest more in the social safety net, establish more progressive tax policies to reduce income inequality, and revamp workforce training and job development programs to link youth to meaningful work.

But the struggle doesn't end with labor-friendly government policies. A robust independent labor movement is critical to the empowerment of the next generation of workers, who will be the chief negotiators of a more just social contract. Contrary to the arguments of corporate lobbyists, it is the low rates of unionization in the U.S.

workforce that erodes labor conditions and puts American workers at a disadvantage in the global economic recovery.

While the economy globalizes, labor must follow suit. With more women and immigrants moving into the workforce, rendering it less white and male than ever, preserving the labor movement for future generations demands we recognize that it will never be the same. The good news is that countless young workers have grown up with this reality and can work within it to effect change, in the workplace, in the public square, even in the statehouse.

According to the Labor Project's report, innovative ideas for organizing youth originate, not surprisingly, with youth themselves. Communications tools like social media may be key to the mass-scale and spontaneous organizing and "rebranding" of unions and worker centers. But more importantly, there are concrete investments to be made in young people as workers, future parents, and global citizens. During the New Deal and Great Society eras, the federal government established a network of workforce development resources, from summer youth employment programs to public works jobs, in response to economic crisis. Public schools were once seen as the seedbed of innovation and intellectual progress, not a boondoggle that "wastes" taxpayer funds on the children of the poor.

This new movement does not come with an instruction manual. But perhaps the main concept to keep in mind is that those who seek to shape a new labor-youth alliance need to get used to being uncomfortable and, indeed, making themselves leave the comfort zones into which many had sunk as they grew accustomed to being permanently relegated to the political margins. Not that conflict is always a virtue: the past century of labor movements in America suggests that indulgent internal antagonism can be about as damaging as consensus for the sake of consensus. But if all sides are genuinely seeking common ground, then honest dialogue is a good place to begin choosing worthy battles.

For the most part, there may be more battles on which we can agree than intractable conflict among us. We recognize social investments that can draw community-wide support: good public schools, fair opportunities for jobs and housing, and an environment we're not afraid to let our children play in. And we recognize the need for both empathy and mutual respect between communities, acknowledging the integrity of differences without letting them turn into insurmountable barriers to solidarity.

Citizenship, locally and globally, demands from each of us an understanding of the importance of collective bargaining and union power, of the right to be free from exploitation and abuse, and of the ways in which global capitalism pits workers against each other across borders, between public and private sectors, between distinctions of "legal" and "illegal" labor. Those currently heading unions and other labor-oriented organizations need to engage youth in a discussion on how the movement can, or should, serve their needs and aspirations. The right people together in a conversation—in a church basement, at the next parent-teacher meeting, or on a Twitter feed—is sometimes all that's needed to catalyze the creativity that shared hardship can unlock. To understand this is the very definition of being young.

BRINGING THE ORGANIZING TRADITION HOME: CAMPUS-LABOR-COMMUNITY PARTNERSHIPS FOR REGIONAL POWER

Nancy MacLean

Let's face it: the old strategies are not up to the scale of the challenge we face. It hurts to recall now the euphoria induced back in 2008 by the slam-dunk "refudiation" of George Bush and election of Barack Obama. It appeared that having worked so hard to defeat the right and elect a former community organizer, labor and social justice activists would finally see progress on our issues after the long conservative regression. And we did, in some areas—especially those outside the klieg lights, such as the staffing and mission integrity of the Department of Labor. But on the terrain-shaping questions of political economy and skyrocketing inequality, the most progressive president possible in today's circumstances has proven unable to deliver. While certainly better than the Republican Party, the Democratic Party at the national level has shown that it is captive to the financial industry and corporate perspectives, captivity that will only worsen as the Supreme Court's *Citizens United* decision opens the spigots of campaign finance. Moreover, one lesson of the death of the Employee Free Choice Act—in which unions and their allies invested so much— is that labor lacks the power to move its national legislative agenda in the face of this extreme corporate power because its own base is so geographically skewed. With a majority of union members confined to six states, very few members of Congress feel accountable to labor.

Any strategy to turn the tide therefore must have a plan to break out of this regional ghetto and rebuild power from the ground up over several decades, much as conservatives did in their era of marginality. They expected fifty years or more; with more popular ideas that advance the interests of the majority (if far less money) we ought to plan for at least twenty-five. As in the Gilded Age, business dominance of national and state government nearly rules out big victories now at those levels. But municipalities and regions are a different story: they are serving as incubators of economic justice initiatives that could spread when changes in the balance of power open broader vistas. In such a long-term, power-building perspective, pro-labor college faculty can play vital roles in the "off" time from teaching and research that we get to devote to active citizenship. Although I will use "we" for the target audience of this piece, faculty and graduate students, I hope that readers in the labor, community organizing, religious, and foundation worlds will also find useful ideas here and reach the other way: for campus partners for their efforts at regional transformation.

The scholarship on where union organizing and economic justice have made headway in the current hostile political economy signals the need for such a multi-constituency strategy. This work demonstrates that labor's failures and successes alike in the last few decades have come from combining intensive rank-and-file organizing with a research-derived corporate campaign strategy and developing community allies for labor, allies who can make a persuasive case for worker justice and bring their power to bear on its behalf. But there's an odd omission in the literature: as the authors inventory potential community partners such as clergy, community organizations, civil rights and immigrant rights groups, political clubs, and consumers, they almost never mention campuses. Even when produced by academics, the authors often overlook their own workplaces. Yet think of the possibilities: students and faculty have at their disposal so much that could enhance the labor-community partnerships we all want to see. Generation after generation of college students has infused hope and untold energy into social movements, from the labor struggles of the 1930s through the civil rights and feminist struggles of the sixties, the environmental movement and the Obama campaign, and the 2011 fights to advance democracy in the Middle East and defend public sector unions in the United States. And lately students have leveraged their home-turf power to help workers in exciting ways: the campus anti-sweatshop movement, the Taco Bell boycotts in solidarity with the Coalition of Immokalee Workers, and campaigns for living wages for campus workers.

Yet faculty, too, can assist the movement with our own distinctive resources. Even folks at the most budget-hacked public institutions could provide speaking and writing talent, research skills, as well as access to library resources, work-study employees, interns, and venues for community forums—to say nothing of public authority when they take a stand related to their expertise. Better-endowed institutions have public policy institutes that could carry out research projects for such partnerships, centers for civic engagement to sponsor student involvement with worker organizations, and offices of media relations to place labor-friendly research in the news and op-eds in the regional and national press. Faculty can also partner with student organizations, as many have for years, to host talks by activist leaders and provide honoraria to help sustain their work. But perhaps most important, faculty can bring the organizing tradition home: we can become self-conscious organizers of our progressive peers as allies of labor. The organizing tradition, as Charles Payne has termed it, puts emphasis on the cultivation of leadership capacity in others and on assisting those thus developed to identify and recruit others in their networks to the struggle, with priority put on long-term collective relationship building for power rather than single-issue campaigns that disperse after victory or defeat. A commitment of even five hours a month from campus-based readers of this piece to reach out to promising peers in this way could materially boost the power of low-wage workers to win better wages and conditions and move a pro-labor policy agenda. If enough of us made this modest pledge, we could help bring about the better future we so desperately want and need.

In this piece, I'll try to explain how. The model presented here for campus-based organizing grew organically from a decade of trial, error, deepening friendship, and ultimately high-impact work among a group of Chicago faculty with a base in the Chicago Center for Working-Class Studies. The argument is simple. But it will entail a radical shift in the way most of us approach work with labor. Faculty and students who believe in economic justice need to stop thinking like individual volunteers and start thinking like organizers. It's a challenging conceptual shift, I know from personal experience: indeed, this piece could be read as a conversion narrative of seeing the light after years of groping in the dark. In some cases, it may even mean continuing to do the same work, but with new emphasis on the relationship-building, leadership-development aspects of it. With such an organizing perspective we can build campus-based communities over the next two decades that make a significant contribution to the building of a vibrant economic justice movement able to change national conversation and policy. Starting small and close to home, we can generate the capacity to make big changes, as this piece will show.

The labor centers that do policy research and development, such as the flagship centers of the University of California system and faculty participation in labor-led "think and act" tanks like the Los Angeles Alliance for a New Economy (LAANE), provide us with a model of faculty and students bringing their research skills and resources to partnerships with visionary labor activists. However, at the moment, campuses themselves are all but ignored as sites of *organizing* potential. There are historic reasons why campuses might be slighted in unions' quest for allies that go back to the devastating sixties-era split between the AFL-CIO officialdom and the antiwar and black freedom movements. Yet that wound has largely healed as all parties have come to see how they contributed to the estrangement and as former student activists such as John Wilhelm and several of the vice presidents of UNITE HERE have distinguished themselves as progressive union leaders. Today, I think what keeps campuses invisible as sources of allies is the persistent mind-set that divides the "ivory tower" from the "real world." That leads us to leave campus as individuals when we seek to make a difference for labor. Off we go, one by one, to enlist elsewhere—away from the potentially powerful networks and resources we could bring to the work. Suppose, though, we tried a different approach, which builds on all that we know about labor's need for vocal public allies and about young people as forces for historic change. In what follows, I describe a new approach that Chicago faculty labor supporters stumbled upon through a decade of working together.

A CAMPUS-BASED STRATEGY BY WAY OF EXPERIMENT IN CHICAGO

In 2001, a group of labor supporters from varied institutions came together to create the Chicago Center for Working-Class Studies (CCWCS). Its aim was to "make class visible" by working with labor and community organizations to build local public dialogue around class issues. The group aimed to enlist far-flung knowledge and skills in a loose network with a broadly defined vision "to promote economic justice and to address class relationships." As its mission language says, "CCWCS' participants are guided by their commitment to strengthen the political, economic and moral power of working women and men, and to expand an understanding of how other identities intersect with class, including race, gender and sexuality" through "five types of activities: Cultural, Educational, Research, Community Organizing, and Union Organizing." It took a few years and some disappointing one-off projects to recognize that being a mainly faculty group need not be understood as a disadvantage. When some members who weren't campus-based quit because they saw the group as primarily academic, the critique helped us clarify the distinct resources and perspectives that faculty could bring to the local labor and community activist scene.

A good example is the most tangible product of the group: the Chicago Labor Trail map. The brainchild of labor historian Leon Fink, it enabled CCWCS to render a lasting service to the labor movement in a way that tapped faculty and student talents. The project documented the city's working-class history through a gorgeous physical map (over ten thousand copies of which are in use by unions, schools, libraries, and heritage tourists), a continuing interactive website (www .labortrail.org), and neighborhood tours led by graduate students who worked on the project, all with funding from the Illinois Humanities Council. "The Labor Trail," as the website announces, "is the product of a joint effort to showcase the many generations of working-class life and struggle in the Chicago area's rich and turbulent past . . . and [the] people—often unsung—who have made the city what it is today." In addition to creating a vibrant consciousness-raising educational tool, the project built relationships among faculty and graduate students and unionists and working-class activists through conversations between individuals and a big public unveiling celebration. As it contributed to labor and community organizations, the project convinced CCWCS participants that we could make useful contributions which were also rewarding to produce.

Another CCWCS initiative was a Young Labor and Community Organizers project we came up with in hopes of pulling these two often separated constituencies into ongoing contact while also leading our faculty group in a more activist direction. We drew a great group of about fifteen young staff from UNITE HERE, the Service Employees International Union (SEIU), and Interfaith Worker Justice's Chicago worker center, on the labor side, and from a variety of community organizing groups, on the other. But after a couple good lunchtime discussions, the busy organizers wanted to see more "value added" from us academics to make coming together worthwhile. That challenge led us to create a more lasting forum: an annual social justice job fair, which Liesl Orenic christened with the winning title "Getting Paid to Cause Trouble: Careers in Social Justice." A three-hour Saturday event held over free lunch in March or April as seniors are looking for work, it features organizers in their twenties and early thirties with eight to twelve varied Chicago labor unions and community organizations. They each talk for five minutes about how they got involved, what they do, why it matters, and what the challenges and rewards are, and then they take questions from audiences that have ranged from thirty to sixty people. At last the young organizers benefited from coming together with us: while winning a new cohort of idealistic students to social change work, they heard helpful reflections by peers from other traditions, and their organizations got a pipeline to new volunteers, interns, work-study students, and sometimes permanent staff. The social-justice-minded students who attend, for their part, finally have an alternative to the narrow business and professional school career support that their schools provide. And the faculty who organize the events (easy to do after the first time) are inspired and reenergized by the organizers and students. That something so simple to pull off could offer so much to so many keeps all parties eager to repeat the event year after year.

The young organizers' project and the Getting Paid to Cause Trouble events made it natural for UNITE HERE Local 1, whose staff had participated in both, to contact CCWCS steering committee members in May of 2006 when the union launched an ambitious comprehensive campaign linking workers' power and sophisticated industry research to determine vulnerabilities with community partnerships: Hotel Workers Rising. By coordinating hotel contract expiration dates across thirteen North American cities, the union aimed to lift standards for organized workers while leveraging these workers' power to win card-check bargaining rights for the as yet unorganized. The union reached out to potential allies with a persuasive case about how improving the wages and conditions of hotel work could achieve shared goals. Clergy joined in big numbers: some four hundred in Chicago alone signed a statement of commitment and many led delegations to the hotels. So, too, did some community organizations locally; nationally, such groups as the National Organization for Women and Parents and Friends of Lesbians and Gays got on board. Local 1's community organizer enlisted a few CCWCS members and we in turn organized colleagues into a Faculty Support Committee.

Solidarity with hotel workers was an easy connection for academics to make because we travel so often to convention hotels, because some of us share neighborhoods with hotel workers and their children, and because we understood that improving standards in place-anchored jobs that could not be shipped overseas would help lift the floor across the city. We first circulated a letter of support among faculty on our campuses. Those conversations helped us identify whom to invite for a "faculty briefing" organizing meeting at Local 1 headquarters, which twenty colleagues attended. That group became the core of a team that engaged in various activities to support the workers, who had voted to strike if necessary in proportions consistently over 90 percent across hotels. We staffed phone banks to alert convention planners and association leaders of the impending showdown and urge them to voice their concern to hotel management and move their meetings if needed. We joined delegations of clergy to hotel management. We attended a big rally where Danny Glover and John Edwards spoke alongside hotel worker activists from across North America, and later marched through the downtown hotel district with workers in a communal show of strength. And we partied with hotel workers and clergy and union staff after the big contract victory.

Truth be told, members of the Faculty Support Committee (FSC) had a blast—we built ties we would never have enjoyed otherwise and had fun working together and getting to know the workers and union staff and clergy. By backing up rank-and-file workers who were well organized on the shop floor and ready to strike, we helped convince hotel negotiators to avoid a public fight and grant unprecedented contracts—which included card-check at new hotels to enable organizing and big gains in wages and benefits, especially for housekeepers, mostly women of color and immigrants. Throughout North America, the 2006 fight was a sweeping success and the union profusely thanked community allies for their contributions to it. Other Chicago campaigns in cooperation with Local 1 followed, including support for the long-running strike against the Congress Hotel, assisting boycotts with letters and delegations, joining the fight to enact a "big box ordinance" that would require Wal-Mart and others to pay living wages, turning out voters against aldermen in hotel districts who sided with Wal-Mart, and lobbying our congressional representatives against a Gold Coast antilabor hotel that had enjoyed federal tax subsidies designed to benefit poor neighborhoods.

But the biggest-impact role for the FSC so far came about serendipitously: when some students freshly seasoned as field directors in the Obama campaign returned "home" to Northwestern and launched a living wage struggle in the fall of 2009. Now in its second year, the Northwestern Living Wage Campaign is the best-run and most vibrant student organizing I've ever encountered. It builds on the impressive labor-support work that students on campuses around the country have done in the anti-sweatshop campaigns and earlier living wage struggles at dozens of schools including, most visibly, Harvard and the University of Miami. Like those, this one taps the electrifying force of moral fraud to enlist support as universities claim to uphold the highest values, yet then hide behind the legal subterfuges of sweatshop employers by pretending that jobs outsourced to firms such as Sodexo and Aramark are beyond their control. The

Northwestern student leaders were trained in the relationship-based organizing tradition by United Farm Workers veteran Marshall Ganz and enjoyed day-to-day mentoring by a former student activist on staff at UNITE HERE, Kyle Schafer. Moreover, as a generation exposed to class, race, and gender analysis, they early on reached out to faculty in African American studies, Asian American studies, Latina/o studies, American studies, and gender studies, from which the core support has come. In the fields that emerged from the struggles of the sixties and seventies, the campaign found allies who were often younger and closer to students than faculty in traditional disciplines and who quickly understood the case for winning better conditions for subcontracted Sodexo and Aramark workers, so many of whom are women, African American, or immigrant. As the faculty pressured the administration through their channels, many students became worker organizers, committing ten to fifteen hours per week to help bring more workers into the fight and build their confidence. With the possibility of a strike looming and nearly two thousand students and faculty vigorously engaged, the Sodexo workers won a contract in September 2011 that included the largest single-step increase in wages in the union's history for the lowest-paid workers as well as new health insurance and pensions, amounting to an annual commitment of $6 million on the university's part.

Being part of the process in which once-silent campus workers found their voices to publicly share their stories and lead the fight has proved a life-changing experience for many students. Some seniors are bypassing the usual career paths to enlist in other organizing drives with UNITE HERE—and working to bring more students into the movement. What started at Northwestern spread to other Chicago campuses, moreover, including DePaul, Loyola, and Dominican. Successes there, in turn, led to organizing at other Catholic universities which proclaim a social mission, including Georgetown. All told, the Chicago experience calls to mind the advice of the legendary SNCC organizer Bob Moses: "Everything starts at your doorstep. Just get deeply involved in something. . . . You throw a stone and the ripples spread."

ADAPTING THE CAMPUS ORGANIZING MODEL TO OTHER CONTEXTS

Suppose that faculty in a half dozen other cities threw a stone; might the ripples spread? It's not hard. Just look around, identify a few promising colleagues (the kind of people you'd like to know better anyway), and have lunch one-on-one. Get in touch with the more progressive and active unions in your area and see what they're working on and how you might connect. Come up with a modest project and see where it leads, as you keep deepening these core relationships and reaching out to new partners. UNITE HERE is so confident that campuses can play a pivotal role in nurturing a new worker-led social movement that it is devoting staff to work with and help train faculty and students who want to organize. In 2011, it fielded summer programs in twenty-four cities to train student leaders in movement building and ran an institute to train students as researchers for comprehensive campaigns, and it's planning bigger programs for 2012. The union is also expanding its immigrant rights organizing and voter registration efforts, projects for which students and faculty could prove crucial partners.

Don't be too ambitious at the outset. Remember that real organizing starts small, as we know from history and from the testimony and research we have on what is working today. It begins with organizers identifying existing leaders, reaching out, listening, *hearing*, and patiently pulling them into the cause. "Organizers learn to tell a story of hope," explains the veteran teacher of organizing Marshall Ganz, "that answers the questions Why now? Why us? and, for those whom one hopes to mobilize, Why you?" Many people come intuitively to this—the ones who get called "natural leaders." But organizing skills can be learned and honed. "Ask questions," Ella Baker regularly chided the young staff of SNCC, "we've had too much of the mesmerizing type of talking." "What is needed," she explained, "is the development of people who are not interested in being leaders as much as in developing leadership in others." For those who aren't sure how to do this, UNITE HERE runs organizer training sessions that would welcome faculty supporters' participation.

If the campus model is best suited to partnership with worker-led union and community organizing, its core elements could likely work in less supportive conditions, even in right-to-work states where unions are weak. In college towns with nonexistent labor movements, new forms of organizing such as worker centers could prove the most promising partners. There are well over a hundred worker centers in operation now, more than half in the South and West. Serving, in particular, unorganized low-wage immigrant workers, often women, the worker centers use direct action, advocacy, and litigation to tame the new jungle created by the growing numbers of low-road employers. Like the settlement houses developed during the Gilded Age, they fill the vacuum created by unrestrained corporate power, a weak labor movement, and an indifferent national government. We won't know how successful such partnerships can be without unions in the mix until we try.

Another strategic partner is likely to be campus religious groups. As late as the 1980s, many students came to the labor movement via some version of socialism, but today that path carries few travelers. Student activists for economic justice are now more likely to come to the work from faith. After all, faith is the lingua franca for progressive ethics in a nation with a historically weak left and national leaders who run from the label "liberal," much less anything more radical. Today justice-seeking clergy are leading the way in developing a popular frame for why economic justice matters in a country in which some 90 percent of people believe in God. Progressive people of faith abound: the most faithful African Americans remain the likeliest Democratic voters; Catholic clergy and laity are in the forefront of the immigrant rights struggle; Jewish students and their campus rabbinical supporters are leading in some living wage fights; and, all the media attention to the likes of James Dobson notwithstanding, even many white evangelicals know that Jesus never mentioned abortion or homosexuality, but he stood with people in poverty and urged all believers to be in solidarity with them. Indeed, notes the evangelical scholar Randall Balmer, "the Bible contains something like two thousand references to the poor and the believer's responsibility for the poor." Thus, reaching out to religious students and colleagues to build a pro-labor organizing base on campus makes sense; bringing a representative of Interfaith Worker Justice, which works closely with unions, to speak could be a big help.

In time, the presence of such a local campus-community-religious pro-worker partnership might reduce the geographic isolation of the labor movement that undermines efforts at national labor law reform. If, say, food service workers were to win contracts on several campuses in some of the more promising right-to-work states, other unions might be more inclined to gamble on organizing projects that could help move state politics in more progressive directions. This is not pie in the sky. Democratic victories in 2006 and 2008 in longtime Republican-held areas have drawn foundation interest to the upper South and Southwest. The Open Society Institute, for example, has a new initiative, the Democracy and Power Fund, to support progressive organizing in North Carolina and Texas. Both the SEIU and UNITE HERE have enjoyed some success in Texas, and UNITE HERE at least plans to expand organizing in both states and Florida. "As the most conservative section of the country," note Amy Dean and David Reynolds in their survey of regional organizing, "the South is an obvious choice for strategic investment by labor and foundation circles." In short, the national political map is dynamic. Even what at first seems a very limited campus-based organizing initiative could start what such strategists call "a virtuous cycle of deepening relationships" that leads to more union and national Democratic Party investment that in turn produces public policies more conducive to organizing and economic justice.

A BOLD BUT FEASIBLE GOAL

Bringing the model of campus organizing outlined here to the support of labor-community partnerships, activist faculty could, over the next two decades, help to build a thriving network of regional laboratories of democracy, to borrow Louis Brandeis's phrase. After all, we know that labor's greatest successes in recent years, as in his time, have been geographically tethered to a select number of places where visionary labor leaders have employed a multiprong approach that enlists strong community alliances, clergy backing, and policy research and advocacy to make big gains for all. Among unions, UNITE HERE in particular has led in regional power-building initiatives that have won impressive gains for working-class communities, especially the low-income workers who need them most. In Los Angeles, San Jose, New Haven, and some other cities in recent years, savvy labor leaders such as Miguel Contreras, Amy Dean, Maria Elena Durazo, and others enlisted area resources to rebuild power for economic justice in the post–New Deal economy. They led their local unions and labor councils to develop "deep coalitions" with community partners, which produced their own visions of a local social contract in the form of "a regional policy agenda." The partners then worked together to win municipal living wage ordinances and card-check and community benefit agreements in tax-subsidized new economic development to meet needs such as more jobs, affordable housing and child care, and public transit, while also engaging in "aggressive political action" to elect progressive leaders committed to sustainable development with broadly shared benefits. "Rebuilding labor's power at the regional level," Dean and Reynolds argue persuasively (at least to those of us who remember how Gilded Age and Progressive Era regional successes influenced the New Deal), "is essential for rebuilding the progressive movement—and for rebuilding American democracy." Why not expand this model to include campuses as organizing bases to enhance it where it's already working and spread it to new sites, which in turn could contribute to state- and ultimately national-level change?

The bottom line is this: we need more faculty labor supporters to become self-conscious organizers of our peers. Faculty and students alike need to see our home turf as a vital strategic front of the real world struggle and identify potential leaders in our networks and cultivate their capacities. Together, we need to develop our own local visions of what we can do and then make it happen. And we need to prioritize long-term relationship building for worker justice over any particular issue or campaign that arises. Indeed, the model itself comes from the best of labor's traditions from the Gilded Age and Progressive Era as passed on to and developed by the community

organizing that came out of the CIO era and the civil rights and feminist movements.

The first task, then, for those who want to be part of the change is
to survey their home terrain for leaders who could be allies and cultivate relationships that build toward feasible but meaningful projects
or actions that slowly build a power base—even if they only involve
a handful of people at first. Over time, these handfuls can become
locally anchored networks that support workplace and community
organizing. The most obvious example is to assist organizing among
campus workers, such as the outsourced food service workers who
are now the focus of ongoing worker-led UNITE HERE organizing
projects in many cities. But where such campus union organizing
projects don't yet exist and in regions with weak or no unions, there
are other possible partners including immigrant worker centers, the
National Day Labor Organizing Network (NDLON), and initiatives
well suited to students such as the research and organizing projects
of the Restaurant Opportunity Centers (ROC) and the dozens of interfaith economic justice groups affiliated with Interfaith Worker Justice (IWJ).

Speaking personally, building such partnerships has been my
most rewarding activity of the last decade. Doing this is not an act
of altruism but of self-interest. You get out of isolation, befriend colleagues who share your core values and are willing to walk the walk,
learn stuff that sharpens your thinking to enhance your research and
teaching, make connections for your favorite students to find meaningful work—and sustain your spirit in the inimitable way participation in struggle does. "Stretch[ing] your perimeter" like this, as the
activist musician and independent scholar Bernice Johnson Reagon
once put it, is vital to our common future in an era in which the right
has us all in its crosshairs: unionists, people of color, feminists, immigrants, lesbians and gays, liberals, users of public services, progressive faculty—and all the multiple intersections of those identities
we share. "If you feel the strain" in your coalition building, Reagon
encouraged, "you may be doing some good work."

So what if academic readers of this piece set a goal that within five years we will have built pro-labor organizing networks on our campuses of three to fifteen faculty? That modest number could accomplish much, between establishing a pipeline for students to work with unions and worker centers, creating a supportive local intellectual infrastructure of media-honed arguments and informational resources to counter the corporate right, and helping organize for a fair regional economy. Between us, the campus-based and the faith-based allies of labor could help change the terms of discussion about labor in our communities. Although separated in recent decades, time and again in American history these natural partners have combined to dethrone the "common sense" that exploitative employers and their political allies try to promote, using straightforward arguments about right and wrong and how we all benefit from economic justice. When linked to a strategy of slow and steady organizing and relationship building with allies in a multiyear perspective, arguments that economic sustainability requires ethics can win in municipal and regional contests. They already have; the challenge is to multiply the sites. This is doable—if a critical mass of faculty in a critical mass of places around the country commits to help. And frankly, if not folks like us, people who care enough about labor to read a book like this, who else can leverage the vast resources of campuses to assist the change we all want and need?

If you agree, here are five simple things you can do to get started:

(1)   Inventory your own networks and other campuses in your area for possible allies. While you'll likely look first to the social sciences, humanities, and interdisciplinary identity-derived programs, don't neglect religious institutions and divinity schools, where often much groundwork is already in place through groups like Catholic Scholars for Social Justice and less formal efforts. When you've identified your likeliest campus allies, make a date for coffee or lunch to share stories and ideas about possibilities, perhaps beginning with a forum like "Getting Paid to Cause Trouble: Careers in Social Justice." They'll probably know others to involve.

(2) Once there are a few of you, reach out to possible organiza-
     tional partners—unions, worker centers, community orga-
     nizations, and interfaith economic justice groups—to find
     out what they're working on and how you might cooperate.
     Could one of their young organizers participate in your ca-
     reers in organizing a forum, for example, to attract interns
     and volunteers?

(3) Contact promising local student groups to see if they're will-
     ing to help with the forum or whatever the project is. In ad-
     dition to groups like the Student Labor Action Project, if an
     affiliate exists on your campus, try African American and
     Latino and women's groups, as well as Hillel, the Catholic
     student center, and any other religious groups that might get
     interested when they understand the ethical values that drive
     labor organizing.

(4) Get in touch to let others know what you are doing so that
     we can create a loose network for discussion and resource
     sharing to advance the work. The Labor and Working-Class
     History Association (LAWCHA), an organization to which
     many labor scholars already belong (and all readers of this
     book should join), is eager to support such work through its
     Labor Activism Committee and its website, www.lawcha.org

(5) If you are interested in becoming part of the Faculty-Labor
     Organizing Network that is movement building on cam-
     puses with UNITE HERE, contact me at nancy.maclean@
     duke.edu.

If Bob Moses was right in teaching would-be organizers that
"everything starts at your doorstep: you throw a stone and the ripples
spread," see what yours can lead to.

Part Two

Place Matters

American students of labor have always understood that the place of work is one of the central factors for how workers develop class consciousness and strategies to organize. Thanks to the pioneers of the New Labor History in the 1960s, there are hundreds of studies of immigrant communities, urban neighborhoods, and rural industrializing towns. Much attention has been paid, appropriately, to the transitions and transformations of people's lives as their work shifted from the farm, home, and artisan shops to the factory throughout the nineteenth century. As new places of work emerged, such as in the modern department stores and service industries which began to take shape in the early- and mid-twentieth century, scholars have noted the differences in relationship to work in those places. But recent trends in work have shifted again, and we are now watching as work and work relationships have become more diffuse. Part-time, contingent, contract, temporary, and domestic work are becoming ever more central to the new economy. The scholars collected here challenge us to understand the new workplace and new workers in ways that offer a strategy to organize and connect them to other workers. This section suggests that the physical spaces and places workers toil in are critically important for the modern labor movement, as important as it was in the age of industrialization. While many of today's workers toil in isolation, some workers have found ways to connect meaningfully that offer models for others.

Andrew Herod offers us a theoretical framework in which to place labor, paying attention to the "material geographic contexts" of where workers live, work, and travel through. Workers are affected by the space they labor in, but they also give shape or give meaning to that space. Herod reminds us that while labor organizations often need to match spatial scale with capital (often mirroring the structures of the companies they seek to unionize), labor's source of strength is often rooted in local circumstances that provide a basis for both power and authority. We must pay attention to "spatial fixes," the system whereby modern neoliberal capitalism remakes or shapes the place and geography of work in ways that advantage management over labor. Yet, as Herod notes, workers do have a certain agency to find ways to resist these fixes locally; history is full of such examples.

Eileen Boris turns our attention to nannies and home health care aides, whose place of work is other people's homes. They work in "private" settings, isolated from other workers. Yet they have been organizing. Domestic Workers United and other organizations have found ways to connect these mainly new immigrant women and have led to some reform in New York State. Boris reminds us that we need to pay attention to the new methods of organization, as well as to these new leaders and the rank-and-file culture, because they collectively offer an example for the rest of labor.

Richard Greenwald's essay looks at freelancers, those workers who move from gig to gig. His focus on the formally white-collar professions, such as graphic design and journalism, which have been reconfigured and outsourced. Understanding the economic insecurity, isolation, and slipping class status of these workers, he argues that the journalist now has much in common with the day laborer. This essay looks at how economic circumstances transform the thinking about work for these workers. It also looks at how these groups, such as the Freelancers Union, have developed promising strategies to organize these scattered workers.

PLACING LABOR

Andrew Herod

[S]*pace is a (social) product.* .... [It] serves as a tool of thought and of action. .... [I]t is also a means of control, and hence of domination, of power.

—Henri Lefebvre

The central matter upon which the essays in this collection focus is that of labor's place in contemporary society and what place it should occupy in the future. When pondering this subject, many will take it to mean, I suspect, "what is labor's situation within our broader society?" or, perhaps, "where do we locate labor in explanations of wider socioeconomic and political transformations?" or, even, "what position does labor now occupy within the political economy of present-day, postindustrial capitalism?" Interestingly, all of these key nouns or verbs—"place," "situation," "locate," "position"—are geographical terms, as is the questioning term "where." However, they are all used in such questions in rather figurative ways. By way of contrast, in this short essay I want to argue that, rather than thinking in such meta-phorical terms of labor's current place/situation/location/position within capitalism, we need also to pay attention to the material geographical contexts within which workers find themselves and over which they struggle, for place, situation, location, and position are not merely descriptive terms. They are, in fact, material conditions of workers' lives which shape their very existence and the possibility that they can create more emancipatory landscapes within which to live.

MAKING GEOGRAPHY

In *The Eighteenth Brumaire of Louis Bonaparte,* Marx famously observed that "men [sic] make their own history but not under the conditions of their own choosing." Here I want to argue that people also make their own geographies, though likewise not under the conditions of their own choosing, that the making of such geographies can be the object of intense political struggle between workers and bosses, and that such geographies, once made, play central roles in shaping the political behavior of both. The idea of "making geographies" will perhaps seem unusual to those accustomed to thinking of geography in terms of knowing the names of the state capitals or that corn comes from Nebraska but that cotton comes from Georgia. However, workers must in fact every day confront the geographical aspects of their lives. After all, they cannot be everywhere simultaneously and it takes time to physically cross the economic landscape as they move from place to place, perhaps from home to work to union office. Such geographical realities shape in dramatic ways the possibilities for workers' political practices. Indeed, the central element in workers' lives, one that comes before all others, is to ensure their own social and biological survival on a day-by-day and on a generational basis, and this requires making certain that the economic landscape is made in some ways and not in others—as a landscape of employment rather than unemployment, for instance.

The issue of how geography affects the possibilities for workers' political organizing and how workers' political organizing shapes the geography of capitalism has been extensively explored by a number of labor geographers. However, for purposes of exposition in this brief essay there are four issues upon which I want to focus. The first is that how work is arranged geographically has definite consequences for workers' organizational capacities and strategies. In particular, whether work is concentrated in space or is dispersed geographically can have implications for the types of strategies in which workers may choose to engage and how they go about developing institutional architectures of representation. For instance, the construction in the early twentieth century by the Ford Motor Company of the massive River Rouge facility, the world's largest vertically integrated factory in which all of the production process, from refining iron ore and generating electricity to assembling cars, was done in this single plant, may have provided certain economies of scale for Ford but it also provided an opportunity for the one hundred thousand or so workers who toiled in the Rouge to come together physically to talk union. Indeed, perhaps as a lesson learned from this, Ford later began spatially decentralizing its operations, building smaller plants across the United States. In fact, the reality that bringing workers together in the production process may create opportunities for them to interact has been clearly recognized by many capitalists, who have subsequently sought to break up the work process spatially so as to isolate workers geographically by locating an assembly plant here, an office there, and a components manufacturing plant somewhere else, even if it may make coordinating the firm's overall operations more challenging. Significantly, this latter geographical tactic on the part of employers may not only make it more difficult for workers in the same firm to unite but it also encourages a degree of "commodity fetishism" which may make it more difficult for consumers to choose to purchase goods from those companies which respect workers' rights and to avoid those produced by companies that do not. This is because if a product comes from a great distance away it is usually harder for consumers to know who made it and under what conditions than if it is manufactured much closer to home, a fact which can lead companies to engage in the practice of what might be called "geographical subterfuge"—they can literally try to hide in far away and isolated communities various parts of the production process, especially those in which workers are particularly exploited or exposed to noxious chemicals.

Equally, contemporary changes in the geography of capitalism have played a role in shaping workers' identities and thus the possibilities for their political praxis. As Richard Hyman has suggested, "the spatial location and social organization of work, residence, consumption and sociability have become highly differentiated" during the past few decades as many workers have become suburbanites. The result has been that the average employee today "may live a considerable distance from fellow-workers, possess a largely 'privatised' domestic life or a circle of friends unconnected with work, and pursue cultural or recreational interests quite different from those of other employees in the same workplace." This spatial "disjuncture between work and community (or indeed the destruction of community in much of its traditional meaning) entails the loss of many of the local-ised networks which [previously] strengthened the supports of union membership (and in some cases made the local union almost a 'to-tal institution')." The upshot of such geographical transformations is that whereas in the past many workers' identities "were reinforced by the broader networks of everyday life . . . the possibility and character of collectivism are today very different when work and everyday life are increasingly [spatially] differentiated." This, of course, can affect workers' ability to unionize, given that unionization often emerges not just out of the conditions workers endure at work but also out of the kinds of social networks which they are able to build outside the workplace—at church, the neighborhood bar, where their kids go to school, the local ballpark, and so forth.

Having said all of this, though, it is important to recognize that being geographically isolated itself does not necessarily render work-ers impotent. Thus, miners who dig metals that are crucial to various production processes can often exert great power within an economy because of the critical importance of what they mine, even if the com-munities in which they toil are in out-of-the-way places. A good exam-ple of the latter are the miners who dig the iron ore in the Pilbara in Western Australia who, in the 1970s and '80s, managed to build pow-erful unions in what are considered by many to be fairly isolated rural communities. Indeed, their ability to do this has more recently led the mining companies to shift from a model of production wherein min-ers lived close to the mines in remote rural country towns which they largely controlled politically to a "fly-in/fly-out" model of labor supply, with miners living in fairly cosmopolitan places like Perth (1,600 ki-lometers away) and other regional centers in Western Australia or even in Sydney, Melbourne, and Auckland (New Zealand) and being flown in for set periods of work, after which they fly home. This spa-tial strategy of geographically distancing miners' homes both from the places where they work and from each other has played a central role in breaking the unions' grip on the Pilbara. Equally, new forms of production such as "just-in-time" (JIT) assembly can mean that workers who are physically isolated may nevertheless be able to bring an entire production chain crashing to a halt, given how increasingly dependent upon regular deliveries of parts JIT makes assembly operations. The end result of all of this, then, is not to argue that workers' geographical isolation will automatically limit the possibilities for their organization but, rather, to understand how their geographical interconnection (or not) with other parts of the production process or other places opens some opportunities for organizing even as it may shut off others, depending upon a host of contextual factors (like whether workers are employed in companies using JIT).

If understanding how work is arranged spatially and how this impacts the possibilities for workers' organizational activities is the first point to recognize when considering the making of geography, the second is to understand that whatever else it is, capitalism as a political economic system is deeply geographically structured, for the economic landscape as a whole has to be spatially organized in particular ways if capital is collectively and individually to reproduce itself and survive. To take a simple example, in order for accumulation to occur, certain animate and inanimate objects—workers, capital, raw materials—must come together in particular places at particular times. They must be configured, in other words, into what David Harvey calls "spatial fixes." Hence, sufficiently skilled manufacturing workers must be coincident in space with the raw materials and tools they will use to fashion completed commodities. Likewise, certain types of infrastructure must literally be set in place so that office workers or stock brokers can organize the myriad pieces of paper which show that billions of dollars have been invested near or yon— there must be office buildings in which they can work, there may need to be roads or train tracks which allow them to commute from home to their place of work, and so forth. Equally, capitalists must collectively ensure that the economic landscape is made in such a way that profit can be not only generated but also realized, a fact which also requires organizing the landscape in particular ways. Hence, as Harvey argues, in order for surplus value to be extracted and realized, capital must collectively invest in "factories, dams, offices, shops, warehouses, roads, railways, docks, power stations, water supply and sewage disposal systems, schools, hospitals, parks, cinemas, restaurants—the list is endless." This means that the unevenly developed economic geography that is emblematic of capitalism—regions of wealth in some places contrasted with those of poverty elsewhere—is actively brought about rather than simply given. Thus, whereas prior to the twentieth-century maturation of capitalism nature and geology played a large role in shaping the economic landscape, such that the early industrial geography of the United States could largely be explained by the location of raw materials like coal and iron ore, as capitalism has developed this is no longer the case. Hence, in the past fifty years much manufacturing in the United States has been drawn by lower wages and antiunion legislation to the Southern states, often some considerable distance from the sources of the raw materials it requires. What increasingly determines patterns of economic development as the productive forces of capitalism develop over time, then, is not so much nature and geology but patterns of capital investment—as the recent growth of banana cultivation in Iceland, thanks to the application of advanced greenhouse technology, attests!

In considering how certain spatial fixes are produced so that capitalism as a system can reproduce itself, though, it is important to bear in mind three things. Firstly, not all capitalists necessarily favor the same spatial fixes. What is good for one may not be good for another. Hence, the highway that allows one manufacturer to better access far-off markets may also allow another's poorly paid labor force to more easily commute to other opportunities in the next town or region down that same road, leaving such an employer with a dearth of workers. Secondly, it is not just various capitalists who have an interest in ensuring the landscape is made in certain ways, but it is also workers. Thus, workers who are spatially trapped in a particular community because they have no opportunity to commute to other job options that may be too far away and who therefore are forced to work at whatever wages and under whatever conditions the employers in that community dictate may also favor the construction of roads which break down their geographical isolation, thereby quite literally opening up new horizons for them. As is the case with collective capital, however, different groups of workers will likely prefer diverse configurations of the economic landscape, depending upon the specificities of their work, political ideology, and so forth. Thirdly, the spatial fixes that were physically emplaced in the economic landscape as a result of the struggles and compromises within and between various capitalists and workers at one historical moment do not necessarily facilitate the reproduction of capital and labor at another. For instance, the cities built around the use of the railroad to transport goods and people in the nineteenth century had to be refashioned in the twentieth century to make them work in the context of the automobile. Thus, as Harvey has put it, whereas "capital builds a physical landscape appropriate to its own condition at a particular moment in time," it may "have to destroy it, usually in the course of a crisis, at a subsequent point in time."

The third way in which geography affects the possibilities for workers' political organization relates to how they are able to come together across space, either through migrating from one place to another or through practices of trans-spatial solidarity, as well as how they might be hampered in coming together. This is because, as Humphrey Southall states, developing worker solidarity is ultimately "a process of coming together, of organizing over space," such that how workers make common cause over often great distances is central to their abilities to pursue their interests. Likewise, employers' abilities to limit such trans-spatial contact and interaction may give them advantage in any particular dispute. One such example of how workers sought to move across space to develop solidarity, together with how employers and the state sought to stop them, comes from the British coal miners' strike of 1984–85, in which the National Union of Mineworkers (NUM) sought to stop the closure of myriad coal mines proposed by Margaret Thatcher's government. In particular, during the strike the NUM dispatched hundreds of striking miners as "flying pickets" to connect struggles in different parts of the country—miners from one region of the country would travel to another to support strike efforts there. The Thatcher government, however, ordered the police to set up roadblocks at county lines to limit the pickets' geographical mobility. This was part of a deliberate spatial strategy to contain the strike's geographical spread. In particular, the government sought to limit the movement of pickets into the coalfields of Nottinghamshire (central England), where the majority of miners had continued working despite the NUM's national strike call, thereby preventing them from being "infected" by the pickets coming from outside the county. Not only did this spatial strategy draw upon biological metaphors of disease through which the government attempted to convince the public that a cordon sanitaire was necessary to prevent "radical, Trotskyite unionists"—referred to as "the enemy within" by Margaret Thatcher—from contaminating the supposedly healthy body politic of the Nottinghamshire coalfields, but it also played into ideologies of localism and local rights (those of the Nottinghamshire miners, who chose to ignore their national union's instructions). Significantly, the Thatcher government's earlier introduction of laws making secondary boycotts illegal had likewise been about limiting the ability of workers in one location to spread a dispute to others situated elsewhere.

Finally, there is the issue of how ideas—like those related to unionism—spread across the economic landscape even if workers are stuck in place. In this regard, Jane Wills has shown how a dispute in one place can have a "demonstration effect" elsewhere without the need for the physical movement of organizers themselves—success in one place may serve as inspiration elsewhere. Concomitantly, failure in one place may have a "dampening effect" elsewhere, perhaps reinforcing local quiescence. The key here, though, is understanding how ideas are translated across, and constituted in, space and how the ways in which this occurs can shape workers' activities, perhaps encouraging workers in one place to become more militant or, alternatively, less militant than they have been in the past. Clearly, ideas of militancy or quiescence or anything else do not float in the ether but are grounded in particular places—they "take place" in specific locales—and their diffusion across the economic landscape is shaped by how different places are connected geographically. Six elements shape this process: the nature of the idea itself; the idea's place of origin; the nature of the landscape over which the idea diffuses; the paths by which an idea disperses from its point of origin; the idea's ultimate destination; and the time it takes to get there. Importantly for the argument here, all but the first of these elements are directly shaped by geography. For instance, depending upon the social context and time period, the paths by which ideas about unionizing can be spread will be quite different. Thus, whereas in the nineteenth century the geography of idea diffusion over long distances generally followed the routes of the telegraph lines or railroads linking together far-flung places (it is really no surprise that the railroad strike of 1877 was the first national strike in the United States, as it spread from its point of origin in Martinsburg, West Virginia, down the train tracks until some one hundred thousand workers across the country became involved), the rise of wireless communication technologies like the radio brought about new geographies of diffusion, as people who were physically distant from telegraph lines could now have the same degree of access to information as did those living in communities located along the telegraph's path. Equally, the nature of the landscape over which ideas travel shapes how they diffuse—some landscapes' physicality makes them more difficult to traverse than others (interaction is likely to be more difficult in mountainous regions than in flat plains), whereas in other cases it may be political limitations which hinder ideas' spread from one place to another (some countries or regions may be quite successful in keeping various union publications from crossing their borders, for example). Even in this day and age of supposedly instantaneous communication, then, there is a geography to how ideas spread, and this shapes workers' organizational practices.

HISTORICAL-*GEOGRAPHICAL* MATERIALISM

So what does all this mean? Well, from an analytical point of view it means that any exploration of labor's contemporary condition and prospects for its improvement must rely upon investigations that are grounded in a historical-*geographical* materialist approach. However, the conceptual issues explored above also have normative implications for considering what is to be done to facilitate worker power—that is to say, what is to be done to build more emancipatory landscapes, whether these are still within the confines of a capitalist economy or perhaps under some other, post-capitalist, form of organizing human and other life. As geographer Jane Wills has argued: "[b]y drawing new contour lines on the map of class power, workers' activity can shape the terrain in which economic processes and social relationships unfold." This declaration, though, should be understood not merely in metaphorical terms but also in material ones.

How, then, might workers actually go about drawing new contour lines on the map of class power and so begin building more emancipatory landscapes in which to live? One key element in this must be their being conscious of how the processes and institutions in which they are embroiled are spatially organized and constituted. If workers are to be successful in improving their lot, they must think strategically about making deliberate interventions into the economic landscape so as to facilitate their own social reproduction and, perhaps, to undermine the ability of those with whom they are in conflict to facilitate theirs. One example of this has been the "Mapping Supplier Chains" project initiated by the International Research Network on Autowork in the Americas, a grouping initially founded by academics but which subsequently took on the role of fostering cross-border union networking and, ultimately, that of a national forum for Mexican auto unions. The network has seen as one of its primary tasks the mapping of "the changing contours of this supply chain, from vehicle assembly plants, to in-house suppliers of major components including drive trains, to outside suppliers responsible for the manufacture of integrated systems, to commodity suppliers and job shops contracted to deliver parts and small components to other plants in the chain." This may seem an obvious thing to do, but it is remarkable how few workers know much about how their workplace is networked into the broader economic landscape. For instance, in the celebrated 1990–92 Ravenswood, West Virginia, dispute between the United Steelworkers of America and a global aluminum-smelting corporation that had locked them out of their plant—a dispute heralded by Tom Juravich and Kate Bronfenbrenner as marking "the revival" of the U.S. labor movement—before the steelworkers could even launch their campaign to pressure the end users of the aluminum produced by the scab labor hired to replace them they had to spend considerable time and energy simply following delivery trucks leaving the plant to discover who these end users actually were. They had, in other words, to construct, practically from scratch, a cartography of the plant's distribution system. Knowledge of the spatial structure of a corporation and the location of its customers (whether other firms or members of the public), then, is crucial if workers are to make well-considered incursions into the landscape to disrupt capital's spatial fixes.

Equally, building more emancipatory landscapes involves understanding how the resources of place can reinforce union praxis and identity and how practices of spatial engineering can play important roles in reconfiguring labor relations and shaping labor's organizing. By way of example, in his analysis of militancy in Merseyside (northwest England), Ralph Darlington took issue with Huw Beynon's celebrated notion of "factory class consciousness" to argue that worker power had not emerged exclusively from conditions on the shop floor but had also been fed by the broader relationships between workplace organization and the particularities of the local community, such as a history of aggressive political agitation in many of the city's working-class neighborhoods around rent issues. This created a political habitus that has outlived its original 1930s creators (principally Communist Party organizers) through being nourished over decades by the resources of place. It is the connections—social *and* spatial—between workplaces and the broader community within which these workplaces are located that have been central to sustaining such a habitus, he suggests. The result, he concludes, is that, given the right resources of place, "it might be possible for industrial and political traditions and patterns of behaviour predisposed to adversarialism, which have been initiated and sustained within certain spatially bounded communities, to be reproduced through time and continue to have a long-term influence on industrial relations—even in the context of dramatic changes in the structure and pattern of employment overall." Places like Merseyside, then, can often serve as geographical reservoirs of militancy and so as bases out from which new rounds of organizing might diffuse. Hence, Darlington's study poses questions concerning how traditions of militancy or quiescence are produced in particular places, how workers are socialized within those places, and how such traditions can be geographically transmitted from place to place. Again, the notion of sustaining such a habitus that connects the workplace with the community may not seem that remarkable an insight, but it does run counter to much of the U.S. labor movement's twentieth-century organizing strategies, which have generally focused organizing activity upon the workplace because of the belief that working-class consciousness largely originates there.

In related terms, another key element in facilitating union strength is understanding how the way in which the landscape is geographically structured can facilitate (or undermine) efforts to develop contacts across space between workers. If we are to accept that unionization is indeed a process of bringing workers together over space à la Southall, then we need to understand how this is enabled or constrained by geography. For example, the fact that it takes time for workers to cross space—and that different groups of workers have varied capacities to do so—shapes where various types of workers can be at particular times of the day and hence their capacities for action. Thus, many women's domestic responsibilities lead them to work closer to home than do their husbands, but this varies considerably by race/ethnicity and age—black and Hispanic women tend to commute just as far as black and Hispanic men and spend more time commuting than both white men and white women, whereas younger women often expect their husbands to take a larger role in domestic chores than did their mothers or grandmothers, which can impact their ability to commute across space. Consequently, the planning of union meetings or other activities needs to take into consideration men's and women's and different racial/ethnic and age groups' disparate abilities to cross space and may result in having to develop new locational strategies—perhaps having such meetings in decentralized local community settings or even workers' homes rather than in the more traditional, centralized union building setting. Changing the spatial context within which workers exist, in other words, can play an important role in allowing them to come together geographically and so to coordinate actions. Likewise, in developing means to link workers across space it is important to understand how the geography of information dispersal and access can shape the likelihood of success. Indeed, despite claims that we live in the age of ubiquitous e-mail, social networking, and instant messaging, with some seeing new communications media like Facebook as potential panaceas for unions, there is a distinct spatiality to people's accessibility to such technologies. Even in a highly computerized country like the United States, there are significant geographical variations in home access to the Internet—rural areas and the Southeast tend to lag behind other parts of the country—such that strategies of information dissemination which assume a geographically level playing field when it comes to using these technologies to bring workers together are likely to fail.

Such geographical considerations can play a significant role in crafting a successful campaign. For instance, it is frequently assumed that, in the age of globalization and transnational corporations' geographical spread across national borders, unions must match the geographical scalar organization of their employers if they are to be successful—in a world of global corporations, it is often argued, unions must of necessity develop global campaigns and structures. Certainly, in many instances this will undoubtedly be the case. Hence, in the Ravenswood situation referenced above, it was through its ability to cross space to make connections with workers and others in various countries around the world, thereby mirroring the organizational structure of the corporation with which they were in conflict, that the union was able to secure reentry into the plant after twenty months of being locked out. However, in other instances it may not be necessary to cross space transnationally but may be possible to use the local resources of place so as to build a campaign against a globally organized corporation. For instance, in the case of the 1998 dispute between the United Auto Workers and General Motors, union workers were able to bring GM's North American operations, together with some of those in Asia, to a halt by striking at just two plants in Flint, Michigan. This is because the highly geographically integrated structure of GM, with its reliance upon "just-in-time" delivery systems, meant that disputes at these two plants quickly had a ripple effect across the company's corporate configuration. Whereas the Ravenswood example, then, was a case of workers crossing space to achieve their goals, the GM dispute was a case of, for want of a better word, workers "digging in" in place and striking key choke points which were highly connected to myriad other plants in the production chain. The key to workers' success, of course, is to know something about a company's geographical structure and points of control so as to know ahead of time what types of strategy are likely to be most efficacious.

Finally, in creating a landscape that is supportive of unionism, it is important to consider the ways in which the landscape may be manipulated to reinforce worker/union identities, out of which a sense of collective experience can emerge. For example, unions' abilities to colonize particular spaces, to make of them "union spaces" through occupying them on a temporary or more permanent basis through marches, the flying of banners, the posting of billboards, or even the construction of memorials and the renaming of streets and buildings after important union-related events and people, can play a significant role in creating a physical milieu and habitus supportive of unionism. In this regard, in their work on the U.S. civil rights movement, Derek Alderman and Owen Dwyer have shown how renaming streets and buildings after prominent figures or events associated with that struggle and the siting of memorials are important material elements in creating particular public memories about the past from which contemporary struggles can draw sustenance. As they point out, much of the struggle in the post–civil rights South has been about erasing from the landscape visions of history which lauded the Confederacy through monumentalization and naming practices and replacing them with a physical and semiotic landscape that presents a quite different vision—in New Orleans, for instance, Jefferson Davis and Robert E. Lee have been removed as names from schools and have been replaced by prominent African Americans. The creation, then, of physical "memorial arenas" in which images and ideas about unions and working-class struggles can be transmitted to new generations of workers and citizens, and through which new geographies of memory can be created, is likely also to be significant in fostering a supportive environment for union activities for, as Maoz Azaryahu has commented, place names and monuments "merge the past they commemorate into ordinary settings of human life" by creating highly visible public texts that can be read by people in their vicinity.

Practices of molding the built environment in certain ways to attain specific social goals—what Robert Fishman called putting "social thought in three dimensions"—link the economic landscape's physicality with its symbolic dimensions and are central to what Henri Lefebvre has termed the "production of space." For Lefebvre there are three deeply intertwined elements to this production and all three warrant consideration by unions seeking to improve their lot. They are:

Spatial practice, which is the social activity through which economic landscapes are physically made and restructured geographically;

Representations of space, which are produced by urban planners, architects, engineers, artists, and so forth using verbal and non-verbal signs and images—maps, models, plans, paintings—and which guide how the built environment is conceptualized and subsequently constructed; and

Spaces of representation, which are the material spaces in which life is lived and in which symbolic meanings are both enacted in spatial form and drawn from the built environment, as through murals, billboards, vernacular architecture, and the like.

All three of these elements have bearing on union efforts to produce space in a way that creates more emancipatory landscapes. Hence, not only are workers and their institutions spatially embedded and must engage with the economic landscape's highly spatially differentiated form, therein seeking to actively shape it in particular ways, but they must also play roles in guiding how that landscape is represented and conceptualized. For instance, they must pose the question of whether people have a right to live in an economic landscape that is one of employment (and, if so, how such a landscape might be constructed) or whether they are to be condemned to live in landscapes of unemployment. They must likewise ponder how workers might engage in the creation of symbolic meanings in the landscape which help to create a supportive milieu for their actions.

A geographical sensibility, then, is essential if workers are to be successful in pursuing their political ambitions, for it allows us to understand how the various elements of capitalist production are interlinked and how workers might therefore engage with each other and with those with whom they are in conflict. But such a sensibility requires understanding how various parts of the economic landscape are functionally connected across space, even as they may appear quite isolated. Hence, the region of the Pilbara in Western Australia, hundreds of miles away from Perth and in the wilds of the Outback, is frequently viewed at first glance by many as being thoroughly geographically isolated—until, that is, it is remembered that the capital which funds the mining operations there is largely controlled from London, the product of the mining goes to fuel China's insatiable factories which flood world markets, and the workers who work there have homes and families living right across Australia and beyond. From this perspective, the Pilbara is not, in fact, isolated but is at the heart of the contemporary global economy. Strategizing about developing greater worker power, then, requires viewing places not simply as unique locations on the surface of the globe in which things happen but as nodes within networks which may stretch near or far, such that the consequences of an action in one place may flow to others quickly or slowly, depending on how it is spatially connected to the broader economic landscape.

In contemplating how economic landscapes can be made in ways which facilitate worker power, however, it is important to recognize—adapting one of Marx's maxims—that the landscapes made by all the dead generations weigh like a nightmare on the possibilities for action of the living. Thus, workers and unions do not have a completely free hand in building more emancipatory landscapes, for how economic landscapes were made in the past will continue to shape the possibilities for making economic landscapes in the future, even as the making of such new landscapes erases the hold that past ones have on us. Nevertheless, such spatial struggles are important, for as Lefebvre argued in his analysis of how the survival of capitalism is dependent upon the making of its geography in particular ways, because "every society produces a space, its own space," all "new social relationships call for a new space, and vice versa." Given this fact, any future emancipation of workers, then, will be at least partially a geographical project in which workers and their institutions must play a significant role. Workers cannot afford to be ignorant of the geographical possibilities and challenges ahead of them, for the making of the geography of capitalism is much too important a task to be left to capitalists alone.

HOME AS WORK

Eileen Boris

For six years, they petitioned, marched, and lobbied the New York State legislature, often with sympathetic employers, sometimes with their children. Nannies, housekeepers, and elder care providers demanded protection under the labor law like other workers, even if their place of employment was the private home and their bosses were housewives. Members of a vast, unrecognized labor force, in 2010 some two hundred thousand in New York City alone, these predominantly Caribbean, Asian, and U.S.-born women of color made it possible for other women to go out to their jobs by cleaning houses, cooking dinner, bathing children, and aiding the aged. They organized themselves into the multiethnic Domestic Workers United (DWU) to push for decent treatment, higher pay, and fair working conditions. Finally in June 2010, the political stars aligned and New York passed the Domestic Workers Bill of Rights, becoming the first state to establish a framework for dignity and justice for paid household labor. Domestics gained coverage under existing laws against sexual harassment and for temporary disability benefits, and became eligible for unemployment insurance and overtime. They won a set workweek with a day off for live-ins. But indicative of the forces against this move, the enacted bill allowed employers to fire workers without adequate notice and provide less paid vacation than DWU proposed. Whether the New York Department of Labor could enforce these rights remained in doubt, but mobilized workers and their allies were ready to hold the department accountable.

In Geneva, another milestone in the struggle of domestics for labor rights was under way. DWU belonged to a global movement of household workers who demanded access to decent work. They pushed for an international labor convention through the auspices of the International Domestic Worker Network (IDWN) and abetted by trade union delegates to the International Labor Organization (ILO), a tripartite (government-employer-labor) standards-setting institution. Since 1948, this United Nations agency for global governance has investigated the plight of domestics, but home-based workers remained a low priority for governments and unions. By the late twentieth century, migrant women themselves were making this invisible workforce visible through their own organizing, sometimes in unions (as in South Africa) and often through feminist NGOs (as in Hong Kong). They demanded the same rights as any other laborer, that is, as a Mexican worker delegate explained, "non-discrimination and equal opportunity, meaning a decent wage, decent conditions regarding occupational safety and health, stable employment, nonviolence and access to social security, so that we have somewhere to live, health care, and a decent retirement" but also "recognition of freedom of association and the right to organize." At its June 2010 meeting, the ILO adopted such standards for domestics. But since it took two rounds to approve a convention, employers and hostile nations (among the most vocal were Bangladesh, India, and several Arab countries) still had time to weaken or torpedo this global effort at social justice.

Such activity on labor standards for home-based workers makes me feel somewhat like an academic prophet. While other labor historians wrote about unionizing the factory or women's entrance into male occupations, I steadfastly have explored the home as a workplace for paid as well as unpaid labors. For the last thirty years, I've had only two topics, home and work, and for the most part, they have been the same. Workers once at the margins of production, no less than scholarship, today stand at its center; home laborers—whether domestics, health aides and attendants, or sweated manufacturers—are crucial to today's global order and the carework economy that generates low-wage jobs in a transformed and feminized U.S. labor market. Given the transnational flow of people and goods from the global assembly line to the outsourced household, it's not surprising that the study of domestic labor now seems so pressing. For their organizing is crucial if we are to build a society which understands—and values—our interdependence.

In this regard, history and feminist theory have much to teach us not only about the commodification of such home labors, their partial removal from the home, and their reprivatization, but also about what we need to do to make the promise of fair labor standards for home-based workers a reality. It isn't that domestic and other household laborers haven't resisted low wages, long hours, and arbitrary treatment, but industrial unions dismissed them as unorganizable when they bothered to notice their protests. Denying their status as worker, law and social policy allowed employers to hide behind notions that the cleaner or aide is "one of the family." It's taken the willingness of more privileged women and men to see the advantages of paying a living wage. It's taken coalition politics and large movements for civil and women's rights to bring about improvement. It's taken trade unions to recognize that home-based workers are workers and thus potential union members. And, most of all, it's taken individual courage and collective action of those who do the world's dirty work and intimate labor to demand justice.

Still, home laborers continue to baffle. Do they add value? Does their product count? Can their work be considered similar to other jobs? Such questions of definition and classification lie at the heart of the quest for labor standards, as well as my research. I continuously ask, "What is work and who is a worker?" because the answer has consequences for ending exploitation on the job.

Each of my major projects has explored an aspect of that question. My first book on the arts and crafts movement of the early twentieth century explored what activities count as work in analyzing the relationship between art and labor. Gender and the state moved to the center of my subsequent book on the politics of industrial homework. In addressing the "problem" of the wage-earning mother, I challenged the division of home from work, private from public that the existence of paid labor in the home denies. Going to India in 1989 as part of a consultation sponsored by the ILO and the Ford Foundation on home-based labor shifted my analysis, as did meeting the activists who created the Self-Employed Women's Association (SEWA) and who confronted the global politics of women and development in their daily work. I subsequently co-edited a collection on homework around the globe as an intervention into ongoing debates over global-ization and as an expression of transnational feminist praxis.

After a series of articles and related research on what I've named the racialized gendered state that reconsidered fair employment, equal opportunity, and affirmative action as part of labor standards, I returned to home labors through two collaborative projects. With sociologist Rhacel Salazar Parreñas, I introduced the concept of inti-mate labor to invite feminist scholars to explore the connections be-tween domestic, care, and sex work. By intimate labor, we refer to a range of activities that entail touch, bodily or emotional closeness or personal familiarity, or close observation of another and knowledge of their personal and daily details. The joining of the terms "intimate" and "labor" challenges a series of separations—home from work, love from money, and productive from reproductive labor—that capitalist globalization has intensified. With historian Jennifer Klein, I've given home health care a history, showing how social policy from the Great Depression to the twenty-first century created a new occupation, the home aide or attendant, as a form of precarious employment for poor women, who became neither nurses nor maids but rather the linch-pins of America's piecemeal and inadequate system of long-term care. But we also found that by transforming private matters, located in the home and involving intimate issues of bodily integrity and family, into public concerns, government set the stage for union organizing, the growth of a militant disability rights movement, and other forms of political contestation. I'm now returning to the gendered promo-tion of handicraft and cottage industries as a part of ILO and UN eco-nomic development initiatives in the post–World War II world, when the "Third World Woman" served as Western feminism's other.

Throughout my work, I've been influenced not only by current struggles but also by feminist theories that have developed to make sense of those conflicts. The interdisciplinary literature coming out of women's, gender, and feminist studies (the issue of naming in this still emerging field remains up for grabs) also has proved invaluable. Whether speaking of double days or care deficits, feminist research-ers have stressed the importance of domestic labor for the overall working of the economy as well as the maintenance of daily life. The process of "housewifization" that Maria Mies identified over two decades ago continues to obscure the centrality of the household for capital accumulation by naturalizing labors in the home, devaluing their worth, and perpetuating the myth of the lone male breadwinner and unproductive homemaker. Conflating the wife with the domestic and both with womanhood itself, gender essentialism has obscured the growth of low-wage household labor that has intensified divisions among women as well as among nations. In undertaking such work, immigrants across the world continue to release the labor of citizen women for better-remunerated jobs, but find their own chances for economic rights and social benefits restricted.

From socialist feminism, I had learned that it wasn't enough to speak about class without considering male domination or patriarchy. The concept of social reproduction, the making of people through institutions of the family, school, and culture, provided a key to understanding structures of power and authority at home and abroad. But as a U.S. historian and an antiracist activist, I could not ignore the originary role of slavery, segregation, and racism to the creation and persistence of inequality. Teaching for over a decade at Howard University also shaped my standpoint. I embraced the intersectional standpoint pioneered by women of color theorists because ideas of multiple and complex identities explained more than any single factor by itself could. I sought to make such terms real through archival research, historicizing the notion of racialized gender to explore differences within racial or gendered groups within class society.

From these perspectives, I engaged with the new labor history and joined with other women's labor historians to question its narratives of working people that left out what most women were doing—cleaning, washing, cooking, sewing, and caring—whether for a wage or not. In excavating the history of home labors, we historicized vibrant debates over housework between the sexes, classes, and races. We looked at the politics of housework, inspired by Pat Mainardi's observation that "men have always had servants (us) to take care of the bottom stratum of life while they have confined their efforts to the rarefied upper regions," the political economy conclusion that the housewife under capitalism worked for both the husband and his boss—what was known as the domestic labor debate—and testimonies that women as the managers of household workers have used class and race privilege to abuse other women. Those of us fleeing from housework were convinced of the significance of domestic labors, but we tended to view the labor of women's sphere, whether chosen or coerced, as we might have phrased it then, as exploitative. Certainly the double day seemed unfair and schemes for cooperative housekeeping or domestic professionals either utopian or flawed.

But older working-class women made us take pause, to the greater gain of scholarship. Many complained about not having time for housework or being unable to stay at home with their children. We further heard the call of the National Welfare Rights Organization to reward the labor of care, to end the historical degradation of poor, single, disproportionately black women's motherwork. In learning about the centrality of the Mexican American mother, some of us remembered the immigrant experience of our own families, the pooling of resources, the unpaid tending of stores or restaurants engaged in by mothers and their children for the family business, the obligatory handing over of wages as part of the family economy. And discovering women's labors under slavery, colonialism, and imperialism, we were sure that they offered an arena for resistance and not just more profit for masters.

Feminist historians of labor engaged in field reconstitution as we returned to those household labors easily conflated with the obligations of wives and mothers, but also performed by women from ethnic and racial groups with less power than their employers and subject to larger market forces. Earlier books by Tera Hunter, addressing the period directly following Reconstruction, and by Elizabeth Clark-Lewis, on the 1920s, unearthed distinctions between the washerwoman, nanny, and cook, or those who lived in and those who went out. Phyllis Palmer and Dorothy Roberts separated the spiritual and menial in housework, a chasm between the housewife and the domestic. Pioneering studies of household labor by Susan Strasser and Dolores Hayden recognized the rise of for-profit cleaning companies before Barbara Ehrenreich discovered the Merry Maids. Sue

Cobble, Sonya Michel, Catherine Choy, and Kathy Barry, among oth-ers, charted the transformation of women's work in the service sector, whether for waitresses, child caretakers, nurses, or flight attendants. They have historicized the insights of sociologist Arlie Hochschild on emotion work and the idea of affective labor illuminated by critic Michael Hardt central to the service sector, whose products are often intangibles, in which what is produced is feeling, belonging, com-munity, or connection. Sara Ahmed's concept of "affective economy" is proving essential to trace the commodification of caring labor and revealing the work that emotions perform in the larger political economy.

Against an earlier scholarship that told a progressive story of women moving from the home to other workplaces, then, a nonlinear one has emerged that tells of the reprivatization of reproductive la-bor under neoliberal restructuring, the devolution of welfare states, and the pain of uneven and unequal development dependent on ra-cialized gendered divisions of labor and ideology. In identifying the home as a site of labor, women's historians of the United States ini-tially forged a parallel narrative of domestic service in which African Americans trade living-in for living-out, immigrants move to better jobs, and their predominantly white employers turn to household ap-pliances. But housework, as we all know, never withered away nor did men take up the slack. Instead, a burgeoning service sector emerged at the same time as new transnational migrants entered homes to cook, clean, and care, especially for dual career families. The famil-iar narrative of domestic service also assumes that household labor was unorganizable, as if state policies and private markets did not organize the labor, setting the framework in which workers joined to-gether in associations and unions, albeit with less success than more concentrated workplaces. Meanwhile, social institutions outside of the family—education and medicine particularly—sought to inter-vene in social reproduction, intrusively as with incarceration or eu-genics when it came to those judged deficient by race, class, morality, or culture.

Something happened in the 1970s: while the number of domestic workers steeply declined, not only did domestics become employees

of for-profit agencies but the number of other household laborers began to grow in such fields as child and health care. Behind this trajectory lay numerous social, cultural, economic, and political factors
that we are just beginning to understand. By the 1980s, home care
had taken off, thanks to an aging population, the unavailability of
women family members now in the labor force, and new federal and
state funding streams. Today, home care is one of the fastest growing occupations—one that still hovers at the minimum wage. These
predominantly African American, Latina, and immigrant women,
who do the public work of the welfare state by caring for disabled and
elderly public assistance clients at home and who a decade ago gained
the largest increase in union membership since the 1930s, illuminate
the transformation of domestic labor over the last half of the twentieth century. Cultural understandings that conflated household labor
with family work, service with love, certainly has led to the under-
valuing of home care—but so have characteristics of the worker as a
poor woman of color, often an immigrant. The burden of the home as
a workplace and the place of women of color there continue to haunt
the very definition of work and worker, reinforcing the feeling that
this isn't real work. Meanwhile, as Laura Briggs shows, dirty wars and
economic readjustment abroad have led to a market in both household workers and transnational adoption, sometimes of the very children of women migrants.

Indeed, when private household workers finally won coverage
under the Fair Labor Standards Act (FLSA) in 1974, home care workers lost out. As Jennifer Klein and I document, even home aides employed by private agencies, previously included in the law, became
reclassified as elder companions under Department of Labor regulations in 1975. By this sleight of hand, the carework of adult women
became equated with that of teenage babysitters and elder volunteers
and relegated to the low wages of the contingent economy. For over
two decades, the Service Employees International Union (SEIU) and
advocates sought to overturn this harm. During the Clinton years,
they almost succeeded, but the victory of George W. Bush blocked
administrative change. The SEIU turned to the courts, but the Supreme Court upheld the validity of the regulatory process and thus

the exclusion of home care workers from overtime and even minimum wage (which remains elusive because home attendants and
aides often work longer than they are paid for, especially at night, and
are uncompensated for travel between client homes). The congressional stalemate that soon engulfed the Obama administration has
all but closed the door to legislative remedy. By 2010, only new rules
issued by the Department of Labor, now a pro-worker entity under
Hilda Solis, a daughter of immigrants, offered hope that those who
tend to senior and disabled people would receive fair treatment.

What can the victory of DWU in New York, despite the continued
exclusion of home care workers from the FLSA, tell us about strategies for organizing today's expanding carework and service economy,
of which home-based labor plays such a vital part? Certainly the scale
of the effort impacted the outcome: DWU worked at the grassroots,
citywide, and statewide level, focusing on legislatures, while the SEIU
confronted national politics and the Supreme Court in seeking to
overturn the FLSA exclusion. But both have recognized that old models of unionization, developed for fixed and central workplaces and
with the male industrial worker as the ideal worker, fail to reach the
immigrant and female home workforce. They discovered that ethnic
associations, community-located strategies of mobilization, and the
issue campaigns of social movement unionism can succeed. Allies—
churches, progressive employers and clients, and feminist and ethnic
groups—have proven crucial. More than generalized concepts of social justice motivate coalition partners. As the SEIU learned in organizing home care workers, finding mutual interest between workers
and consumers or employers in the realm of intimate care helps build
power to lobby governors and legislatures. Struggles over bills of
rights or codes of conduct are potent mobilization devices.

Both domestics and home care workers found themselves relying on elected officials and state agencies to devise rules of inclusion
and develop mechanisms for improving labor standards, like the
public authority that serves as an employer for collective-bargaining
purposes, offers training, and provides a registry of available home
care workers. Private household workers, however, receive payment
from individual families without benefit of state subsidies—monies

that child and home care providers depend upon. Who pays the bills distinguishes these forms of home labor and, during a period of fiscal strain, when the social budget is under attack and state spending shrinking, lobbying for state reimbursement for welfare services, like home care, requires more than deals between politicians and union leaders. It requires a committed and mobilized rank and file and fired-up beneficiaries of their work. For when politicians are unable to deliver, unions and worker associations need more than ever strong member participation and a democratic culture to push through their demands and regroup to continue the fight another day.

What can we take away from these efforts by home laborers? By appealing to the central role of reproductive labor in capital accumulation, and the need for someone, if not the state, to care for the dependent members of all families, the movement is more likely to succeed when the message is about us all, not just individual workers. Home health care becomes about the direct care needs of an aging society; domestic service is not merely a mechanism for mothers to go out to work, but a crucial input to the larger economy; and child care—whether at home or a center—becomes social nurturance, part of the shaping of the next generation. The actions of actual workers reinforce this politics of mutuality. Home care workers often are reluctant to strike; 1199 and other SEIU locals have no-strike clauses because they see themselves as representing larger interests. So they win legislative and community support against employers because they appear as acting in the interests of us all in providing a vital service.

From the study of these workers we learn of the necessity to cultivate multiethnic coalition building as a tool to advance support for public carework. Back during the Great Depression, the Domestic Workers Union Local 149 of New York's Vivian Morris urged "Rabbies [sic] in the various synagogues, and white clergymen, that they should stress to their congregation that they should stop hiring the girls from the slave marts at starvation wages, and have an organization set up and supervised by the church members in the church, or some community house in the neighborhood, and let the girls come there and wait for jobs." In recent years, clergy-headed marches of home health care workers and Jews for Racial and Economic Justice educated New York employers of domestic labor and organized them to lobby the legislature with DWU.

Even so, domestic workers, their advocacy groups, and their allies can't achieve victory by themselves, even with a winning message. Those paid directly or indirectly by the government, like many home aides and child care providers, need to join with public employees to defend the public sector. The trade union movement, despite its decline, remains the most effective countervailing force to the politics of inequality. Rather than relics of the past, domestic workers are here to stay and represent an important constituency for organized labor if only unions would embrace the home as a workplace. If so, then the old slogan "Every home a union home" will have a broader meaning.

CONTINGENT, TRANSIENT, AND AT-RISK: MODERN WORKERS IN A GIG ECONOMY

Richard A. Greenwald

America is transforming before our eyes, and with our focus on the short-term economic crisis, we are blind to what might very well be the most fundamental economic shift of the past fifty years: the nine-to-five, forty-hour-week job with benefits and some security is fast going the way of the compact disc. It still exists, barely, but is more of an echo than a modern reality.

According to a recent Bureau of Labor Statistics report, almost 30 percent of all Americans work contingently as free agents, contractors, day laborers, or consultants or are self-employed. They don't have long careers with companies that provide employer-based benefits, such as health insurance, sick time, retirement plans, and paid time off. Nor are they unionized or protected by most state and federal labor laws. The America of today is simply much riskier economically than that of our parents' generation—maybe even riskier than that of our grandparents. American blue-collar workers have known this since at least the late 1970s and the rise of deindustrialization and manufacturing job loss. In fact, few young workers today may ever know a work life with the kind of stability enjoyed by their parents. Pundits have bemoaned the decline of stability and the stress it places on American families. Clearly they are right. There is a mature literature on deindustrialization and globalization and its effect on the social fabric of America. But frankly, we might be wasting our time pining for a return to the past, or a new New Deal, or an effort to stop the slide because we are now living the new normal.

A recent cover story in *Bloomberg Businessweek* entitled "The Disposable Worker" describes the future as it now appears: businesses are "making the era of the temp more than temporary," as firms are outsourcing many more functions to consultants and freelancers, who have little legal standing or economic stability. For Fortune 500 companies, these so-called permatemps, freelancers, and consultants are often the first choice for getting work done. While good for business, because they limit risk, the new freelance army faces mighty hurdles. They live assignment to assignment, gigging. They have no security, and, like one freelancer I spoke to, their health plan is "Let's hope I don't get sick." Welcome to the gig economy, the world in which more and more Americans will work on a contingent basis as a permanent way of life, where nine-to-five jobs will become a thing of the past for many. For nearly a generation, this was something that affected only factory or service workers. But, now, the so-called middle class is just like the working class in terms of risk and the economic burdens they carry. One could say, in all honesty, we are all workers now.

This transformation of the American workplace will be as profound for the twenty-first century as the Industrial Revolution's shift from farms to factories was for the nineteenth century. One of the fastest growing contingent worker groups today is college-educated, white-collar professionals. They grew up thinking they would lead lives of economic security and corporate advancement. Now they jump from job to job, career to career, and project to project working as consultants. Current estimates predict that this trend will only continue to increase in the coming years. Imagine, by 2020 maybe as many as 50 percent of all collars, working on a contingent basis, with a growing majority of them consisting of college-educated, white-collar, and professional classes. What was the old middle class, as confusing as such terms can be, may just become part of the new working-class majority. If once secure workers become both socially and economically marginalized, how will this affect the way they see themselves? What might this mean for labor? Will these once middle-class freelancers see themselves as workers, exploited by the same system that exploits day laborers? Will they unionize or join with other blue-collar workers? And, more importantly, will they develop a political sensitivity that will produce a workerist worldview?

WELCOME TO THE NEW NORMAL

Current political debates about health care, tax policies, job creation, and economic revitalization, for instance, must address the new fact that a nation of freelancers is not served either by the current employer-based health care system or by the W-2 focused tax code. A recent survey found that a significant number of "new jobs" created were in fact freelance positions. Yet the current policy discussions about job creation do not take them into account. These workers, for instance, do not benefit from payroll tax deductions. If benefits such as workers' compensation and unemployment insurance are employer-based, then the "1099 nation" (the now 30 percent of the national workforce who must use the 1099 form to report income from multiple employers) are truly disadvantaged. Freelancers are not eligible to collect unemployment insurance, workers' compensation, and long-term Social Security disability, to name just a few. They have for the most part failed to see themselves as consciously exploited workers and hence do not yet see unionization, or at least organization, as a successful strategy for improving their lives. And more importantly, they do not see kindred spirits in day laborers or other blue-collar workers. They remain isolated. Yet they are increasingly working in public view.

We also need to reshape our current economic thinking about work beyond matters such as tax codes and government benefits to think hard about public space, such as libraries and cafés, which are no longer just places of learning or leisure but now also function as workspaces and as such sites for possible unionization. The public debate in the 1950s and 1960s over the role malls played (public commons or private retail property) in American society was the last time America seriously considered how complicated the definition of public/private space is—that debate looks simple in comparison to our post-nine-to-five world. Many workers today think of commercial spaces (e.g., a café) the same way we as a society used to think about the town square: simply put, they are our public commons. We expect not only free and uninhibited access, but also certain amenities, such as clean restrooms, air-conditioning, and Wi-Fi. The army of laptop-tapping latte sippers working in the corner café is not a quaint blip of recently unemployed job seekers or college graduates, but instead is a permanent feature of the new American workforce. The closure of a neighborhood café, changes in library hours, or charges for Wi-Fi have an economic impact greater than mere coffee sales. Such changes can displace a growing contingent workforce. Hence, Starbucks' recent return to free Wi-Fi can be seen as an important recognition of the role it plays in the economy as a new workspace. Local governments have also come to realize the importance of this mobile workforce. But because this is where workers are, if these workers are ever to see improvement in their lifetime, we need to find a way for them to organize; this is where unionization needs to start.

The shift from nine-to-five jobs to a gig economy has fundamentally forced us to rethink our relationship to work and the centrality work plays in all our lives. This sea change has brought with it a new work ethic that values multitasking, embedded communities of workers, the blending of leisure and work activity, and the rise of creativity and independence, along with money as co-measures of success. We seem to be returning to a craft sensibility as workers blend leisure and work and work harder, faster, and longer, but also find time to squeeze in a social life too. To older workers, they might seem lazy, because they do not keep traditional hours. Yet they *constantly* work, as defined blocks of time are meaningless for them. They might work all night to free time during the morning. This squeezing in, mixing, or blending completely blurs the lines between the social world and work. Most accept this quickened pace because they get some enjoyment out of work by finding ways to make a living doing things they are passionate about. They are combinations of nineteenth-century craftsman, outworkers, and high-tech gurus. They struggle in what they may not yet fully understand as a continually shrinking economy.

HOW DID WE GET HERE?

The last time we witnessed such a massive shift in the way we work and think about work was the 1950s. In 1956, no book better depicted the new development than William Whyte's *The Organization Man.*

America was becoming a nation of white-collar workers, leaving behind its blue-collar roots. Whyte, a sociologist whose book catapulted to the bestseller list, captured the angst and compromises that accompanied the mid-twentieth-century world of the white-collar workers. Most had been raised with a blue-collar ethos rooted in the Great Depression, and many still clung to what Whyte called an antiquated attitude toward work that would get them nowhere. Whyte argued that the Protestant work ethic, which was the predominate ethos of the previous one hundred–plus years, was dead by the 1950s. He identified a new social compact that had recently developed but was previously not, he said, defined:

> By social ethic I mean that contemporary body of thought which makes morally legitimate the pressures of society against the individuals. Its major propositions are three: a belief in the group as the source of creativity; a belief in "belongingness" as the ultimate need of the individual; and a belief in the application of science to achieve the belongingness.

Most Americans seemed content in trading some individuality for increasing economic security—especially following almost a generation of depression and war. While Whyte worried that we as a society gave up too much in our new corporation-based culture, sacrificing our sense of being individuals, the system he named became our socially accepted norm. Yet, for all his concern, what was centrally important for his book was his naming the system. In naming it, Whyte facilitated a comprehensive public discussion of this fundamental shift. The name he gave it, "the organization man," entered our lexicon and has become shorthand for that period's professional, middle-class workers (and mindless office work) ever since. Whyte's thesis is still the basis of our way of describing this work culture. It is so pervasive that even many reviewers of the recent TV show *Mad Men* used the phrase to describe the office culture depicted in the show.

Whatever our thoughts about Whyte and the 1950s, we all must agree that the organization man is certainly now dead—as dead as the

Protestant work ethic seemed in 1956. And just like Whyte's generation, today we are witnessing a yet-unnamed transformation in the
way we both work and think about work. A replacement social ethic
is clearly emerging. One could say this is the age of the freelancer
except that this shift is not, like the one in the 1950s, solely a male
thing, as women are a major part of the micropreneurial-class story.
Micropreneurs process an entrepreneurial spirit, but on the micro
scale, where what is being sold is the person's skills. This sense that
they are the business and they need to hustle is at odds with their ability to see themselves as exploited. There is a well-established industry of seminar and workshop leaders, authors, and other gurus who
claim to have the magic bullet for freelancers. This has led many of
them to internalize their economic insecurity. Rather than blame an
economic system that is structured against them, many blame themselves. If only they worked harder, faster, smarter, they would have
more security. This mind-set keeps them from organizing.

As security is fleeting, the micropreneurial age is based on assumed risk, flexibility, and a perpetual hustle. Today's new workers
are less loyal to any firm or business, do not trust institutions or large
organizations or leaders, but are part of loose communities of freelancers that are built on mutual support. They value independence
and creativity as much (or perhaps more than) financial success
(maybe because many do not have it); they blend work and life rather
than balance them; and they participate in a perpetual hustle from
gig to gig. We need to understand the culture, mores, and ethos of the
emerging micropreneurial class because, whether we acknowledge it
or not, each one of us is increasingly likely to join it.

Today, work is becoming all about flexibility, risk, and smarts.
Those of us not prepared will be destined for perpetual struggle. The
well-known management guru Tom Peters argues that "work today
is about two things: talent and projects." And because work is now
increasingly project- or task-based, businesses can more readily hire
the necessary high-level talent while management merely has to organize, synthesize, and consolidate the myriad projects that are the
work of a corporation. Jim Collins, author of *Built to Last, Good to
Great*, and *How the Mighty Fall*, recognized something many smart

CEOs already knew: business success often requires hiring smart people and giving them freedom to be creative. Freedom, creativity, and flexibility are the hallmarks of the new business environment, and they are also the key components of freelancing culture. That is not a coincidence. What is good for business may not be good for the new economy's workers.

The business press, led by *Fast Company, Businessweek, Fortune, Harvard Business Review, Inc.*, the *Wall Street Journal*, and others, has of course heralded this shift toward flexibility as nothing less than the embodiment of the American entrepreneurial spirit, while writers such as Robert Reich and Barbara Ehrenreich have declared this a signal of American decline. When sociologists C. Wright Mills and William Whyte wrote in the 1950s about the new "white collar" and the "organization man," many Americans had defined benefit and pension systems—and most paid nothing (or little) for full medical coverage. Junior executives made peace with the organizational model, trading independence for security.

Today, whether one works for a corporation or on a contingent basis, workers pay an increasingly large share of any benefits they might have, if they even have them, as 401(k)s replaced pensions and organizations shift health care costs increasingly onto employees. We are much less economically secure as a workforce. As the political scientist Jacob Hacker reminds us, American workers (of all collars) are without a safety net.

We are in a transitional zone between two coherent systems of work or economic regimes, and we must understand what is happening in order to actively shape the trajectory rather than passively watch it play out.

CULTURE MATTERS

There is a pressing need for a historical understanding of this shift that can build on social scientific literature but that speaks to a larger, general audience. As humanistic academics have given up their once important cultural spot as interpreters of social trends (and Whyte, despite being a sociologist, was a humanist), journalists have begun to carve out this niche and to frame many of the key questions we now ask about work. First, few journalists see freelancers as workers. They instead see them as what Richard Florida calls "the creative class." Yet these white-collar folks are workers, albeit hidden for the most part, but much separates them from blue-collar workers: culture, education, race/ethnicity, community, status, and above all economic and cultural expectation. And, in the new economy, collar doesn't signify class the way it once did. The new divide may be between the salaried and the freelancer rather than blue and white collar, or between creative and noncreative classes or groups of freelancers. I believe that freelancers, as a group, are shaping the way we view work and therefore class relationships. In short, how freelancers see themselves signals much about our culture as a whole today as well as where it is going.

Journalists and business writers, who are either unabashed cheerleaders for the new economy or ideologically critical of it, are shaping our larger cultural understanding of the freelance economy. And, truth be told, these journalists are increasingly often freelancers themselves, further complicating the narrative.

The reality is much more complex than this journalistic literature reveals, and the current lack of nuance should worry us all. Micropreneurial is both low-wage and lucrative, both dead-end and limitless, depending how one focuses the lens and what skills one possesses. Who wouldn't want to be their own boss, control their career, and pursue their creative talents? Yet few Americans can position themselves to take advantage of the new situation. This means that a whole new army of workers is being created who do not recognize their class status and therefore are cut off from labor and working-class organizational traditions. They do not even have an echo of memory of labor activism. The biggest hurdles they face deal with having them recognize that their economic insecurity is a result of larger economic and structural forces that, as individuals, they can not surmount. They need to realize they are not alone and the only way out, the only way to a decent and secure life, will be the result of structural changes, and that will only come through organized political pressure.

LISTENING TO FREELANCERS

I recently met a twenty-seven-year-old photographer from Brooklyn, a graduate of Bard College. James was a tall, serious young man who had dreamed all his life of being an artist. When I interviewed him about his work life, it was hard for him to sum it all up without writing it down on paper. He was doing what he loved, he was creative, and he didn't need to depend on a corporate job or wait tables to support his passion. He worked as an assistant to a relatively famous photographer for an hourly wage one or two days per week. He also worked in an art gallery a day a week. And he "took independent work" on the side, as he told me, shooting PR photos for bands and B-list celebrities. In addition, he worked as a set photographer for film and television production companies in New York City. During the interview, I asked him to count the number of hours he worked in a typical week—he said it hovered slightly over sixty on "a good week." Sometimes he had nothing, and he meant nothing—no work whatsoever. Last year his income was under $40,000. He said he lived dorm-style, like so many other young freelancers, with three roommates in an apartment in Williamsburg, Brooklyn. He had no health insurance, retirement benefits, or savings, but he hoped to "get some soon." Yet he seemed happy and successful, and he said he felt lucky. He was pursuing his passion and making a living at it. I asked him if he felt exploited and he looked at me with a puzzled face as if he never heard about the word. I also asked him if he imagined a time when he had security and wouldn't have to work so many hours. His answer was interesting. He told me he believed that if he could hone his skill and improve his portfolio, he would advance. Maybe he is right, but he failed to see the gerbil wheel that was his work life. He did not recognize that the reality of the new political economy would make his ascent difficult. Rather, he took personal responsibility for his economic position. His inability to advance was all his fault. This individualization makes it difficult for him to connect with others, to discuss economic matters, or, more importantly, to join collectively to improve his life.

Yet for all their seeming economic isolation, freelancers are also more politically engaged than others in their age group, though they are more independent as voters than their parents' generation. Yet this political sensibility does not yet extend to unionization or even support for labor unions. The freelancers I have interviewed were deeply involved in the first Obama campaign, but they did so as individuals, not as a collective. A hopeful example might be the Freelancers Union (FU), which has over 140,000 members, and dedicates itself to providing health insurance, retirement plans, and political advocacy. Their promotional material states:

> Independent workers make up 30% of the nation's workforce. We are freelancers, consultants, independent contractors, temps, part-timers, contingent employees, and the self-employed. Despite our contribution to America's economy, we're often left out of the social safety net. Most freelancers can't access affordable insurance, are taxed more than traditional employees, and have limited access to protections such as unemployment insurance, retirement plans, and unpaid wage claims.

The indefatigable Sarah Horowitz, founder of the FU, who has a picture of Sidney Hillman, founder of the Amalgamated Clothing Workers of America, in her office, specifically used the word "union" to name her organization. When I asked her in a recent interview why she choose the name "union" for her organization she told me it was because that was the name that worked best in focus groups. The FU may not be a union in any traditional sense. But it knows what it is and what it wants to be. It sees its role as educational and political. Yet it recognizes that what brings in members are the services it provides (health insurance, mainly, and also retirement plans and other discounted group services). Horowitz's hope is that once in the FU, new economy workers will come to the various educational outreach workshops. Building on her hero Sidney Hillman, Horowitz—whose own grandfather was a garment worker union leader—recognizes the importance of educational outreach, meeting her members where they are and carrying them forward.

Because of its size and vision, the FU has become a political player in New York City, where it is headquartered in a chic DUMBO loft, has its own political action committee, and engages in get-out-the-vote and intensive lobbying efforts. It has already helped change city and state tax codes to be more favorable toward freelancers. But can it truly organize these workers, and build a true union out of them? That remains to be seen. But they are not alone.

As I write this there has been a resurgence of activism around the Occupy Wall Street movement. This movement, leaderless, socially networked, and multigenerational, is emblematic of the labor movement today. It started not with unions, but with loosely connected bands of individual organizations. It seems to have included many young people who fit the freelancer profile. Unions have started to pay attention, joining the daily protests. Where this might lead, we cannot know. But one thing is clear: there is a resurgence of activism around economic issues and traditional unions seem not to be able to organize around it.

Freelancers and the protesters, unlike autoworkers in the 1930s, do not all work in large factories that can be targeted by organizational drives at the factory gates. Rather, they are disparate collections of often unconnected individuals. What seems to be emerging is not a leader-centered movement, but rather a new political sensibility, as many of this generation are leery of organizations and leaders. What remains to be seen is if one structure that speaks to these newly socially active citizens can emerge that captures their attention. It seems not to be the labor movement. The hope for American workers is in the ability to connect these protests with an organization that can live beyond these protests and provide a vehicle for lasting political change. The historian Arthur Schlesinger Jr. has written about political cycles in American history. Others have spoken about periodic realignments. We seem to be living in one of these transformational political times of party realignment. It might be possible that what we are witnessing with the Occupy Wall Street movement is what the former secretary of labor Robert Reich has called "only the tip of the iceberg."

It seems that many, including freelancers (this growing group of once privileged and educated workers), might now be recognizing the structural and economic issues confronting them. They are joining with unionized workers in a movement. What comes out of this could be very interesting. I am excited to watch and hope.

Part Three

State and Policy

The state—through legislation, court injunctions, and the use of force—has always been important for working people, either in the suppression of labor rights or the encouragement of union building. When railroad workers from Maryland to Missouri walked out and demonstrated over drastic wage cuts in 1877, President Hayes used federal troops to augment local and state militias, killing scores of workers, to end the first nationwide general strike in the United States. But sympathetic politicians at times supported labor and refused to use force against workers on strike. Michigan governor Frank Murphy not only refused to oust the autoworkers who sat down in the General Motors plant in Flint in 1937, he ordered in the National Guard to protect strikers from local police. The Sherman Antitrust Act of 1890, which was designed to constrain the power of large corporations, was then used to limit the ability of unions to organize, strike, picket, and boycott. The promise of the Clayton Antitrust Act of 1914, as an amendment to Sherman, to protect labor rights was short-lived but created a precedent leading to state and eventually federal recognition of union rights. The National Labor Relations Act of 1935 ultimately established the framework for modern American labor-management relations. While a boon to workers in many industries for decades, the national labor law ignored others. And revisions to the law have made it increasingly difficult for organized labor to operate within its confines.

This complex relationship between the state and workers' rights provokes questions about what, how, and to what extent workers and unions can make demands on the state. Is the labor law salvageable and what should unions be demanding in terms of reform? How do workers make demands in such a way that the state responds? What are the limits of American labor law's reach? Which historic models of labor's struggles and achievements serve us best going forward today? And how do we think about those workers who have been left lagging behind?

David Brody, a founder of the New Labor history, implores the labor movement to make labor law reform the singular, pressing concern of the movement. He reminds us that the yellow-dog contract, an agreement employees were forced to sign agreeing not to join a union, was once a great obstacle to union organization before it was banned in 1932 through the Norris–La Guardia Act. Brody argues that section 8(c) of the Taft-Hartley Act of 1947, which gives employers enormous advantages of "free speech," has constituted another yellow-dog-contract moment, making it all but impossible for unions to engage in free and fair elections. The repeal of this onerous section would create possibilities for organization that just might change the political system and could lead to one of the most important changes affecting labor in the twenty-first century.

Jacob Remes looks at grassroots organizational strength as a tool for workers to make credible demands on the state. Looking at the historic response of workers to disasters in the absence of the state, from the Halifax explosion in 1917 to Hurricane Katrina in 2005, he argues that it is often an organized working-class community that commandeered rescue and recovery operations. Relying on pre-disaster social networks, ordinary people took care of one another in acts of solidarity that can serve as models for workers in times of calm as well as during disasters that are sure to come.

Leon Fink's study of maritime workers offers us a powerful example on how the United States could affect the conditions of workers globally through domestic legislation. Merchant mariners, who traveled the globe in the late nineteenth and early twentieth centuries, were an international labor force working in a global economy. Working on ships registered under many national flags, traveling through international waters, they were subjected to harsh working conditions, including corporal punishment and bans on shore leave, without the protection of states or other legal authorities. But the La Follette Seamen's Act gave rights to workers on any ship entering American ports, regardless of their citizenship status. Fink argues that this example could be the precedent the United States needs to regulate a globalized economy through tools we have always possessed but have forgotten to use.

Jefferson Cowie cautions us to resist hoping for another New Deal as a solution to labor's problems today. The era in which a strong centralized federal government spent money and passed protections for nonelites was born out of the Great Depression. Rather than look to the 1930s as a model period, he suggests we look further back into the Gilded Age and Progressive Era, in which income distributions and overwhelming corporate power are more analogous to conditions today. Local and state governments' experiments with reform, regulation, and labor rights during the 1900s and 1910s, while chaotic, made them laboratories of change that we would do well to emulate and mine for new solutions.

Kimberley Phillips reminds us that while labor unions have been important, they have not always been the singular force for progressive change in workers' lives, and that many have been left out of the American dream. The struggles of working-class African Americans too often took place outside of the halls of labor, and more times than not were resisted by labor. African American workers' struggles have been deeply rooted in a complex relationship to the state. Civil rights efforts for social and economic justice were principally aimed at federal legislative reform, though the results have been mixed. Even now, blacks have access to few good union jobs and are becoming poorer at a faster rate than whites. Phillips argues that if labor wants to speak for all workers, it must address the structural racial and economic inequalities in the American political and social systems.

POSTMORTEM: YELLOW DOGS AND COMPANY-DOMINATED ELECTIONS

David Brody

Hardly anyone remembers the yellow-dog contract. In the old days, before the New Deal, employers commonly required workers, as a condition of employment, to sign documents warranting that they were not union members. The courts regarded these yellow-dog contracts as a lawful exchange of considerations: the employer proffered the job, the employee handed over his freedom of association. The surrendered worker's right became, in effect, the employer's property and—so the Supreme Court declared in *Hitchman Coal & Coke v. Mitchell* (1917)—entitled him to an injunction against any union trying to organize his workers, that is to say, inducing them to breach of contract. In the wake of this monstrous decision, wide swaths of American industry became off-limits to union organizing. It was something to behold when one of New York's principal subway systems sought an injunction barring the entire American Federation of Labor (AFL) from approaching its workers.

Sound incredible? Yes, but it's true and worth recalling, because in this distant past are lessons for our own time.

The simplest way to describe the modern labor law is that it offers a state-administered channel by which employees can move to collective bargaining. The simplest way to describe what ails the law is that this channel has become so constricted that what had once been a torrent of workers has slowed to a trickle. An authoritative analysis at M.I.T. of twenty thousand petitions for National Labor Relations Board (NLRB) elections between 1999 and 2004 reveals that a union (invariably starting with strong employee support) stood only one chance in five of ever getting a first contract; if the employer committed an unfair labor practice, the odds came closer to one in ten. So the basic process established by our labor law is effectively going out of business. In 1970, 7,733 NLRB elections brought collective bargaining to a quarter million workers. Thirty years later, for the period surveyed by the M.I.T. study, only one-third as many elections were held and the thirty thousand workers who made their way annually through "The Eyes of the Needles"—the apt title of John-Paul Ferguson's study—were statistically trivial in a labor force that normally grows by 1.5 million or more a year. More recently, as unemployment soared after the financial meltdown of September 2008, the number dwindled to about 22,000. Union density in the private sector is down to 6.9 percent, the lowest it's been since Sam Gompers rolled cigars for a living, and, for the first time, a majority of union workers are public employees.

So the country has arrived, slow motion, at another yellow-dog moment, when the dissonances are so jarring, the consequences so unpalatable, that something must be done. The question is whether today's labor movement is up to the challenge. And the answer, if we go by the failed 2009 campaign for the Employee Free Choice Act (EFCA), is that it is not.

The obstructions are in themselves not mysterious. First, employers violate workers' rights with relative impunity. In representation campaigns, according to the most recent available NLRB data analyzed by Cornell's Kate Bronfenbrenner, 34 percent of employers fire workers and over half threaten them. To end this lawlessness, the EFCA called for stiffer penalties and, for serious offenses, fast-track mandatory injunctions. Second, many employers defy the mandate to bargaining in good faith. According to Ferguson's findings, 62 percent of all newly certified unions lacked a contract after a year and 44 percent failed altogether. To overcome employer recalcitrance, the EFCA sought to impose mandatory arbitration after 120 days of unresolved negotiation. Finally, there was a democratic process at the core of the law: workers would choose by majority rule whether they wanted union representation. For NLRB certification, the law has ever since the Taft-Hartley Act of 1947 required a secret-ballot election (although it's the employers' choice; they can grant voluntary recognition without an election if they accept a union's demonstration of majority support). The secret ballot is itself unimpeachable, but it is premised on a formal campaign, normally lasting around forty days, in which employers are fully entitled to participate. Ever since the 1970s, when resistance to unionization markedly stiffened, employers (or the consultants they hire) have become so effective at intimidating workers that only unions with the strongest rank-and-file backing venture into the process, and even so, according to Ferguson's research, two-thirds either give up midway or lose the election. For this core problem, labor's remedy was that, as an alternative to the election, the NLRB would grant certification by a showing of signed authorization cards—the so-called card check.

And it is here, on the issue of card check, that the battle over labor law reform was joined. This was, in its way, curious, because of the bill's three proposals, card check was least satisfactory for its purpose, which was to shield workers from employer interference. In the union-avoidance industry—the outfits that specialize in union busting—card check inspired much talk of continuous "education" programs, trigger-ready responses, and closer surveillance. We can be sure, from Nelson Lichtenstein's recent book on the company, that Wal-Mart would not be stymied. At the first sign of union activity, management teams would have been flying in from Bentonville. And while card check was better than nothing, it was not better, not more effective, than the EFCA's sanctions against unlawful dismissals and threats. Yet employers were mum about that provision, and for good reason: enforcing labor's rights is hard to argue against. Card check, on the other hand, is easy. All that needed to be said was that Big Labor wanted to deprive workers of the "basic, democratic right" to the secret ballot, which employer groups did, incessantly. The labor side offered no effective response. There was vague talk about "leveling the playing field," a lot about "rescuing the middle class," and a sad effort at renaming card check to "majority sign-up."

The best union strategists could have hoped for was that, as an issue, card check wouldn't register with the public. In fact, they were mostly right. A blitz of business-funded television ads targeting key Senate races in the 2008 campaign was shown by a Peter D. Hart survey to have left voters unmoved. It made for an arresting visual, but why was that actor, familiar to all viewers of *The Sopranos* as a Mafia boss, handing a paper to a cowed worker and saying: sign here?

If public bemusement counted as a plus, however, what did that say about the AFL-CIO's strategy? It said that labor law reform was not an issue to take to the people (and, in fact, the EFCA never even came up during the presidential debates) but a deal to be made on Capitol Hill.

After the 2006 congressional elections, when the Democratic tide was running, the AFL-CIO put forth its bill, signed on a raft of co-sponsors, and awaited the presidential campaign. In the primaries, all the lead candidates attracted union support, but the powerhouse Service Employees International Union (SEIU) committed to Barack Obama early, before he caught fire. After his nomination, the entire movement, the AFL-CIO and Change to Win, went all-out, pouring money into the campaign and providing the boost among male white workers, where Obama was weakest, that enabled him to carry the key industrial states. If ever labor's political moment had come, this was it: an indebted president, a strongly Democratic House, even a filibuster-proof Senate.

For any normal law, the gambit might have paid off, but labor law is not like other laws. It touches the most sensitive of employer pre-rogatives: the power they hold over employees. There are still plenty of unionized firms, but labor law gives off a whiff of class conflict, and they stand aside. So, to begin with, the EFCA faced opposition uniquely united, and, by way of explanation, uniquely motivated by hostility to collective bargaining—hence the fevered talk of Arma-geddon, or similar hyperbole, at the prospect of the EFCA's passage. These people are not kidding. In a notable piece of investigative jour-nalism, *Harper's* Washington editor Ken Silverstein recounted the lobbying juggernaut in high gear—the "fly-ins" of local business leaders to lobby on Capitol Hill; the united front of big companies and trade associations led by the U.S. Chamber of Commerce and called, if you can believe it, the Coalition for a Democratic Workplace; the paid-for findings from conservative think tanks that labor law re-form is a "job killer"; antiunion front organizations galore, includ-ing the mysteriously financed Center for Union Facts for the hatchet work, plus at least 126 registered lobbyists working the Hill, includ-ing, on the Democratic side, the former legislative director for Rahm Emanuel, President Obama's first chief of staff, and the brother and

sister-in-law of John Podesta, the head of Obama's transition team and
a top party influential. In Washington, money can buy you anything.

All this ferocious energy funnels into a dysfunctional political
system. On Capitol Hill, a Democratic sweep translates into a progressive House of Representatives. Not so the Senate, where even a
big victory at the polls is diffused by equal state representation and
by arcane rules of delay and filibuster. As for the president, well, any
president, no matter how beholden, has a lot on his mind and, as the
Chamber of Commerce functionary who organized the Arkansas
"fly-in" observed, an ambitious incumbent like Obama will think
twice before "sink[ing] a lot of political capital into a radioactive issue
like [EFCA]."

The gentleman had it right. The new president made many
gestures—appointments, executive actions, access (the SEIU's Andy
Stern was reportedly the White House's most frequent first-year visi-
tor), but on the EFCA Barack Obama was not to be counted on. At
a lengthy preinaugural meeting with the *Washington Post* editorial
board, the president-elect said he favored the bill, but believed both
sides should sit down and agree on its terms—this despite conceding
that one side considered the EFCA "the devil incarnate." And he signaled that job creation, not the EFCA, was his main priority, because
if employment was plummeting, "there are no jobs to unionize."

The White House was, in any case, probably not decisive. On the
EFCA, senators from Arkansas don't listen to the president; they listen to Wal-Mart. And they were joined by half a dozen other Democrats from Nebraska, Virginia, Delaware, even Dianne Feinstein of
California. As it happened, it was the lone Republican co-sponsor,
Arlen Specter of Pennsylvania, who broke ranks first because, so he
said, he valued the secret-ballot election too highly. This was where
card check came in handy, as cover for senators like Specter (who was
trying to fend off a right-wing primary challenge). And, while the industry side was getting mobilized, the unions were dismantling their
formidable network of campaign workers. Whatever momentum
the EFCA had going in was overtaken by the economic emergency
and then, after Specter's defection, by dispiriting efforts at patch-
ing together a compromise—the talk was of fast-track elections and

watered-down arbitration—that might hold the sixty votes needed for cloture. And then there weren't sixty. In a special election in early 2010, the Republicans unexpectedly captured the Massachusetts seat long held by Ted Kennedy, who would have led the fight had he lived, and it was over.

This was not labor's first failure at labor law reform, only the last in an unbroken record of defeats going back to the Johnson administration, each marked by the inside-the-Beltway tactics that failed the EFCA.

So let's return to my starting point, the yellow-dog injunction. If the odds seem bad today, consider how much worse they were seventy years ago, when labor lacked any apparent political recourse because the Supreme Court had not only upheld the yellow-dog contract but barred any contrary legislation, state or federal, as unconstitutional infringements on liberty and property. Labor injunctions seemed nearly as unassailable, resting as they did on judicial equity powers, initially by the state courts, and then, in a series of increasingly draconian decisions, by the Supreme Court as well. As for the political landscape of the 1920s, although differently configured from our own, it was if anything bleaker, with the Republicans dominant, the Democrats regionally divided, the AFL of small account politically, and labor's troubles of little public interest.

And then something changed. It was as if a slow burn took hold of the country, fed in part by labor's defiance of the injunction—being in contempt of court became more or less a trade-union rite of passage—and, more fundamentally, by a growing revulsion at the yellow-dog spectacle. By the end of the decade the New York courts were declining to enforce yellow-dog injunctions. Wisconsin passed a new anti-yellow-dog law in 1929, defying the Supreme Court, and four other states soon followed. When Hoover nominated Charles Evans Hughes in early 1930 for chief justice, Senate insurgents noticed that, in private practice, this distinguished ex–New York governor, ex–associate justice, presidential candidate, and secretary of state had represented only corporate interests. Did the nation, thundered George W. Norris of Nebraska, want someone with his "one-sided life" in service to the rich to be "supreme and final arbitrator" over the

lives of "the men who toil and the men who suffer?" Hughes's nomination got through, but only after a fight that stirred the country.
Then President Hoover nominated John J. Parker and all hell broke
loose. In the infamous Red Jacket decision of 1927, Judge Parker had
approved the yellow-dog injunction closing the coalfields of southern West Virginia to union organizers. Parker's only defense was that
he was bound by the Supreme Court, but it wasn't enough to save
his nomination. In a close vote, the Republican-controlled Senate rejected Judge Parker, something that hadn't happened in a generation.

In the meantime, a legal strategy had emerged, not from the AFL,
which was gutsy enough to defy the injunction but not smart enough
to find a solution. That was the work of an expert team, including Felix
Frankfurter, assembled in May 1928 by Senator Norris, who chaired
the Judiciary Committee. In a few days, they sketched out what would
become the Norris–La Guardia Anti-Injunction Act. Drawing on congressional authority to declare public policy and define the jurisdiction of the federal courts, they wrote a constitutionally defensible bill
that defanged the labor injunction and pronounced the yellow-dog
contract unenforceable in the federal courts. They could well have
stopped with the injunction, because, without it, the yellow-dog contract was unenforceable, or rather, it was enforceable only by a right to
dismiss that employers had anyway. But confronting the yellow-dog
contract provided the occasion for a public policy statement asserting that "the individual unorganized worker is commonly helpless to
exercise actual liberty of contract." With that phrase, "actual liberty of
contract," Norris–La Guardia repudiated the doctrinal basis for the
nation's labor jurisprudence.

It took one final, disastrous nomination, this time the Seventh
Circuit Court appointment of the Chicago federal judge who had issued the injunction breaking the 1922 national railway shopcrafts
strike, to put Norris–La Guardia over the top. Republican opposition
crumbled, the bill passed both houses overwhelmingly, and Hoover
reluctantly signed it on March 23, 1932. Almost miraculously, a century of court oppression had been lifted from labor's back.

It would be convenient, for purposes of this essay, to stop at this
point, because the battle for Norris–La Guardia offers a template for

what it will take to succeed where the EFCA failed. But history did not stop, and what followed, triumphant on its face, helps explain labor's current malaise.

Norris–La Guardia not only swept away the old order, it opened the new by asserting that "actual liberty of contract" required

> that [the worker] have full freedom of association, self-organization, and designation of representatives of his own choosing, to negotiate the terms and conditions of his employment, and that he shall be free from the interference, restraint, or coercion of employers, or their agents, in the designation of such representatives or in self-organization, or in other concerted activities for the purpose of collective bargaining, or other mutual aid or protection.

It was unclear just how, or even if, these grand words would be implemented, but when the New Deal swept in, there they were, in Section 7a of the National Industrial Recovery Act, FDR's misbegotten effort at reversing the deflationary spiral by cartelizing industry. For two years, the meaning of Section 7a was contested, primarily over whether it permitted employers to set up their own unions. In the end, they lost that battle and, under the aegis of Senator Robert F. Wagner, Congress passed the National Labor Relations Act in 1935. What was transformative about this law was that it linked self-organization to a right to collective bargaining, coupled (the second key innovation) to an employer duty to bargain, a duty triggered (the third innovation) by a democratic vote of workers. These innovations, embodying the right to "representatives of their own choosing," created the state-mandated channel by which, over the next two decades, millions of workers gained collective bargaining.

But there was a contradiction at the law's core: self-organization by definition excluded employers, while any formal system implementing "representatives of their own choosing" invited them in. Senator Wagner was alive to this danger; he had been schooled in it by the National Recovery Act battles over company unionism. And he was aware of a long history, about to be illuminated by the La Follette

Civil Liberties Committee, of employer spying and other dirty tricks aimed at penetrating and disrupting labor's organizing efforts. But the National Labor Relations Act was a product of the Second New Deal. Having witnessed the invalidation of much of Roosevelt's hastily written original program, Senator Wagner wanted a statute that would survive Supreme Court scrutiny, and that led to a decision, despite his fears, not to address the free-speech question: the word "influence" was stricken from the designated list of prohibited employer actions. Instead, Wagner handed the issue off to the NLRB, which, understanding his concerns, enforced employer neutrality.

But the board was on exposed ground. The Supreme Court— after 1937, Roosevelt's court—might well have rejected the employers' First Amendment claim had the constitutionality of a provision of the act been at stake. But with no legislative mandate to push up against, the Supreme Court equivocated, at once denying, in *NLRB v. Virginia Electric & Power* (1941), that the company was enjoined, either by the act or by the board's order, "from expressing its views on labor policies," while endorsing an earlier court opinion that employer speech was inherently coercive. The court resolved its indecision by remanding the case of the board, with instructions that the employer's speech be placed in a broader course of coercive activity (which the NLRB duly did). Two years later, the Supreme Court left standing a lower court ruling explicitly acknowledging a constitutional right, provided that employer speech met the course-of-conduct test (and in this case, where no other coercive acts were alleged, reversed the NLRB order).

From these inconclusive beginnings, however, the jurisprudence on employer speech was swept up by a revolution in judicial activism, in which championing property rights gave way to championing civil liberties. For liberal justices, the lodestone was Justice Holmes's famous postwar dissents in defense of political speech. Employer speech ultimately fell within that ambit, but in a case unrelated to the Wagner Act. *Thomas v. Collins* (1945) involved a Texas licensing law for union organizers. In striking down that law as a free-speech infringement, the court declared *in dictum*, with nothing in the case requiring it, that employers were equally as privileged as union organizers under the First Amendment. Especially in the concurring opinions called forth by this gratuitous step there stood revealed the court's discomfort with what it regarded as an illiberal feature of the Wagner Act. "Speech of employers otherwise beyond reach of Federal Government is brought within the Labor Board's power to suppress by associating it with 'coercion' or 'domination.' " Thus wrote Robert H. Jackson, applying the formulation Justice Holmes had invoked against wartime legislation meant to stifle disloyalty to a labor law meant to secure the associational rights of workers.

Justice Jackson's solicitude, of course, played into the hands of employers gunning for the Wagner Act. Indeed, *Thomas v. Collins* offered a template for what was the essential premise of Taft-Hartley two years later: that employers and unions stood equally before the labor law. It followed, with employer speech rights vindicated, that the representation election be reconstructed so as to give full play to employers as participants. Taft-Hartley also defined coercive speech, something the sustaining case law had skirted (or, in the case of *Thomas v. Collins*, couldn't have addressed because there was no employer speech to define). Under section 8(c), employers committed an unfair labor practice only if their speech contained a "threat of reprisal or force" (or promise of benefit). And what constituted a threat? Under current case law, that it be more than a prediction. Employers cannot threaten, but they can predict, dire consequences—a distinction, of course, beloved by lawyers but lost on workers listening to lawyer-crafted "predictions." Another line of case law, based on employer property rights, has over time reversed all the ground rules initially promulgated by the NLRB: employers can hold captive-audience meetings, interrogate individual workers, and exclude organizers from company grounds. Today, workers hopeful of gaining union representation truly have to go through—to use Ferguson's metaphor—the eye of a needle. This grotesque reality has not, however, dimmed enthusiasm on the bench for employer free speech. In 2008, in an opinion written by John Paul Stevens, one of the court's liberals, the representation election was still being celebrated as a process of "uninhibited, robust, and wide-open debate."

Now we know the derivation of the card-check provision. It arises from a perception of obstacles too deeply embedded in the law's juris-prudence to be challenged. But the card-check stratagem has failed, and labor has to confront employer speech. The reader understands by now why I started with the yellow-dog contract. It demonstrates how, in the face of long odds, labor can win. What is wanted is a cam-paign that holds the corrupted representation election up to public contempt, and as the history of the yellow-dog contract shows, the public's contempt can move mountains in the nation's capital. The situations are of course not strictly comparable. As a delegitimizing phrase, "yellow-dog contract" can't be surpassed. The best equiva-lent I can come up with is "company-dominated election." Employer domination is a potent concept in the labor law—it renders company unions unlawful—and applying it to elections might one day come in handy in court (the argument would be that employer speech is a form of company domination), but as a rallying cry, it's not up there with the yellow-dog contract. On the other hand, the labor movement has at hand, thanks to Norris–La Guardia, a language of labor rights not available to the old AFL.

An advantage is only as good as the uses to which it is put, how-ever, and, as the EFCA campaign showed, the American labor move-ment is clumsy at such talk. (I even wrote a historical essay in *Dissent* once explaining why.) But it knows how to take a stand. And in this instance, that means the Employee Free Choice Act should have called for the repeal of the Taft-Hartley 8(c) employer speech provi-sion. What a howl that would have raised! All the better. How more effectively to focus the minds of people who work for a living than to have the corporate side fulminating about its rights? What about em-ployees? Isn't the purpose of the labor law to protect their rights? Put these simple questions to the ordinary citizen: *Would you personally be willing to go up to your supervisor and say you thought this place needed a union? Would you feel coerced if your employer told you that collective bar-gaining would lead to job cuts and maybe a closed plant? or ordered you to attend captive-audience meetings where you could not speak up (because, as an employee, you have no free-speech rights)? or interrogated you about how you felt about union representation? In sum, do you think, although the labor law says you have this right, that you and your coworkers could have a union if you wanted one?* Employers do not want these questions asked and, thanks to labor's reticence, they have been given a pass. But they are extraordinarily sensitive about it, hence their furious opposition to the labor lawyer Craig Becker's nomination to the NLRB. He serves, at this writing, as a recess appointee—one of the president's gestures—but is unlikely ever to be confirmed. Employers say Becker is out of the "mainstream" or an "ideologue" when what they mean is that he once wrote a law-review article arguing against their right to participate in representation campaigns.

Calling for repeal of section 8(c) is a provocation, yes, but also the starting point in any long-term battle against the company-dominated election. Repeal would nullify the permissive Taft-Hartley definition of coercive speech and restore to the NLRB and the courts the task of setting the coercive/noncoercive boundary line. This would open a path, if cleverly exploited, for bringing into play the case for employer neutrality. Moreover, repeal of section 8(c) would, on a smaller scale, be comparable to Norris–La Guardia's declaration of public policy, conveying congressional disapproval of the court's employer free-speech doctrine, and if joined to a well-developed case could persuade a future court to revisit the foundational employer free-speech decisions.

If it did so, the court would find them substantively empty. This is perhaps not surprising when we consider that in the 1940s, at the crest of CIO power, it was not far-fetched to regard employer speech as just a component of robust workplace debates over representation. Thus the easy equivalence in *Thomas v. Collins*: in protecting the freedom of organizers to address workers, remarked Justice Jackson, we are applying "a rule the benefit of which, in all its breadth and vigor, the Court denies to employers in National Labor Relations Board cases. . . . The remedy is . . . to apply the same rule and spirit to free speech cases whoever the speaker." Neither Jackson nor his fellow liberal justices took any notice of the employment relationship itself, nor of its foundation in master-servant doctrine (the basis on which the NLRB recently found university teaching assistants not to be employees and not eligible for labor-law coverage), nor of the futility of distinguishing employer speech as the expression of opinion and employer speech as the exercise of economic power. It was easy enough, the distinguished jurist Paul Hays acidly remarked, for judges "safely ensconced in their chambers" not to feel threatened by an employer's artful prediction of lost jobs, but "he doesn't fool his employees; they know perfectly well what he means."

Before it can be a legal problem, however, the company-dominated election has to be a political problem, and before it can be a political problem it has to engage public opinion. The case for the yellow-dog contract collapsed when people ceased believing that it was a fair exercise of liberty of contract. The case for the company-dominated election will collapse when people cease believing that it provides— to use Oliver Wendell Holmes's famous words—"a free marketplace of ideas." The labor movement is clumsy at making that disbelief happen—hence the failed Employee Free Choice Act—but in the right circumstances it knows to take a stand. Who would have thought that the shellacking (as the president put it) taken by the Democrats in the 2010 elections would have produced the right circumstances? Or that the precipitating event would arise in the one sector not afflicted by the company-dominated election?

Wisconsin was one of the dozen states that changed hands in 2010. The Republican governor, Scott Walker, belonged to a new generation of arch-conservatives, inflected by Tea Party rancor, riding into office on a populist rhetoric for cut-down governments and balanced budgets, and capitalizing on popular resentment at public employees who seemed shielded from the economic vicissitudes buffeting the country—"a new privileged class," Indiana's Republican governor Mitch Daniels called them. The subtext was everywhere that the public employee unions needed reining in. But Wisconsin was unlike other Midwestern states caught up in the Republican counterrevolution. It had deep progressive roots, a tradition of open and fair-minded politics, and a record of pioneering public-employee unionism. Wisconsin was, in fact, where the movement had first taken root and where, in 1959, state employees first won collective-bargaining rights. Wisconsin was different also because of the ham-handed governor it had elected. Under the guise of a rather modest "budget repair," and with no forewarning during the campaign,

Scott Walker sprung a bill on February 11, 2011, intended to break the public employee unions. The budget repair bill cut state wages (by mandating increases in health insurance and retirement payments), limited future bargaining strictly to wages (with anything above the cost of living requiring a referendum), and, having stripped public employee unions of their functions, inhibited their ability to collect dues and required elections every year confirming that a majority still wanted union representation. Totally barred from collective bargaining were the state universities and university hospitals and, cruelest of all, home health care and child care workers only recently delivered from the bondage of private service.

Wisconsin unionists flocked to Madison to testify at legislative hearings, and from that initial action a remarkable popular movement sprang up. Young people brought in sleeping bags and occupied the Capitol. Day after day demonstrators, ordinary citizens from many walks of life, crowded Capitol Square. On Saturdays, they exceeded 75,000. Even off-duty police and firemen, although exempted from Walker's bill, marched. Democratic state senators decamped to Illinois, depriving the bill of the quorum needed for consideration. And recall campaigns began against eligible senators. The country watched in amazement. Governor Walker accomplished single-handedly what the labor movement had signally failed at for half a century: he made collective-bargaining rights a national issue. In the end, the Republicans muscled his bill past the quorum requirement by stripping out the budgetary side of it, rushing the bill through with so little regard for the legislative rules that its legality was immediately called into question. But in the meantime the Wisconsin drama had revealed something about the country. Consistently, across all the national polls, Americans believed in collective-bargaining rights by a two-to-one margin.

On March 8, seven Republican senators led by Jim DeMint of South Carolina introduced the National Right to Work Act. Now why would they want to do that? Taft-Hartley already permits the states to pass right-to-work laws. In the nation's conservative belt, they generally have, and right-to-work is a live issue in Midwestern states caught up in the post-2010 Republican resurgence. DeMint's crew are states' righters; they should, philosophically, be fine with the Taft-Hartley status quo. Besides, they don't actually expect a national right-to-work bill to be passed. No, this is about something else. It signals anxiety that Governor Walker's antics, although confined to the public sector, may have opened a national debate over collective-bargaining rights. If the worst happens, and Americans begin to think seriously about our national labor law, the employer side wants to be prepared. It wants the debate to be framed by individual liberty—an old ploy, tried and true—and not by freedom of association. That's the point of DeMint's right-to-work bill.

One of the co-sponsors was Orrin Hatch of Utah. Senator Hatch had been a rare voice of candor in the earlier debate over the Employee Free Choice Act. In a Senate speech greeting the bill in June 2007, he gave short shrift to arguments about the sacred secret ballot and all that, already the standard Republican line. What labor finds objectionable, Hatch argued, is not the form of the vote, but "that ever since the 1947 Taft-Hartley Amendments, the law allows employers to communicate with their employees about union organization." Labor wanted to reverse Taft-Hartley, and card check was just a backdoor way of doing it. Hatch's speech vibrated with hostility at the notion that the upper hand that employers enjoyed (although he did not quite put it that way) might in any way be diminished. "If they thought they could get way with it," Senator Hatch concluded darkly, "unions would have Congress repeal employer speech rights altogether." Exactly right, on both counts. The unions didn't dare. And employer speech is the real issue. If it is not confronted, if the company-dominated election is left unchallenged, private sector collective bargaining will simply fade away, whatever its fate in the public sector.

There, in states with well-rooted public-employee movements, collective bargaining will survive. Wisconsin's grassroots backlash has spread to Ohio, Indiana, and other states where emboldened Republican administrations had pushed through, in a variety of guises, union-busting legislation. Almost overnight, the center of gravity of progressive politics seemed to shift, as organized labor and its allies redeployed their energies to state battlegrounds. There will be wins and losses, but one way or the other, collective bargaining will have entered politics, where it belongs. And, as an ongoing state issue, it will feed a national discussion, which the country sorely needs.

The notion that they have collective-bargaining rights is, of course, unreal to working Americans who have spent a lifetime in an antiunion environment, although a recent NLRB order that those rights be posted in every workplace (over bitter Chamber of Commerce objections) is a brave try. But something else has happened. *Citizens United* (2010) famously overturned long-standing doctrine limiting corporate spending in political campaigns on free-speech grounds. That reasoning, it turns out, applies also to the provision in the Federal Election Campaign Act that shields rank-and-file employees from political advocacy by employers. It can be anticipated that companies will be emboldened. Wal-Mart, indeed, jumped the gun in 2008, and, in the wake of *Citizens United*, the right-wing Koch brothers, financiers among other things of Scott Walker's Wisconsin run, sent partisan political mailings to all their employees in this country. Ultimately more and more workers will be subjected to the same kinds of employer coercion in high-stakes political elections that they routinely experience in union representation elections. Only the resonance, once the reality of company-dominated politics sinks in, will be different, because while collective-bargaining rights might seem unreal to most employees, the freedom to vote as they please is not unreal.

And then, if organized labor drives home the link, the notion that corporations enjoy a free-speech right to intimidate employees—to collective bargaining no less than at the polling booth—will lose credibility. It will be laughed off, just as the yellow-dog contract as an employer liberty-of-contract right was once laughed off. Collective-bargaining rights, now that Wisconsin's attack on public-employee unions has captured the country's attention, should stay right there, implanted in the national debate, with this as labor's message: the surreptitious denial of collective-bargaining rights embodied in the National Labor Relations Act is a stain on America.

When I began this essay, I never imagined that we were on the cusp of another yellow-dog moment, but maybe we are, and one day, after a long slog up to the Supreme Court, we will be rid of the company-dominated election. At the first opportunity, Senate Democrats should call Orrin Hatch's bluff: they should introduce a bill repealing the Taft-Hartley section 8(c) employer speech provision.

SOLIDARITY, CITIZENSHIP, AND THE OPPORTUNITIES OF DISASTERS

Jacob A.C. Remes

After the landfall of Hurricane Katrina in the late summer of 2005, New Orleans lay flooded, the poorest of its population seemingly abandoned. The entire state seemed to have collapsed with its ill-maintained levees. Left in their rubble, we were told, was a city disintegrated into chaos, the police fleeing their jobs; looters, murderers, and rapists running rampant; and poor people seemingly inexplicably attacking the very people who tried to help them. The *Washington Post* banner headline that Friday linked two states that were, it implied, intimately related: New Orleans was now "A City of Despair and Lawlessness." Only a week later, though, a different story began to trickle out of New Orleans, one that inverted the roles played by authority figures and those stranded in the city. This one told of spontaneous organizing by people who remained in New Orleans, working together to try to find food and a way out of the city. In the second story, it was not poor survivors who were the sources of murder, rape, and mayhem, but rather the police and National Guard. Indeed, gang members organized to break into abandoned stores and find supplies: clothes, food, and water for those who needed them. They even wore uniforms to identify themselves. Katrina, it seemed, proved the opposite of what the mass media told us in the first week. Left to their own devices, poor and working-class New Orleanians practiced solidarity with each other, and indeed the state that remained in the city—in the form of the police and National Guard—did its best to break up those very bonds of solidarity.

How odd, then, that there is no mention of this sort of grassroots solidarity among the "quality values for all individuals regardless of their race or religion" that the Foundation for a Better Life promotes on billboards, television advertisements, and movie trailers. The foundation, financed by billionaire Philip Anschutz, instead spends

$3.3 million a year encouraging values capitalists would like to in-
still in their workers, including ambition and hard work. Values that
could be political are carefully defined in less dangerous ways: caring
becomes "feeling concern" for others, but not acting on it; "helping
others" and "making a difference" are limited to volunteerism and
charity; loyalty, bizarrely, means "being faithful to commitments";
and most perversely of all, unity is interpreted as patriotism and illustrated by a little girl waving an American flag. Anschutz's values, it
seems, all emphasize hierarchy and submission. None of this should
be surprising, of course, since his money also promotes such values
as conservative propaganda (via the *Washington Examiner* and the
Weekly Standard), homophobia (via Colorado for Family Values), and
creationism (via the Discovery Institute).

As flooded New Orleans shows, Anschutz's individualistic values
are a dangerous lie. The left needs to promote its own, truer "quality value": solidarity. As a descriptor, solidarity summarizes what
happened in New Orleans; as an aspiration, it points to a new, less
hierarchical, and more democratic form of citizenship. In stark contrast to Anschutz's version of "helping others," which emphasizes the
"others" and suggests an individualistic and hierarchical notion of
charity, solidarity is mutual and reciprocal. "I'll be there," promises
the solidarity pledge promoted by Jobs with Justice. "During the next
year, I'll be there at least five times for someone else's struggle, as well
as my own. If enough of us are there, we'll all start winning!" Notably,
the pledge is not just to help others, and certainly not in the supposedly selfless way of charity, but also to help oneself. The pledge signer
promises to be there for others, but he or she also promises to be there
for his or her own fight. At the heart of the Jobs with Justice pledge is
the promise it makes about the power of solidarity: that, if carried out,
"we'll all start winning." That is, of course, just a different phrasing of
the first verse of "Solidarity Forever": while there is "no force on earth
[that] is weaker than the feeble strength of one," with solidarity "there
can be no power greater anywhere beneath the sun."

But solidarity is critically important beyond our battles against the
greedy parasites on the shop floor, in the mall, and at city hall. In 1919,
Christian novelist Basil King defined "active brotherly kindness" in

terms strikingly similar to what we would recognize as solidarity. *City of Comrades* is a novel about an architect destroyed by drink who reclaims his proper standing in life by way of the "Down and Out Club," a house on the Bowery where drunks and former drunks help each other find sobriety. "It's the fact that so much heart's blood goes into this work that makes it so living," the club's leader says. Each task a man performs to help his fellow, each donation, is a prayer. "Prayer is action," he explains, "only it's kind action." What makes the Down and Out Club successful—so successful that the architect's sidekick, a more committed dipsomaniac, fears going because he knows he will be cured—is the spirit of solidarity in which it operates. The club receives no outside funding, and its leaders are themselves former drunks, not professional do-gooders. The mutual aid is successful precisely because it is not charity, but rather because it is solidarity. King, with his "active brotherly kindness," understood that the solace comes jointly and inseparably from the aid offered and from the relationship with the person or organization who offers it.

When Basil King adapted *City of Comrades* for the screen— he wrote under contract to Samuel Goldwyn—he shifted the plot slightly. In the original novel, the now-sober architect proves himself in World War I and returns to New York to convince America to join the war and a young woman to marry him. In the film version, the architect enlists but makes it only as far as Halifax, Nova Scotia, where he proves his worth—and is blinded and nursed to health by the love interest—in the midst of a terrible, true disaster there. In December 1917, a munitions ship exploded in Halifax Harbor, killing two thousand people and destroying roughly a quarter of the city. King appropriately shifted his novel about solidarity to Halifax, since it is in the aftermath of disasters that we see solidarity's full blossoming. Indeed, when King wrote his novel, the phrase "City of Comrades" appears to have been exclusively associated with the Halifax explosion.

This comradeship was a solidarity conditioned by Haligonians' relationships and social networks from before the disaster. Middle-class college women volunteered at unheated hospitals literally flooded with blood and gore. Working around the clock in conditions that would challenge even trained medical workers, these women were certainly impressively altruistic, and for the most part they helped people they did not know. But they went to hospitals with their friends, supporting each other in their unfamiliar and frightening work. Their work was shaped and conditioned by the daily patterns of solidarity from their ordinary lives. Men likewise volunteered. The soldiers and sailors who had swollen Halifax's wartime population flocked to their adopted city's devastated area to help dig out injured and dead bodies. Although their officers later took credit for this work, contemporary descriptions made it clear that the soldiers were working of their own accord and without orders. Well trained in preparation for the trenches, they exhibited impressive esprit de corps, with enlisted men pressuring each other to work harder. "Wherever you went there were half-a-dozen boys with hands out to help you," reported Mrs. J.G. MacDougall, a nurse. She told the story of an American sailor, sent ashore from a visiting ship, who hid on a window ledge in order to sleep. He was "dragged out of it by a mess-mate who abused him for disgracing the U.S. Navy." Like the women who went together to hospitals to volunteer there, these sailors and soldiers were reenacting their daily patterns of solidarity to their neighbors and to their fellows.

Most of all, the people most directly affected by the explosion relied on their pre-disaster social networks. Survivors went to the places they were accustomed to going for succor: the convent, doctors' houses, local hospitals, drugstores, even barbershops. Mothers, fathers, daughters, and sons left the factories, offices, and barracks to run home or to school and check on their relatives. Neighbors went next door to check on each other. Usually they were the first to arrive, the first to notice their loved one bleeding or in shock or in need of rescue from under fallen stoves. They provided rescue, food, warmth, and comfort. Sarah Ellen Powell took into her mostly undamaged home three of her married sisters and their families, a total of seventeen people. In ordinary times, an unrelated family boarded with her, so she was used to sharing her home with others. But more important is that Powell's husband, a stove fitter, died in the explosion, and we can imagine that the busyness and bustle of her sisters and their families may have distracted her, and their presence provided her emotional support. This support may have been particularly important to

her, both emotionally and practically, since her six-month-old daughter, Hilda, never fully recovered from a cut on her face she received in
the explosion and died about four months later. In the face of this un-
derstandable grief and depression, the presence of Powell's family became all the more important. Her tight mesh of social relationships
meant that the categories of benefactor and recipient were not cleanly
distinct, and, as Basil King would have recognized, neither were the
categories of material and emotional aid.

These moments of solidarity expose what is always there, even in
ordinary times. Anarchists find in times of spontaneous order evidence that it is the state that holds back a true flowering of humanity.
To quote anarchist writer Colin Ward's famous metaphor, "Society
which organizes itself without authority is always in existence, like
a seed beneath the snow, buried under the weight of the state." The
reciprocal solidarity shown by Sarah Ellen Powell and her relatives, or
the women who worked in hospitals, or the sailors who forced their
buddy to work harder all demonstrate and display the bonds that were
always there. It may have taken the extraordinary circumstance of
the explosion to expose it in these particular ways, but the impulse to
solidarity, and the spontaneous order it created, were always there. Alternatively, of course, disasters may expose what is already not there.
Once we understand how disaster survivors rely on their friends,
neighbors, and daily patterns of solidarity, it explains why, as sociologist Eric Klinenberg has demonstrated, neighborhoods with less
social capital have significantly higher death rates in heat waves.

Solidarity in the aftermath of disaster relies on what existed before, but it also builds new connections, new forms and structures.
The women who volunteered in hospitals had to negotiate and rene-
gotiate social expectations and hierarchies while in the midst of difficult, stressful, and unpleasant circumstances. There were arguments
about who should help whom and which tasks were appropriate for
which kind of people. But for the most part, arguments were settled
and agreements reached, either explicitly or implicitly. A medical
student named Florence Murray was amazed by what she called the
"organization without any organization," the way in which her fellow volunteers found useful work with a minimum of instruction

or argument. Something similar happened in the devastated area. Charles Burchell, a leading lawyer, recalled a few weeks later that he "had" a soldier and sailor as his "helpers" in gathering the wounded in his automobile, but as a civilian he could not have had command over them. Rather, the three of them must have implicitly or explicitly negotiated the system in which they would work: Burchell drove the car and the soldier and sailor stood on the running boards and loaded the wounded into the car.

The Halifax explosion suggests what sorts of solidarity are possible, even in extraordinarily bad situations. To adopt solidarity as our major and public value is not a pie-in-the-sky utopia. Rather, our job as organizers and teachers on the left must be to help our neighbors, coworkers, students, and friends rediscover the capacity and need for solidarity they carry around with them. But disasters also create new forms of governance, new opportunities and dangers. As Naomi Klein has argued, disasters can be particularly dangerous moments of increased militarism and neoliberalism. But it need not be this way. Since disasters are also moments of solidarity and creativity, they can be opportunities to craft new forms of citizenship.

This is a particularly important moment to consider the dangers and opportunities of mass disasters, because we are about to see many more of them—and by "see" I mean both experience and witness. In the twenty-first century there will likely be a sharp increase of meteorological and seismological disaster. Global warming will mean more and worse floods, heat waves, and droughts. Although scientific disagreement persists about the effect of climate change on the frequency and intensity of hurricanes, there is mounting evidence that it increases the proportion of storms that are particularly violent. Moreover, the chronic effects of global warming, especially coastal erosion, mean that coastal communities are less able to withstand storms and floods.

While there is no reason to believe that there will be more or worse earthquakes this century, the human cost of seismological disasters will almost certainly grow. In the twentieth century, urbanization in relatively rich countries led to a decline in the fatality rates of earthquakes, thanks to improved building codes and other infrastructural advantages of cities. But urbanization in poorer countries has not been accompanied by stronger buildings and better infrastructure. To the contrary, globally poor cities are marked by construction that even in ordinary times is shoddy and dangerous and by infrastructure that is inadequate even absent a disaster. The continued and accelerating massive growth of cities in poor, seismically active countries will almost certainly lead to an increased rate of fatalities per earthquake. Port-au-Prince is not particularly large by global standards, but its earthquake in January 2010 presaged the sorts of catastrophic earthquakes we can expect in coming years. As always, the social effects of all these types of "natural" disasters will be felt most by the poor, both globally and within developed countries.

New communications technologies make disasters all the more relevant for crafting a movement and a culture based on solidarity. With the growth of global mass media and the increasing development of Internet-based many-to-many communications platforms, those of us who do not directly experience a disaster are increasingly affected by it. Disasters thus become moments of global empathy and solidarity. The massively successful charitable donation drives that followed the Port-au-Prince earthquake and Tohoku tsunami in March 2011 suggest how globally distributed television footage and, especially in Japan, new technologies that allow individuals to post amateur video and short-form reporting have made the world smaller. But charity is not enough to relieve disasters effectively or ethically or, especially, to minimize future ones. Successful disaster relief, like a broader movement for global justice of which it should be a part, must be based on solidarity. The trick will be to create transnational polities that respond not only with empathy but with true solidarity. This project will be particularly important as we seek to mobilize a global citizenry to respond to and avert the coming disasters associated with climate change.

The Halifax explosion points again to an example of how transnational giving can create transnational polities. Much as in our own time, in 1917 and the years that followed, working-class Haligonians were increasingly squeezed out of politics in favor of an ideology of technocratic expertise. Throughout North America, the ideology of governance increasingly emphasized good government, expert knowledge, and managerial authority. As in Klein's account of disaster capitalism, the explosion was a catalyst for the growth of the technocratic state. The Canadian federal government established the Halifax Relief Commission to distribute relief funds, compensate people for lost property, and rebuild the destroyed parts of the city; the commission was developer, city planning authority, landlord, employer, court, and relief agent all in one. But union and working-class voices were excluded from the commission, which claimed to act on behalf of the undifferentiated people of Halifax, but without representation. Almost immediately after the explosion, an international cadre of disaster experts converged on Halifax, bringing with them models of relief, organization, and governance developed in disasters in Galveston, San Francisco, Dayton, and Boston. Their ideology emphasized the power and knowledge of experts like themselves and proclaimed that disaster relief was part of a larger Progressive reform project. Social workers and other relief experts, wrote the author of an American Red Cross manual that the Russell Sage Foundation sent to Halifax just after the explosion, should use disasters as an opportunity to reform city charters and insert themselves into families' legal affairs, their parenting, their education, and their employment. "There will be families to move to cleaner and better houses, housewives to instruct in purchasing and preparing food to better advantage, others to be taught needed lessons in infant hygiene, men and women to arouse from the apathy and despair into which their misfortunes have plunged them and to be heartened to face the future with hope and courage."

The disaster experts who converged on Halifax brought with them ideas, forms, systems, and a lot of money, including an eventual $700,000 donated by Massachusetts residents. But they were not the only ones carrying their ideas across the border. So too did working-class people, whose transcience created transnational political communities that contested and resisted the new technocratic state. The Massachusetts money came from ordinary residents, many of whom had direct cultural and migratory connections to Nova Scotia. By donating, they created a transnational polity. People who had given money wrote to the Halifax Relief Commission, objecting that their friends and relatives back in Halifax had not gotten an appropriate amount of the donated aid. Mrs. A.E. Anderson, for instance, complained that her friend Levinia MacKenzie was threatened with being sent to the poorhouse and noted that she had contributed her share of money because she had friends in Halifax. Haligonians, too, wrote to the authorities, complaining that their friends had given money and so now they were owed more relief. These letters were successful in getting social workers and other officials to reopen files and reconsider, and sometimes they worked to extract more money from relief coffers. Nova Scotians used their transience to demand more aid—demonstrating their new expectations of the state—and with that to craft an alternative form of citizenship that spanned international boundaries.

In other ways, too, Haligonians experimented with different forms of citizenship after the disaster. The city's unions became increasingly willing to organize across lines of skill, race, and gender. By the end of 1919, the Halifax Trades and Labour Council counted eight thousand members, making it the fourth-largest labor organization in all of Canada. Even with that expansion, unionized workers realized they needed a broader base politically, so in January 1920 a newly revived Halifax Labour Party welcomed membership from all "workers, whether organized or unorganized, mental or manual regardless of race, sex, creed or vocation," and its platform was endorsed by the Great War Veterans Association. The provincial Independent Labour Party's platform reflected this breadth; it included not only production-related planks about the eight-hour day and reforms to workers' compensation, but also reproduction-related planks on school reform and housing. That year, workers tried to fight a two-front battle at the shipyard and at the ballot box. The Marine Trades and Labour Federation, an umbrella organization of skilled trades unions, struck the city's largest employer, the Halifax Shipyards. The rest of the province's labor movement, understanding that a loss at the shipyards would be catastrophic for everyone, provided the strike fund, countenanced a low level of violence, and even considered a general strike. Four weeks into the strike, a provincial election was called. Unions formed a coalition with rural workers and mounted a joint Farmer-Labour ticket across the province, campaigning on the reproductive question of housing, not the productive question of labor rights. The campaign ended the same week as the strike, and in the end, Halifax's labor movement failed. The shipyard strike collapsed, the company blacklisted union men, and the closed shop ended throughout Halifax. In the vote, although the Labour candidates did well in working-class neighborhoods, they could not win a single seat in Halifax County. More broadly, however, the Farmer-Labour coalition was quite successful, and it became the official opposition with eleven of forty-three members of the House of Assembly.

Though the Halifax working class did not ultimately achieve its alternative vision of citizenship, we can see how, in the aftermath of disasters, opportunities abound for radically reimagining the relationship between state and citizen. In the contemporary period, perhaps the best example is the Common Ground Collective in post-Katrina New Orleans. In the early days of the flood, Common Ground began as a small group of anarchists working with a local Black Panther veteran on radical relief. They confronted government officials demanding evacuation, set up a triage and first-aid center, broke through military lines into the cordoned-off city to find survivors in their attics, and helped local blacks defend themselves against gangs of white vigilantes. They were self-consciously radical, operating from an ideology of "solidarity not charity" that drew from Black Panther survival programs, Zapatista ideas about "leading by obeying," and the experiences of veteran community and global justice organizers. At the heart of their notion of solidarity was the understanding that outsiders, no matter how well intentioned, could not know what was best for the community, and that work must be directed by the people being helped.

In the years since, Common Ground has institutionalized, even while trying to preserve its decentralized structure and radical ideology. The devastation of the flood created an opportunity for radical activists and their neighbors to create the community they desired. Common Ground participants work to rebuild a new New Orleans, not only with new power relations but also a different material and built environment. The group has expanded into home rehabilitation, wetlands rehabilitation, legal services, a long-term medical clinic, and community organizing and activism. Because its short-term volunteers, who have totaled about thirteen thousand since 2005, are mostly middle class and white, Common Ground tries to use their race and class privilege "tactically . . . to bring resources into the city and redistribute them to the communities most in need." Educating these volunteers is also part of the mission, and when done in New Orleans, these newly radicalized youth return home to organize in their own communities. Common Ground continues to struggle with questions of race and class privilege, with the difficulties of remaining outsiders "serving" a local community, and with questions of gender dynamics and sexual violence within the organization. But it suggests the ways disasters can be generative moments, and how they can encourage people to experiment with new ways of being urban citizens.

Perhaps the only upside of the coming era of disasters—of climate change, of heat waves, floods, and storms, of terrorism, of increasingly fatal earthquakes, of austerity riots—is that it will provide more opportunities to reimagine citizenship the ways Common Ground participants did explicitly and the way Mrs. A.E. Anderson did implicitly. A movement based on solidarity as a value, ideology, and method need not rely on the state or electoral politics—nor must it be based in existing unions, legally recognized as exclusive bargaining agents. "Workers, whether organized or unorganized, mental or manual regardless of race, sex, creed or vocation" can build solidarity themselves, in their organizations, in their daily lives, and in their response to local, national, and international disasters.

THE HOUR WHEN THE SHIP COMES IN

Leon Fink

For labor-oriented progressives, "globalization" is something of a curse word. There is no doubt that the pressures of the competitive, international marketplace have again and again proved a scourge to community- or nation-based norms, standards, and rights secured—often after decades of struggle—by worker-centered social movements. The negative impact of globalization—at least on developed-country working-class living standards—poses a continuing political dilemma on issues ranging from trade to immigration to social welfare legislation. Moreover, it seems, out-and-out opposition to globalizing economic forces risks not only likely failure but a revanchist, protectionist, and likely racist reaction among peoples as well as nations. So what's the alternative?

As it happens, the history of merchant shipping, the industry with the longest track record of the commercial crossing of borders as well as one of the most international of labor forces, may provide a partial answer. Research for my own just-completed book, *Sweatshops at Sea: Merchant Seamen in the World's First Globalized Industry from 1812 to the Present* (Chapel Hill: University of North Carolina Press, 2011), points to two powerful historical precedents that could conceivably serve as a broader wedge to radical economic reforms.

THE POWER OF PORT CONTROL

First, there is the idea of the expansion of domestic workplace standards to encompass foreign workers and thus prevent the super-exploitation of all workers. In a nutshell, this was the key concept behind the once-famous (though now largely unknown) La Follette Seamen's Act of 1915.

American workers shut out of an ever-widening, ever-cheapening global marketplace. Sound familiar? Such was the state of the U.S. merchant marine at the turn of the twentieth century. Indeed, by the mid-1880s, official estimates indicated that a mere 15 percent of American oceangoing commerce was carried in U.S.-flagged vessels. Not only was the cost of construction (especially after the arrival of the age of steam) uncompetitive with British and other carriers, but also American seamen's wage norms dwarfed those of their competing British and Swedish counterparts. At the same time, conditions for the seamen themselves remained miserable: in addition to low wages and the ever-present occupational risk to life and limb, maritime workers endured coercions and tyrannical control found in few other ostensibly "free-labor" settings. Though flogging had been proscribed at mid-century, the holding of miscreants in stocks and other forms of physical coercion remained in practice. Moreover, abuses also continued at the recruiting end, where "advance wages" often ended up in the hands of saloon owners or boardinghouse bosses as a payment for previous debts. But likely the most notorious of the occupational inequities was the effective "inability to quit": mariners the world over were "bound" to their employment contracts (or "shipping articles"), commonly extending from one to three years' time, on penalty of criminal punishment, including imprisonment at hard labor as well as forfeiture of wages. In addition to rendering sea workers the effective vassals of their masters, the sea captains, the prohibition on leave-taking gave each seafaring nation (or "flag") a weapon of control over a labor force that might otherwise have regularly escaped its economic authority as well as its geopolitical reach. That's where the La Follette Act came in. Dreamed up (and fought for over ten years) by International Seamen's Union (ISU) president Andrew Furuseth and his legal advisers before receiving crucial backing from Wisconsin progressive senator Robert La Follette as well as President Woodrow Wilson's secretary of labor and former miners' leader, William B. Wilson, the act aimed to use leverage over commerce in U.S. ports to transform the entire global maritime labor market. Important sections of the act gave seamen the right to leave their contracts at any port without sanction in exchange for half their wages earned to that point in their voyage. In addition, it banned all forms of corporal punishment (replacing them with a graduated code of punishment for disorderly conduct) and limited the payment of advance wages to the sailor's immediate family. Third, as a measure outwardly justified on grounds of safety but inwardly fueled by fears of cheap, foreign (read Asian) labor, the act required the crew to speak and understand the language of the captain. Finally, in perhaps its boldest but least advertised move, the authors of the act specified its application not only to all U.S.-flagged ships but also to "foreign vessels"; any treaties to the contrary, moreover, were to be abrogated in short order.

The authors of the La Follette Act fully realized that only by extending the jurisdiction of U.S. law to foreign shipping (and specifically the conditions of foreign seamen on foreign-flagged vessels) could they affect the maritime labor market in any significant way. As a remedy, the act posited a single world market for seagoing labor in the foreign trade, effected by allowing seamen legal right to "jump ship" at any American port and negotiate the next leg of their journey at the prevailing "local" wage rates. As the ISU elaborated in 1914: "If conditions can be brought about whereby the wage cost of operation will be equalized, the development of our merchant marine and our sea power will be unhampered. The remedy is to set free the economic laws governing wages." Once the world's merchant marine (or at least any part of it that passed through a U.S. port) could demand, via the right to quit, comparable pay and conditions, foreign captains would have to hire new crews, or rehire their old crews, at the wages then prevalent in a given port. Moreover, to secure their crews, they had best make such adjustment well in advance of arrival in U.S. waters, thus at least theoretically creating what, in modern-day parlance, might be termed an economic "race to the top." "Just as sure as the United States passes this law," Furuseth thus told a congressional committee, "European nations will have to follow you, because you will take from them the cream of their seamen until you can develop your own. . . . The result will be, as a whole, the rebuilding of the [American] merchant marine." In addition to its immediately felicitous impact on "150,000 American seamen," Furuseth modestly predicted that the legislation would also benefit the rest of an estimated two million other seafarers "throughout the world."

As the eminent maritime authority Elmo Paul Hohman later summarized, the La Follette Act rested on "a theory of wage adjustment
which aimed at nothing less than a worldwide equalization of wages."

It is clear, moreover, that at least some contemporaries fully
grasped the innovative ambition and potentially radical reach of the
seamen's legislation. Prior to the passage of the bill, a House of Representatives minority report christened it "the most extreme and
revolutionary in all probability that has ever been favorably reported
to this House." Likewise, the Senate Republicans' foreign policy
doyens Henry Cabot Lodge and Elihu Root protested the bill's "ar-
rogant indifference to the interests and even the prejudices of other
nations." On purely economic grounds, Georgia's Democratic senator
Hoke Smith worried that the legislation would scare off the foreign
tramp steamers that carried his region's cotton to market. Support
for the La Follette Act likely caught the Progressive Era at its reform
zenith. To understand its very "possibility," we have to reckon with
two strong currents—one enabling, one disabling—affecting state-
making and political culture in this period. On the positive side, the
appeal for an economic readjustment on behalf of American sailors
wrapped itself tightly in nationalist bunting. Furuseth, for example,
invoking the classic text of Admiral Mahan, labeled his analysis of the
legislative saga "American Sea Power and the Seamen's Act." Other
commentators connected the reform effort not just to workers' rights
and welfare but to the revival of an American merchant fleet. The simultaneous invocation of a "reform spirit" with assertion of national
prosperity and power was, of course, a common denominator of Progressive Era thought. The notion of a "fair marketplace"—competitive
but accessible to all participants—ran from Populist granaries and
railroad regulation to Gompers's anti-injunction campaigns through
Theodore Roosevelt's New Nationalism, Wilson's New Freedom, Herbert Croly's *Promise of American Life* (1909), Walter Weyl's *The New
Democracy* (1912), and Walter Lippmann's *Drift and Mastery* (1914).
Like their larger Progressive cohort, therefore, the maritime reformers managed to champion state action while still embracing a competitive marketplace economy. As Croly would put it, there were "two
indispensable economic conditions" to the higher development of

democratic civilization: "the preservation of the institution of private property in some form, and the . . . radical transformation of its existing nature and influence."

That the substantive reach of the La Follette Act proved exceptional even amid other legislative reforms of its day has much to do with the peculiar jurisdiction to which it applied. As a measure affecting a body of workers who had long been regulated, albeit often to their disadvantage, by explicit *federal* authority, the seamen's legislation did not face the legal hurdles that undermined so many other Progressive Era initiatives. To wit, there was no question that Congress could act here regarding a matter of clear, interstate commerce, a situation that also freed legislators from the suffocating contemporary interpretation of the Fourteenth Amendment's "due process" clause, which treated employing corporations as citizens who could not be "deprived" by "States" of their "property" without "due process of law." Uninhibited by the usual federalist or judicial constraints (at least at first) that hog-tied so many contemporary attempts at humanizing work environments or granting union rights, lawmakers demonstrated a penchant for robust regulatory relief on behalf of working people. The La Follette Act surely reminds us that ours is not the first age to confront the debilitating aspects of a competitive global marketplace nor the first to try to do something about it. Moreover, more than mere trade protectionism, the act sought to enlist regulatory reform as well as the logic of the marketplace itself in the pursuit of social justice. For a variety of reasons the La Follette Act never realized either the promise of its proponents or the fears of its detractors. Most significant for the argument at hand, the "international" features of the act were hamstrung both by administrative adversity and ultimately decisive hostility from the U.S. Supreme Court. The Department of Commerce regularly favored the shipowners in its interpretation of the law. Safety inspections, for example, were dropped for foreign vessels whose national laws roughly met American standards. The language provision was similarly weakened by accepting pidgin English and even hand gestures as adequate communication between officers and crew. Forecastle space provisions were deemed applicable only to ships built after 1915. Perhaps most tellingly, the crucial principle of the right-to-disembark at half-wages was vitiated by U.S. immigration policy. Asian exclusion laws confined sailors on shipboard in harbor. Widening the circle of exclusion, alien seamen denied admission under the immigration quotas of 1924 were equally forbidden to land, except temporarily for medical treatment. Meanwhile, other nations determined to hold men on their ships. French law, for example, effectively discouraged desertions by defining the merchant marine as a naval reserve service. Even if Americans declared desertion legal, foreign nations were under no such compunction should the offender ever return to his native soil. Out of both nationalist loyalties and economic calculation (the same attributes that had helped pass the act), even many foreign seamen's union officials "were opposed to the Act, and did not encourage their members to avail themselves of its opportunities." The Great War, of course, utterly upset normal sea commerce for several years running. While the war initially drove up wages (and union membership), a disastrous strike in 1921 brought the ISU back to a low ebb, just as Republican administrations, utterly disinclined to push the regulatory envelope, took over, only to be followed by a long slump in world shipping, and then the Great Depression. In the circumstances, evidence for the wage "equalization" anticipated by the act was spotty at best. Finally, in two judgments in the late 1940s and early 1950s, the U.S. Supreme Court, fearing the unnatural restriction of international commerce, dealt a final, retrospective blow to the international enforcement provisions of the act.

Notwithstanding the limited, real-world reach of the La Follette Act's internationalist, "radical edge," its existence offers a valuable precedent for imaginative labor reformers. For starters, what if the logic of the La Follette Act were dusted off and the United States (as well as other major trading nations) demanded a host of safety and welfare standards—as well as the random cargo inspections currently under way for security reasons—for every ship destined for its ports. As it happens a legislative measure to do just that—giving "port states" the right to compel merchant ship compliance with a host of International Labor Organization standards (bundled together as the

Maritime Labor Convention of 2006)—was due to take effect in 2011. But the same principle could conceivably be further expanded. Just as U.S. law since the Tariff Act of 1930 prohibits the entry of prison-made goods from abroad, why not restrict importation of other products or services dependent upon certifiable human or labor rights violations? The latter would surely include child labor and human trafficking, but it also could stretch to limits on working hours and even the rights to worker association and organization. Though such a unilateral step would likely trigger a collision with the free-trade principles enshrined in WTO agreements (which do allow national restriction of prison-made products), it could set a useful stage for returning labor rights and welfare to the center of global foreign policy debates.

THE FORCE OF GLOBAL UNIONISM

If the La Follette Act demonstrates the potential reach of domestic legislation for progressive ends, then the worldwide enforcement actions of the International Transport Workers' Federation (or ITF) against so-called flags of convenience (or FOCs) show that transnational labor action can extend beyond empty slogans of solidarity into hard-edged bargaining and collective mobilization. Again, let me briefly set the relevant background.

Dating to the 1920s when Averill Harriman sought to evade Prohibition Era restrictions on his gambling ships, the world's shipowners discovered a way around national regulations and labor costs by formally re-registering (or "off-shoring") their vessels in cheaper, low-regulation states. A postwar trickle first turned into a torrent of such FOCs—most famously associated with Panama, Liberia, and Honduras, but since joined by the Marshall Islands, Bahamas, and many others—amid the worldwide competitive pressures of the 1970s. In addition to tax advantages, the shift, of course, also undid national collective-bargaining agreements built up over decades with the maritime unions of the world's traditional shipping powers, including the United States; Great Britain; Germany; Scandinavia (Norway, Sweden); Greece; and Japan. As a logical corollary, the general deregulatory fever of the 1970s led to a mass transfer of maritime employment to Third World crews centered in the Philippines, India, China, and, post-1989, the ex-Soviet republics.

Not surprisingly, the ITF, effectively the world's oldest global union, did not take the FOC threat lightly. An energetic boycott campaign—highlighted by transatlantic job actions among both seamen and dockworkers in 1958—aimed to restore authenticity to the registration of oceangoing ships. The initial campaign, however, met two potentially crippling obstacles. In a crucial 1963 ruling, the famously "liberal" Warren Court (i.e., the U.S. Supreme Court under Chief Justice Earl Warren) ruled that American unions' legitimate activity did not extend beyond the Wagner Act's stated focus on U.S. employment relations to "foreign territory"—in this case a Honduran-flagged vessel chartered by the United Fruit Company. Secondly, the Euro-American-centered boycott interests encountered resistance from Asian seamen's groups determined to hold on to their share of the world employment pie.

Remarkably, for all the challenges involved, the ITF "righted the ship" of union resistance to the FOC onslaught. In a rare combination of political vision and economic hardheadedness, by the 1990s the ITF had restored a multipronged anti-FOC campaign with far-reaching practical effects. Effectively, in a largely unspoken policy shift, the ITF abandoned the aim of abolishing FOCs in favor of "regulating" them along lines of trade union principles. First, within its own global ranks, the ITF hammered out more flexible (i.e., lower) unionized rates for Third World, and especially Asian, crews. The latter move facilitated reconnection to the international union body of its previously disaffected Indian and Filipino affiliates. Through the threat of restored boycott or work-to-rule port action—now concretized in a worldwide circuit of one hundred ITF inspectors—it then reached collective-bargaining agreements with the major international shipowner federations, themselves worried about being undercut by unsafe, cut-rate operators. By 2008, the ITF (representing some 60 percent of the world's 1.2 million seafarers through its affiliates) had won contracts on more than a third of FOC carriers. Moreover, the momentum of the ITF's international mobilization carried over by 2006 into an unprecedented agreement within the tripartite (government, labor, and business) legislative arrangement of the International Labor Organization (ILO) for a Maritime Labor Convention that, beginning in 2011, will mandate labor- (as well as safety-) standard inspections of all oceangoing ships by port authorities around the world. Shipping, in short, will be the first "globalized" occupation subject to global standards of work and pay, as aided by a strong union presence.

LESSONS FROM THE DEEP

Stepping back, it is worth taking stock of the mechanism that has allowed the ITF to defy the generally adverse winds of global marketplace competition. In particular, what, if anything, can land-based workers learn from their brethren on the waters? A crucial node in the ITF network is the role of the global union's munificent Welfare Fund—a $100 million treasury secured from the per-seafarer taxes paid by the FOC operators to obtain their union-authorized right-of-way. That the international federation (not national union affiliates) have control here allows the ITF to deploy a global strategy with uncommon teeth. Distributions from the Welfare Fund clearly help to secure the loyalties of otherwise disparate constituencies—at once melding the interests of Western-state unions (who get a share of the FOC proceeds when the ship in question is declared to be under their state's ownership) with Third World affiliates and tangibly rewarding the solidarity of dockworker unions (who dominate the port-side ITF inspectorate).

Yet the distinctiveness of maritime labor leverage and standards need not remain sui generis. Certainly the exceptionality of the shipping industry as an arena "adrift" from national moorings lessens with each passing year. Various forms of "off-shore" production and services—from telecom call centers to transnational subcontracting in the construction trades—have led to a situation of limited national political sovereignty over affected workplaces. In sector after sector and trade after trade, a neoliberalist globalism threatens traditional nation-centered labor strategies. As state protections for workers and citizens are increasingly weakened or rendered meaningless, what can take their place? The example of the shipping industry suggests that at least something other than a deregulated "race to the bottom" can emerge from the globalized shake-up. In that sphere, as we have seen, a transnational regulatory regime has emerged, combining the powers of government and international agencies, labor unions, as well as employer associations.

For starters, we might imagine new organizing approaches applied to other nodes of the commercial transportation network. As with oceanic shippers, retail-driven manufacturing (à la Wal-Mart) depends on the on-time delivery of diverse products to consumers across the globe. The nexus of land-based warehouses (themselves an industry with a large labor force) from whence universally containerized goods are regularly "shipped" by rail or truck duplicates many of the structural features of the classic port. Could not joint action by teamsters, railway unions, and distributive workers create a wedge into the unorganized depths of the Wal-Mart economy? In world merchant shipping the combination of a union power base together with shrewd political alliances has determined that a "flat" world—in the sense of an ever more competitive commercial playing field—need not abandon standards of "fairness." For organized labor, the trick, it seems, is less to walk on water than to learn to sail on land.

GETTING OVER THE NEW DEAL

Jefferson Cowie

Spilled across the pages of progressive journals a few years ago were demands for a new New Deal, a global New Deal, a New and Improved Deal, a reNewed Deal, and even New Deal 2.0. After Obama's election, political cartoons—most notably, but not exclusively, on the cover of *Time* magazine—featured a jubilant, toothy Barack Obama with a cigarette holder, posing confidently in an open limousine à la FDR. Elsewhere, otherwise sober commentators began speaking of "Franklin Delano Obama." Even before the coming of the Great Recession, but accelerating ever since, the era of Roosevelt has become a metaphor, political principle, and guiding light for all that must be returned to American politics. Then, inevitably, comes the shock of reality: a new Gilded Age of robber barons lording over a world of heightened inequality, working-class divisions, regional tensions, racial animosities, and anti-immigrant sentiments seems to have a lot firmer grip on American political culture than does the hope of a new New Deal. Understanding the ways in which banking on a revival of the New Deal is misguided is important for any path forward.

As a historian and social democrat, this puts me in a bind. I'd love to see a triumphal return of the New Deal. Many of the policies of the 1930s represented the best of what the United States might be as a nation—caring, sharing, secure, and occasionally visionary—while few issues seem more important today than bringing the concerns of working people out of the shadows and into the political and economic light. But bad history makes for really bad political strategy, so we must face up to a key fact: the creation of the New Deal was pretty tenuous to begin with, and the decades following—often called "the New Deal order"—were pretty close to an aberration in American history unlikely to return.

Indeed, the political era between the inauguration of Franklin

Delano Roosevelt through the administration of Richard Nixon, as my co-author and fellow historian Nick Salvatore and I have argued, marks a "long exception" in American political history and culture. During this period, the central government utilized its considerable resources in a systematic, if hardly consistent, fashion on behalf of nonelite Americans. One can visualize the outcome in the statistical graphs as an anomalous historical hump that rises in the 1940s and declines in the 1970s: economic equality improves then tumbles, union density rockets upward and then slowly falls, working people's income goes up before dwindling, and the percentage of wealth possessed by the most affluent dips before roaring back with a vengeance.

While it is useful and hopeful that the United States can achieve such a politics again, we ought not be misled by freewheeling historical analogies. The catalyst for these developments was neither FDR's charismatic personality, the brilliance of his New Deal advisers, nor World War II. Rather, it was the unique circumstances of the Great Depression itself, particularly the ferocious impact it had on Americans over the three years and five months between its start in October 1929 and FDR's inauguration in March of 1933. It was this trauma— at once economic, political, and cultural—that propelled a more activist government intervention on behalf of everyday American citizens than the United States had ever seen before—or since. Even as partisan a champion of the New Deal as historian and presidential adviser Arthur Schlesinger Jr. explained that the dawning of the New Deal was a "unique episode" in the nation's history "which grew out of a unique crisis."

Nothing emerges from nothing, of course, and the New Dealers built upon a number of historical trends: the Progressive reform impulse, Theodore Roosevelt's demand for the regulation of big corporations, and—above all—the massive federal mobilization during World War I. Also, the new corporate paternalism of the 1920s, known as "welfare capitalism," raised expectations of what the employment relationship could and should offer, just before it all collapsed following the economic crash. All that said, and it is admittedly not a short list, the New Deal was as clear a break with policy tradition as any in American history. Harry Hopkins, one of FDR's closest advisers, suggested the degree of departure when he described creating national relief on a blank drafting table "almost as if the Aztecs had been asked suddenly to build an aeroplane."

The rupture with the past may have been real, but the legislative achievements were also more tenuous and brief than most tend to recognize. What historians call the "first" New Deal basically turned the project of recovery over to business itself (along with some substantial relief interventions and dramatic efforts like the Tennessee Valley Authority). Those early reforms ended due to their internal contradictions or the Supreme Court—or both. With the notable exception of Glass-Steagall and other reforms of the financial sector, the first New Deal failed to have a lasting impact. After 1935, the true breakthroughs, known as the "second" New Deal, offered a more cohesive, proto-Keynesian vision for reform and the most substantive parts of Roosevelt's legacy: the National Labor Relations Act, the Social Security Act, the Works Progress Administration, the Fair Labor Standards Act, the empowerment of the CIO, and—above all—the landslide 1936 election that created the "Roosevelt coalition" out of a historically fragmented working class. In sum, not only did FDR inherit a massive three-and-a-half-year-old financial and employment crisis from a discredited administration, but it still took two full attempts to get the New Deal close to right.

Even then, when Roosevelt famously wagged his finger at the "economic royalists" as the people's champion, he did so only briefly and superficially. The window of opportunity for substantive collective economic policies opened in 1935, but it also slammed shut less than three years later. What followed the onrush of reform from 1935 to 1937 were the forgotten years of the Roosevelt administration: the 1938–39 years of defeat and retreat, the return of hard times, and the possibility that the 1936–37 strike wave would be just another failure like 1919 or 1934. As the historian Nelson Lichtenstein argues in the case of the labor movement, "industrial unionism's moment of unrivaled triumph proved exceedingly brief." He notes that it was only a matter of weeks after the CIO's famous victories at General Motors and U.S. Steel in 1937 that "the radical challenge posed by mass unions generated furious opposition: from corporate adversaries,

Southern Bourbons, craft unionists, and many elements of the New Deal coalition itself." As the New Deal's brief window of opportunity began to slip shut, Maury Maverick, an outspoken Democratic congressman from Texas, was one of the few to openly declare the exhaustion of his party's efforts. "Now we Democrats have to admit that we are floundering," he told the House. "We have pulled all the rabbits out of the hat, and there are no more rabbits. . . . We are a confused, bewildered group of people, and we are not delivering the goods."

With the forward progress of the New Deal halted in 1938–39, it took World War II to consolidate existing achievements—especially union strength—while simultaneously marking what the historian Alan Brinkley calls "the end of reform" (which he defines as "a set of essentially class-based issues centered around confronting the problem of monopoly and economic disorder"). Macroeconomic planning for mass consumption and the gradual shift toward genuine support of individual rights trumped the disparate inventiveness of the Progressives and the New Dealers (and, in turn, almost completely ending the Democrats' anti-monopoly tradition). As a result, the nation ended up with a postwar politics that Brinkley calls "less challenging to the existing structure of corporate capitalism than some of the ideas [postwar liberalism] supplanted." Yet we often forget that the path to such a trimmed political vision for the postwar order required a twelve-year-long depression, a false start, surviving a strongly organized counterattack, and a world war before it reached its modern form—a truly extraordinary gauntlet of historical circumstances.

How best, then, to think about the New Deal as it shaped the postwar era from the 1940s to the 1970s? After the war, New Deal alliances seemed like an all-powerful force capable of implementing liberal policy, regardless of conservative opposition. Yet when challenged, this same juggernaut shattered, its central contradictions revealed in its own negotiations with the very real complexities of American history and politics. The divisiveness of race, ethnicity, immigration, and religion all bound up tightly with one of the thorniest problems in American politics—individualism was temporarily mitigated, though hardly terminated, during the New Deal era. The easy answer to the question of American conservatism has been that corporations have exceptional power, but that answer begs the question of the political culture that allows for such power to proceed unchecked.

Black-white race relations were certainly the most salient example of how important—and thin—the New Deal veneer was. While African American voters switched their allegiances from the party of Lincoln to the Roosevelt coalition for good reasons, the price of almost every piece of New Deal legislation was the exclusion of black people. And, while the CIO devoted itself to organizing without regard to race, its project remained hamstrung on the racism of the white rank and file and the political power of the "Solid South." When the Democrats dared to introduce a civil rights plank in 1948, or when they passed the 1964 Civil Rights Act, the entire coalitional edifice shook as the white South bolted from the Democratic Party and the urban North cleaved along racial lines.

The absence of immigration was another decisive factor in both the formation and continuation of the New Deal order. The "culture of unity"—a term used by historian Lizabeth Cohen to describe the shared sense of fate produced by the homogenizing forces of large-scale industry, welfare capitalism, and mass culture—was based largely on the suspension of immigration after 1924. As a result, when the crash hit, nativism was largely at bay (not to deny the repatriation of Mexicans in the 1930s or the internment of the Japanese in the 1940s) and the workers living in this country were here to stay. When immigration resurfaced slowly in the generation after the 1965 immigration reforms, so did the neo–Know Nothings and militant nativism of today, returning *the* working class to historical patterns of internecine hostilities and political divisions reminiscent of the pre–New Deal era.

Like immigration, the divisiveness of religion in American politics also had a reprieve that allowed the New Deal to cohere. Evangelical Christianity, mocked into irrelevance after the 1925 Scopes monkey trial, largely went underground in the 1930s and 1940s, offering limited "culture war" challenges to the rise of the New Deal. Even so, the New Deal had to squeak ahead of Father Coughlin and other religious populists, creating a civic faith that managed to keep ahead of the evangelical tradition. Garry Wills calls the postwar era a "Great Religious Truce," an "interfaith Amity" in which a vague Judeo-Christian faith was enough to define Cold War Americanism. That consensus would finally fall apart in the 1970s, as conservative Christians questioned rendering unto Caesar what was Caesar's when the state was busy intervening in cultural questions like abortion, busing, prayer in school, pornography, and birth control—issues that re-politicized the place of Christian fundamentalism in American life and undermined the New Deal coalition, in the 1970s and beyond.

The ideology, though hardly the reality, of individualism wound around all of these other issues like vines in a political jungle. Roosevelt, despite being the architect of the regulatory state, never quite offered a clear alternative to the individualist ethos so deeply embedded in himself or America's public culture. In fact, so persuasive were FDR's evocations of that American ideology that brain truster Rexford Tugwell thought—even when Roosevelt tried to construct a new vision of individualism suitable for modern, corporate society—that those efforts, too, had "not been immune to our national myths." "Like all of us," Tugwell continued, FDR "had a weakness for what was familiar and trusted which led him to overestimate [the myths'] sufficiency and underestimate their irrelevant antiquity." Even the Great Society and many of the lasting incarnations of the new social movements of the 1960s were based more on expanding long-denied individual rights rather than securing the type of collective economic rights promised by the New Deal. Less about redistributing the economic pie, post-1960s liberalism was more about providing people with the skills to compete for a decent slice: equal opportunity to all to fail as well as succeed.

The labor movement, the backbone of postwar liberalism, followed its meteoric rise with a slow but steady decline after 1955. Following the New Deal, labor never gained another substantive advance in labor law reform despite many attempts to rejuvenate American labor law and, in fact, had to sound several important retreats including Taft-Hartley and Landrum-Griffin. As the economist J.K. Galbraith put it in the late 1960s, "Since World War II, the acceptance of the union by the industrial firm and the emergence thereafter of an era of comparatively peaceful industrial relations have been hailed as the final triumph of trade unionism. On closer examination it is seen to reveal many of the features of Jonah's triumph over the whale." In the 1970s and beyond, the corporations succeeded in their own counter-reformation of capitalism, regaining terrain lost under the New Deal. By the 1980s the organizing advances of the CIO of four decades earlier were being erased. This time, however, corporations were less dependent upon state-led redistribution to boost demand than on a global market for cheap labor and an avidly consuming professional middle class.

The argument here is not that the United States is monolithically any one set of characteristics—or that the New Deal was monolithically their opposite. Rather, all was contingent, in tension, and in play, often tipping in one direction rather than another. FDR, for instance, managed to trump the darker strains of populism of a Father Coughlin. Racially motivated "hate strikes" accompanied the solidarity of the CIO. In the 1940s in Southern California, as Darren Dochuk explains, a struggle erupted between material betterment of working people and the power of blue-collar evangelism—a choice between "Christ or the CIO." King's Poor People's Campaign may have sought collective economic betterment for the poor, but the main institutional legacy of the civil rights movement is the Equal Employment Opportunity Commission, which guarantees individual rights to nondiscrimination on the job. The New Left, despite its collective rhetoric and action, had at its core a search for individual emancipation that would soon mesh neatly with the "bourgeois bohemianism" of the Reagan era. When the ideological revival of individualism took hold in the 1980s, it was accompanied by the massive growth of the state acting on behalf of corporate power.

While many liberals in the Reagan era waited for a return to what they regarded as the normality of the New Deal order, they were actually living in the final days of what Paul Krugman later called the "interregnum between Gilded Ages." In the face of assault, many labor intellectuals of the 1980s and 1990s overlaid the idea of a tidy and respected "postwar management accord" on the complexity of the period in which capital's recognition of labor was more tactical and

uneven than permanent and inclusive. Again turning popular inter-
pretations around, it might be more accurate to think of the "Reagan
revolution" as the "Reagan restoration," a return to a more sharply
conservative, individualistic reading of constitutional rights and liberties, an economic policy in which the state looks after the corporation, and a working class once again fragmented by race, religion,
immigration, and culture. This "restoration" was in no sense a return
to small government as Reagan had so forcefully advertised. The issue was never really whether that government was large or small as
political rhetoric might have us believe but, like the Gilded Age, toward what ends and whose interest those massive institutions would
be driven.

Yet the postwar era is not, of course, a story of decline. The revival
of individualism since the faltering of the New Deal order developed
in a radically expanded and much healthier form. The promise of
constitutional rights and liberties has been made much wider and
more substantial by the social movements of the twentieth century:
there are no segregationist state constitutions, a commitment to gender equality is far broader, and the official forms of Jim Crow are
in their grave. The Civil Rights Act and the Voting Rights Act are
the most important political achievements of the postwar era, and
the transformation in gender relations is the most significant social
transformation of the contemporary age. The current—and perhaps
exhausted—debate between "class politics" and "identity politics"
or "rights consciousness" overlooks the fragility of the onetime leap
forward in class identity and how readily a reformed individualism
adapted to the deeper impulses in American life. Yet a rather enormous problem remains: any understanding of post–New Deal order
individualism must place at the center of the discussion the problems
inherent with the restoration of the nearly uncontestable power of one
set of legally protected, if fully fictitious, individuals in American life:
the corporations.

So if mining the political veins of the New Deal for our historical analogies proves futile, where should we turn? If we need historical metaphors to guide our political activities at all, perhaps the Progressive

Era (1901–19) might prove more helpful. The political hodgepodge of the first decades of the twentieth century contained often chaotic and contradictory claims with regard to community, social harmony, voluntary association, radicalism, and—when necessary—the state. While the pragmatic approach to reform, diffuse leadership, mixed-class alliances, and the lack of a clear left and right dichotomy have been criticized as the era's failures, perhaps they are its virtues. At their best, the progressive reformers appreciated the power of individualism in American political culture, affirmed a vision of democratic life across class (if decidedly not racial) lines, and sought a bridge between that individualism and a common good.

Grasping the import of the Progressive Era requires reversing the diagnosis of its problems. The main limitation of the pre–New Deal reform impulse, according to historian Shelton Stromquist, was its failure to deal with questions of class. "By focusing on the individual and by attacking the environment that limited individual opportunity," argues Stromquist, "Progressives promoted the idea that social differences based on structural inequality could be ameliorated through voluntary action and enlightened governmental social policy." Stromquist is largely right about the spirit of the age, and it may be heresy to say so, but that failure may have been the era's virtue. Progressives' view of class harmony may have been naïve, or it may have inadvertently been the strongest reform tradition that might be expected of a society in which the crosshatchings of religion, race, individualism have served to diffuse the power of class (outside of the great political exception of the 1930s and 1940s). That approach, with all of its mixed potential for results, is worth revisiting to consider if, and how, it might provide insight on the new problems of our own time.

A return to the pre-Depression, pre-trauma outlines of Progressive-style politics, albeit updated for the global age, would suggest a politics of reform and regulation both moral and pragmatic; spurred by local and state sites of innovation; bolstered by cross-class alliances and enlightened elite leadership; focused on immigrant rights, consumer safety, corporate regulation, and occupational justice; advocacy of gas and water (perhaps health care) socialism; and even promotion of the types of militant voluntarism that originally grew in the shadow of a state hostile to the collective interests of workers. Nowhere is this more true than in labor policy, where most union successes appear to lie both outside of the state and inside the broadest of coalitions (a marked contrast to the "industrial pluralism" of the postwar era).

Had it not been for the Great Depression, it is probable that American liberalism would not have taken its modern form; we would have been left with the chaotic brilliance of Progressivism without a cohesive liberal creed. Even the term "liberalism," in its modern definition, arose during the New Deal to distinguish the new politics from the versions of reform that had been discussed a couple of decades before. Obviously the racial politics of the Progressive Era offer nothing but descent into some of the most heinous aspects of American political culture, but otherwise the messy and often irresolute politics of the first decades of the twentieth century might actually be the most promising foundations for new roads to reform. In sum, perhaps the problem is liberalism itself.

The late Tony Judt—in his eloquent defense of social democracy, *Ill Fares the Land*—explains that today's progressives "must take onboard the sheer contingency of politics: neither the rise of the welfare states nor their subsequent fall from grace should be treated as a gift from History. The social democratic 'moment'—or its American counterpart from the New Deal to the Great Society—was the product of a very particular combination of circumstances unlikely to repeat themselves." Historical analogies can empower, but they can also limit. If a path out of our own time is to be charted, and this is the most urgent of projects, it must be done afresh—without stale political metaphors resting on extraordinary historical circumstances.

YOUR AMERICAN DREAM, MY AMERICAN NIGHTMARE

Kimberley L. Phillips

In the weeks before the midterm election, President Barack Obama, the nation's first black president, hoped to shore up support for his economic policies during a town hall meeting in a Virginia suburb adjacent to Washington, D.C. Instead, he heard only skepticism from union members, African Americans, and younger voters reeling from the long recession. One African American woman expressed the collective frustration with government policies that had ignored the plight of her household: "I have been told that I voted for a man who said he was going to change things in a meaningful way for the middle class. I'm one of those people. And I'm waiting, sir. I'm waiting." One man wanted to know if the "American dream was dead." While Mr. Obama attempted to allay the audience's agitation, he also conceded that "even though economists may say that the recession officially ended last year, obviously for the millions of people who are still out of work, people who have seen their home values decline, people who are struggling to pay the bills day to day, it's still very real for them."

The president's response alluded to the hallmarks of the "American dream," a concept that has fueled many Americans' ideals of individual prosperity since the early twentieth century, but he did not acknowledge the two entwined claims suggested in the woman's plaintive remark. The first is that millions of working Americans have experienced little financial stability since the 1970s, and disproportionate numbers of African American households have existed on the nation's economic margins for generations. This latest recession has only exacerbated these trends. The second is that major contestation continues between those who believe the government should ensure and help make it possible for the majority of Americans to have a decent living, good jobs, and opportunities for their children, and those who believe the government should transfer as much money as possible to the already wealthy.

African Americans have long felt that individual and national wealth had come at their expense, thus the current chasm between how they hope to live and how white Americans expect to prosper is unremarkable. Beginning with slavery, black Americans were rarely granted access to the critical components to "attain their stature": equal work, fair wages, the right to vote, and education. In 1855, anti-slavery and labor activist Frederick Douglass reported how African Americans succinctly voiced the structural inequalities that race and class imposed on their labor: "We raise the wheat, dey geb us de corn / We bake de bread, dey geb us de cruss." Blacks' deprivation was seen as the "natural social order." After emancipation, the freed people gave equal weight to their right to labor for equal wages and the right to vote. As black workers sought better wages and work conditions, local, state, and federal policies ensured that they had few political rights. Dispossessed of land and the right to vote, they existed on the margins of the nation's political, economic, and cultural plenty until well into the twentieth century.

Ironically, the concept of an "American dream," which appeared in the epilogue of James Truslow Adams's *The Epic of America*, gained popularity at the start of the Great Depression when unemployment was high and government economic support for most Americans did not exist. Adams posited that the dream was uniquely American where "life should be better and richer and fuller for everyone, with opportunity for each according to ability or achievement." Such a dream, he claimed, would be impossible for the "European upper classes to adequately interpret." In the context of the American grain, this dream did not grasp toward material gain or "high wages," but instead aspired toward a "social order in which each man and each woman shall be able to attain to the fullest stature of which they are innately capable, and be recognized by others for what they are, regardless of the fortuitous circumstances of birth or position." Posited at a time when so many unemployed workers could no longer believe Poor Richard's maxim that industry and thrift made wealth and when an increasing number of Americans demanded steady work and adequate wages, Adams's claims emerged from the hagiography of America's special virtues interpolated in the Declaration of Independence, values that only *seemed* expansive. Adams's American dream did not include a federal government that ensured a Whitmanesque egalitarianism.

As Adams's book became an international bestseller and the concept of the American dream acquired momentum, poet Langston Hughes ruminated over the gaps between the rhetoric of social and economic opportunity and the exclusions ordinary African Americans encountered. As New Deal policies evaded a challenge to America's racialized economic inequalities (and, in some instances, reinforced them), Hughes's 1936 poem "Let America Be America Again" questioned a credo that was not capacious enough to include African Americans. His parenthetical aside at the poem's beginning and end—"America never was America to me"—rebuked and challenged those who excluded black workers from "The land, the mines, the plants, the rivers." Marked as exclusionary, the "dream" had to be reimagined and include the equality of African Americans and the dignity of their labor. Unions that organized all workers regardless of race would "make America again!"

With the exception of some mass industries, Hughes's plea went unheeded and toward the end of World War II 80 percent of surveyed white Americans believed the millions of African Americans who had labored in war industries and served in the segregated military deserved nothing for their sacrifices. In contrast, the majority of whites demanded jobs, homes, and schools of their own, frequently with specific exclusions directed at nonwhites. Private businesses received support from a federal government that also endorsed their discriminatory hiring practices and covenants. African Americans helped provide the tax dollars used to build the suburban dream, but covenants and harassment, including violence, closed their access to these new homes and schools. By the late 1950s, many of the urban factories that precipitated the largest black migration of the twentieth century closed or shed workers. Others followed white workers to the segregated suburbs or left the United States. Ironically,

American-owned factories around the world employed colored workers for jobs denied to black Americans in the United States.

By the 1950s, "the American dream" ceased to include workers'
rights and Hughes's optimism for postwar integration thinned. In
his 1951 collection, *Montage of a Dream Deferred*, black workers figured prominently in these poems, but not the robust roustabouts or
the defiant domestics that appeared in his 1930s poems. Using the
rhythms of bebop—a rhythm Hughes declared came from Northern
police bopping blacks on the heads during the riots of the unemployed
in the 1930s—Hughes detailed how these weary workers in Harlem
and Bronzeville anticipated the next decade's riots with "The boogie-
woogie rumble / Of a dream deferred." Critics described these poems
as "naive," "facile," and "limited" by folk art, yet Hughes's question in
"Harlem"—"What happens to a dream deferred?"—reinforced a critical black lexicon that believed the concept excluded them and came
at their expense. Lorraine Hansberry's 1959 play *A Raisin in the Sun*,
which drew its title from Hughes's poem, critiqued real estate agents'
practice of redlining and white home owners' menace. Frustrated
by the menial work he found and anxious to open a bar, Walter Lee
Younger's anger threatened to engulf his family.

As presidents' administrations and members of the U.S. Chamber of Commerce endorsed deindustrialization and deregulation,
Americans bought bigger cars and workers lost union jobs. If the
American dream existed, it thrived inside the walls built to keep
blacks out of white neighborhoods in Detroit and Cleveland, two cities with high concentrations of black union members. Americans
shook their fists at the newly constructed Berlin Wall and then turned
to reinforce their own.

While the majority of African Americans considered the federal government more helpful than state and local officials, African
Americans still chastised the newly elected President Kennedy for
sending troops to Vietnam, while failing to use the power of his office to stop the violence and economic reprisals civil rights activists
faced in the South. Blacks' support for the president slipped after his
tepid response to the violence against the Freedom Riders in 1961

and civil rights activists in the South more generally. Civil rights and some labor activists urged him "to insure the free exercise of civil and constitutional rights in and around the South," including access to employment in every region. Confidence in federal policies eroded further after he drafted a civil rights bill that failed to include a ban on private employment discrimination. This omission precipitated the 1963 March on Washington for Jobs and Freedom, which linked racial and economic justice.

A quarter of a million Americans participated in the march and urged President Kennedy to draft a civil rights bill that addressed the gross economic inequalities African Americans faced. Placards that demanded "Voting Rights Now!" shared space with signs that called for "Jobs and Freedom." Reverend Martin Luther King Jr.'s speech is now seen as a moving expression of black Americans' aspirations for the American dream, but he began with a rebuke against it and a radical proposal to make it possible for all Americans. Backed by the statue of the president, who symbolized emancipation, black citizenship, and black enfranchisement, King drew upon a century of African American political and theological critique that reached back to the Enlightenment's moral squeamishness with slavery, yet accepted ideas of blacks' racial inferiority. Nearly one hundred years after the promise of full citizenship, King noted how "the Negro lives on a lonely island of poverty in the vast ocean of material prosperity." He honed in on concepts that had undergirded the nation's economic policies but also excluded African Americans. He demanded their expansion and insisted they be understood as obligations both moral and political. "The architects of our republic," he insisted, signed "a promissory note to which every American was to fall heir." Regardless of race (and presumably gender, class, creed, national origin, or sexual orientation), this promise meant all Americans "would be guaranteed the unalienable rights of life, liberty, and the pursuit of happiness." For African Americans, he argued, the nation "has defaulted on this promissory note." He warned that black Americans no longer tolerated their exclusions from their inheritance of racial and economic justice.

John Lewis, who chaired the Student Nonviolent Coordinating

Committee, followed King with a sharper connection between blacks' right to economic and political justice. Civil rights in America meant more than the right to vote—it also meant the right to work, the right to receive fair wages, and the right to access economic policies, such as FHA loans and the GI Bill. These demands, he noted, were revolutionary in a nation that had consigned blacks to poverty. The "nation," he charged, "is still a place of cheap political leaders who build their career on immoral compromises with open forms of political, economic, and social exploitation." Lewis's remarks were edited before he reached the podium and excised from many of the national broadcasts, but the original text circulated in black radical magazines and journals.

Blacks' critique of the exclusionary rhetoric and practices of the American dream continued. Weeks after his break with the Nation of Islam, Malcolm X spoke at Cory Methodist Baptist Church in Cleveland and rejected liberals' claim that the pending civil rights bill would remedy the grave economic, political, and social inequalities African Americans' experienced.

> I'm not going to sit at your table and watch you eat, with nothing on my plate, and call myself a diner. Sitting at the table doesn't make you a diner, unless you eat some of what's on that plate. Being here in America doesn't make you an American. Being born here in America doesn't make you an American. Why, if birth made you American, you wouldn't need any legislation; you wouldn't need any amendments to the Constitution; you wouldn't be faced with civil-rights filibustering in Washington, D.C. No, I'm not an American. I'm one of the 22 million black people who are the victims of Americanism. One of the 22 million black people who are the victims of democracy, nothing but disguised hypocrisy. I'm not standing here speaking to you as an American, or a patriot, or a flag-saluter, or a flag-waver. I'm speaking as a victim of this American system. I see America through the eyes of the victim. I don't see any American dream; I see an American nightmare.

While many Americans ignored the demand that they expand their dreams and abandon racial discrimination in the first half of King's 1963 speech and focused on the second half instead, African Americans listened to Malcolm X's assertion that the American dream was their nightmare.

President Lyndon Johnson's War on Poverty and the 1964 Civil Rights Act partly drew from a half century of black activism for racial and economic justice. The bill did not include fair housing policies, but it did include a ban on discrimination in public accommodations and Title VII, which banned employment discrimination. Pro-business opponents and anti–civil rights legislators argued that the act would undermine free enterprise and hinder employers' right to hire and fire as they pleased. The bill brokered a compromise, making it illegal to deny employment or to fire a worker because of her "race, color, sex, or national origin." It lacked a provision for enforcement. Proponents for federal anti-discrimination legislation rightly argued that the law did not address the absence of work altogether. The Great Society programs established job training, but they did not push job creation. Many black men could only find work on the front lines of Vietnam.

The televised debate between James Baldwin and William F. Buckley at the Cambridge Union Society of Cambridge University in October 1965 occurred in the midst of America's continued intransigence against economic justice and open housing. The dozens of riots that erupted, which began in 1964, formed a backdrop to the debate. Along with too few jobs, poor housing, and segregated schools, the church bombing in Birmingham, the murder of Medgar Evers, and the assassination of Malcolm X also stoked blacks' rebellions. Baldwin prefaced his remarks about whether "the American dream came at the expense of the Negro," with a description of himself as "a kind of Jeremiah." Yet in this description, Baldwin reached toward a more immediate past: America had ignored King's warning two years earlier during the March on Washington.

Baldwin's pessimism about racial and economic justice was significant. Alongside the "bloody catalogue of oppression" that characterized blacks' history in America was a history of their subjugated labor: "From a very literal point of view, the harbors and the ports and the railroads of the country—the economy, especially in the South— could not conceivably be what they are if it had not been (and this is still so) for cheap labor. The Southern oligarchy which has still to-day so very much power in Washington, and therefore some power in the world, was created by [black] labor and sweat." The nation's refusal to make recompense, economically and morally, had consequences. Echoing the claims he made in *The Fire Next Time*, Baldwin proclaimed America needed to abandon its history of inequities, and see black people as Americans with a right to work. "I am not a ward of America, I am not an object of missionary charity, I am one of the people who built the country—until this moment comes there is scarcely any hope for the American dream. If the people are denied participation in it, by their very presence they will wreck it. And if that happens it is a very grave moment for the West."

While African Americans looked to federal, and not local and state, agencies as a bulwark against economic policies that frequently came at their expense, they also agitated for other means to control their economic lives. Point two in the Black Panther's Ten-Point Program demanded the federal government provide full employment and protection from the avarice and discrimination of private businesses. Many African Americans joined unions at a higher rate than other groups of workers. This pattern continues. Even as the number of Americans in unions steadily dropped, African American workers have been 30 percent more likely than any other group of workers to join a union.

Despite their continued efforts to control their own economic destinies, blacks' access to too few, and the decline in, union jobs has significantly eroded an already vulnerable middle class. Between 1980 and 2000, blacks have been three times more likely to be impoverished than whites. While blacks' poverty rates declined slightly between 2000 and 2005, it jumped well over 30 percent in the second half of the decade. As a result, the median income of black households is 1.5 times lower than that of white households ($32,584 compared to $51,861). The loss of jobs, not the cultural inadequacy of black households, has been the culprit. Between 1950 and 1981, employment increased by only 2.8 percent in New England states and by 1.1 percent in central Northeast states. In the Mid-Atlantic states, where even higher concentrations of blacks live, employment opportunities declined by 15.7 percent.

The increased poverty in the Deep South and Mississippi Delta states came into sharp relief during Hurricane Katrina. As U.S. and international audiences expressed shock at the Bush administration's responses—and lack of responses—to the horrific conditions in New Orleans after the storm broke the levees, the U.S. Census Bureau released its yearly data on poverty, which had risen for the fourth straight year. Blacks' high poverty rates in New Orleans were not an anomaly. Long before the arrival of Katrina, New Orleans and the entire Mississippi Delta was a social and economic disaster. Mississippi has the lowest per capita income in the United States; it has one of the lowest-ranked educational systems with one of the highest dropout rates. And it has the highest child poverty rate and the highest infant mortality rate in the nation. Alabama ranks third from the bottom, making these states the epicenter of the nation's poor. Nearly half of the black children in each of these states live below the poverty line. Latino Americans have rates equal to that of African Americans. Only 9 to 11 percent of white children are similarly situated. The anomalies in African American political life have continued as well. One year before an interracial and intergenerational coalition of voters in states outside the South put a black president in office, two-thirds of elected blacks came from Southern states. While restrictions to black voting have been present for decades, it has only gotten worse. Two years after this historic election, 24 percent of African Americans in Kentucky are disfranchised; in Ohio, intricate state laws continue to limit and suppress blacks' voting rights. In Wisconsin, the Republican Party has sent out mailers to black voters, which are then put in a database, and these voters are purged from the rolls. Using a practice called "caging," Arkansas Republicans have targeted soldiers—who vote for the Democrats in increasing numbers—and removed them from the polls. Other states have sent out misleading and incorrect information about the location of polls; officials intimidate voters at polls, close parking lots near polls, and provide broken or too few computers at polls in minority neighborhoods.

Since the 1950s, pollsters have regularly questioned Americans about whether they have attained the American dream or if they have believed it possible to achieve it, but they have given widely different responses, depending on their age, class, and race. In nearly every survey, the majority of Americans believed they have done so or they have had a chance to achieve some semblance of the dream. Few of these early polls surveyed African Americans, but since the 1980s they have been included. As a group and regardless of age, they have typically expressed far less optimism for either question.

This trend has continued in a 2004 survey conducted by the National League of Cities, a nonprofit company, and again in a 2009 survey conducted by MetLife, an insurance company. Both surveys defined the American dream as access to individual home ownership, financial stability, status, and success. In 2004, 53 percent of African Americans told pollsters that they were not living the American dream; by 2010 this percentage jumped twenty points. In contrast, 36 percent of Hispanics and 32 percent of Caucasians expressed the same view. A majority of whites in each poll believed the government has hindered their efforts. Middle-class and upper-class whites in every age bracket wanted lower taxes and little government regulation. Despite abundant evidence to the contrary, nearly half believe the health care reform passed by Congress in early 2010 will hinder their economic advancement.

Not all Americans agree with the narrow definition of the American dream or the curtailment of government's role. Organized workers surveyed by the Change to Win Federation defined the American dream as jobs that pay a living wage, quality health care, a secure retirement, and opportunities for their children. These workers do not want government out of their lives; they expect government to invest in good jobs, health care, and education. They include the right to organize in unions and the dignity of work as key components in their concept of the American dream. These workers make powerful claims but they do so with diminished ranks. *All* workers have seen a decline in numbers, but organized workers have seen their ranks drop to less than 15 percent as employers have launched a relentless assault on their right to organize.

Black unemployment rates continue to climb while the national rate of unemployment inches downward. Overall unemployment dropped to 8.8 percent in March 2011, but black joblessness rose from 15.3 percent to 15.5 percent—nearly double the 7.9 percent white jobless rate. For young black men, the jobless rate is higher. The U.S. Labor Bureau reports that over one-third of black men between the ages sixteen and twenty-four are jobless, a rate that equals the proportions of unemployed African Americans during the Great Depression and is more than three times the rate for the nation's population overall. But black workers, whose ranks include a larger population of young workers than most other groups (Latinos have slightly higher populations of younger workers than blacks), have been hard hit by this long recession.

Low-income and unemployed African Americans and other minorities have borne unevenly the brunt of the recession and subsequent cuts in services and programs. State and federal efforts to reduce the deficit have relied almost entirely on slashes to programs and jobs with large minority populations such as teachers, health care workers, and municipal and state workers. While some progressives consider cuts to prisons a welcome addition to this list, others rightly note that any employment is important to many communities with few other economic opportunities. Calls for massive cuts in Medicare, Medicaid, Social Security, and other programs that address the everyday needs of low-income people are also programs that employ higher percentages of workers of color, particularly women, whose incomes have been historically critical to their households. While Great Society jobs programs did too little in generating jobs in the private sector, programs such as Head Start created jobs in many communities. Whenever Republicans have gained control of state legislatures and Congress, they have attempted, often successfully, to reduce or eliminate these programs. The deficit-reducing proposals in 2011 are similar in their tone and intent: a frontal attack on low-income people who are served and the elimination of jobs of moderate-income people who serve them. These programs, from child care, early education, K–12 education, jobs programs, and food and health care programs, provide a modicum of stability in some households and communities. When done right—and many are done right—they launch individuals and families on the road to economic stability.

The areas where organized labor has been hard hit, such as in the old economy sectors of auto manufacturing and shipbuilding, have had a devastating impact on black communities. Yet service workers and public workers have been equally challenged. The reductions in the number of these jobs have caused equal havoc on black men and women.

The need to assert progressive U.S. labor policy by state and local governments and private and public sector unions to address the overall high black unemployment rates and the decline in opportunities for many of the jobless to find work, particularly veterans and ex-convicts, has never been more urgent. While African Americans have been loyal to unions, they have also seen the federal and state governments as critical participants in making sure labor policy is fair.

For many blacks, access to jobs has been as important as the right to join a union. Since the inception of organized labor in the United States, African Americans have pressed unions to make civil rights integral to the rights and dignity of labor. Black workers and their allies have challenged—with varying degrees of success—the stereotype of the American worker as a male skilled manufacturing worker in a private company. The creation of service and public employee unions with large numbers of nonwhite women has been a victory for labor, and this population of workers has become a formidable component of the labor movement. Along with this expansive view of workers, the demand for work as a right that benefits the individual, community, and nation must remain at the heart of organized labor.

At the same time, organized labor must challenge discrimination at the point of hire. Black workers continue to face particular barriers to employment, especially young black men. Despite education, training, or time in the military, the ability for young black men to find permanent work is little better than for a convicted felon. A recent study by scholars at Princeton University uncovered widespread patterns of discrimination among employers in New York City. Many employers *assume* black men are ex-convicts, a point the Princeton study revealed. Employers were more likely to hire white men just out prison than black men without a criminal record and with education and training.

The U.S. incarceration rate is high overall for men of all races, especially for drug and alcohol offenses, and they all face both the potential to be put in prison and the long-term impact in limited job opportunities once they are released. The high incarceration rate of black men adds to the bleak overall employment picture. A 2008 study revealed that one in nine black men between the ages of twenty and thirty-four were in a state or local jail compared to one in one hundred for white men. Many are in prison for nonviolent crimes. Scholars and civil rights organizations have uncovered abundant evidence about the discrimination in arrests, convictions, and sentencing that account for the high disparities between blacks and all other groups. What happens to blacks after they leave prison is just as discriminatory, patterns only hinted at in the recent Princeton study. Civil rights organizations have addressed the limited employment opportunities African Americans face once they have left prison, but unions must challenge employment discrimination.

The solemn promise of "life, liberty, and the pursuit of happiness" made at the founding of the United States was not egalitarian, yet African Americans have demanded that the nation reconceptualize this covenant with the people. In 1965, James Baldwin assumed the voice of a prophet appointed to confront America for ignoring the uncompensated labor of many of the people even as it has ensured the wealth and political power of others. Baldwin's urgent plea for honesty and honor resonates forty-five years later: "Unless we can establish some kind of dialogue between those people who enjoy the American dream and those people who have not achieved it, we will be in terrible trouble." Baldwin had long challenged the relegation of African Americans to the nation's economic margins. Racial and economic justice in the United States will require systematic change to the structural inequalities that are endemic and threaten to engulf increasing numbers of Americans, regardless of race. Meaningful change in how government and organized labor work for the people and by the people will also require a moral revolution that sees the right to work and the right to vote as inherent and unalienable rights.

Part Four

Political Economy

When workers come together to make demands on their employers, corporate polluters, predatory banks, or the state, they operate simultaneously in both the political and the economic spheres. This is true whether they are acting through formal unions, through worker centers, or in their communities. Workers strike for wages, demand fair housing, insist on environmental regulations, campaign to raise the minimum wage, or fight for equal protection under the law; they are economic as well as political actors. No conflict with management is free of the implied threat that their political allies can limit workers' ability to strike and boycott, and can back up those restrictions with police powers. And as the government has expanded its size and authority over the twentieth century, military contracts, tax codes, and international trade agreements have all shaped the major sectors of the American and global economies.

Until recently, mainstream labor has traditionally defined its role in the political economy narrowly to promote job growth, most often supporting American foreign policy, trade policy, and domestic energy policy without regard to broader social concerns or long-term employment prospects. The authors in this section question that wisdom and suggest models for how labor needs to address the complexities of the American political economy.

Bill Fletcher Jr. argues that labor needs to reassert a role in advocating for the dispossessed, but not as loyal insiders and partners in the political economy. He draws on examples from the early CIO to the rise in public sector unions and militant dissident movements in the 1970s for inspiration. Fletcher suggests that unions need a broader social agenda and a more pointed criticism of neoliberal capitalism to successfully transform the labor movement.

Andrew Ross challenges us to think about the climate crises in the context of union strategy. He argues that labor should embrace a strategy of "Eco-Keynsianism" that supports the development of the green industrial sector through federal funding. At the same time, labor should take that opportunity to build relationships with environmentalists. This would necessitate labor rethinking its industrial policy. He suggests considering historic proposals to assist workers who would be displaced by reducing, even eliminating, the extraction of fossil fuels with money and training.

Our next essay, by economist Marcellus Andrews, reminds us that economics is not always just about markets but is fundamentally about work and the conditions under which workers sell their labor. He brings us right back to the fundamental question of what is the labor bargain and how it relates to labor solidarity. Andrews argues that broad labor solidarity should not be limited to relationships between trade unions, nor should it be merely a tool to garner union support. To do so misses the opportunity to change the labor bargain itself. Unions are a vital part of this, but they are not the only part. They need to make partnerships with organizations and communities connected to workers to unpack what he calls the "veil of ignorance" about the true moral implications of our political economy, which, he insists, needs to be about the substantive meaning of economic freedom, racial inclusion, and social justice.

For Elizabeth Faue, to reverse labor's decline, unions need to communicate to ordinary people what unions are, who belongs to them, and what their potential is for social reform and transformation. She argues for a revived labor press and media to counteract the negative stereotypes and slander about workers and their unions propagated by the corporate-controlled media and their politician allies.

ORGANIZED LABOR: DECLINING SOURCE OF HOPE?

Bill Fletcher Jr.

Though I was never raised to believe labor unions to be a panacea, I am not sure that I was fully prepared for the realities that I encountered when I walked through the gates of a shipyard in 1977 and became a member of Local 5 of the Industrial Union of Marine and Shipbuilding Workers of America. This union, which in the 1930s had a strong national reputation as a progressive union, including in its approach toward the need to combat racist discrimination, had become anything but progressive. The leadership of Local 5 was a clique of older, conservative white men, with the union having the vibrancy of a tree hollowed out by termites. It had no inclination to reach out to any communities and focused itself largely on lobbying for more government military contracts to build and repair ships, rather than thinking through the evolution of the shipbuilding industry and alternative products we could have constructed. To add insult to injury, when we embarked on a strike against a very aggressive employer, the union leadership (at the local and national levels) had absolutely no strategy outside of having us walk the picket lines.

Not only was the union conservative, but it was racially divided. The leadership paid no attention to the fact that racial segregation existed in the shipyard and that workers of color were largely restricted to the dirtiest and most dangerous of the jobs. In fact, workers of color did not see the union as a vehicle to address the racist discrimination that was experienced on a daily basis.

The U.S. labor union movement exists as a contradiction. There is both a radical tradition, which includes fighting for inclusion, reaching out to support workers overseas, and organizing the unorganized, but there is also a more conservative tradition, one most often associated with the founder of the American Federation of Labor (AFL) Samuel Gompers. This latter tradition is one that focuses primarily on the dynamics at the workplace and sees the growth of the union largely associated with the growth of the employer. This tradition is one that sees in capitalism the best of all possible worlds and the union serving as a willing partner, rarely paying attention to the price paid by workers here and abroad for such an alliance.

This contradictory existence that has haunted labor manifests itself in different ways at various moments in history. In the 1960s and 1970s it played itself out in a particular manner that largely reflected the struggles around race and gender, but additionally U.S. foreign policy, which marked that era. For most of the generation energized, and in many cases radicalized, by the social movements of that period, organized labor was largely a nonplayer. While it was true that United Auto Workers president Walter Reuther and AFL-CIO president George Meany—among others in the top echelons of organized labor—supported important pieces of civil rights legislation, it was equally true that most of the official labor movement did little to encourage and support, not to mention unite with, emerging progressive movements, such as the civil rights movement, the women's movement, environmental movement, and certainly the anti–Vietnam War movement. As a result, mainstream unions were, for the most part, discounted as mechanisms for any significant social transformation by younger activists in these various social movements. In some cases, the unions were viewed as obstacles to progress, particularly with respect to their failure, until very late in the day, to oppose the Vietnam War. In fact, insofar as the AFL-CIO and most of its affiliates actively supported the U.S. aggression in Indochina, a wall developed between the movements and made it very difficult to collaborate on matters of common concern.

There were, however, certain important exceptions. Labor struggles in Memphis, Tennessee, with the sanitation workers in 1968 (where Martin Luther King Jr. was murdered); the 1969 hospital workers strike in Charleston, South Carolina; and the radical labor efforts of groups such as the League of Revolutionary Black Workers in Detroit (1968–71), the Harlem Fightback in New York City (formed in the early 1960s), and United Black Workers in Mahwah, New Jersey (formed in the late 1960s), illustrated fascinating and inspiring examples of a symbiosis between the Black Freedom Movement and the workers movement, and, in fact, a demand for a different sort of unionism.

For those pondering fundamental social transformation, the possibilities represented by the examples just cited point to a significant difference from alternative reform or revolutionary approaches offered at that same time. Community-based, non-working-class-focused efforts, particularly in the Black Freedom Movement, illustrated a sometimes opposing/sometimes complementary approach to mobilizing masses for social change. Among more so-called moderate organizations, this could include the Southern Christian Leadership Conference's Operation Breadbasket (which later became Rev. Jesse Jackson's Operation PUSH when he split off from the SCLC). Further to the left could be found the Black Panther Party, which by 1969–70 illustrated this approach of not paying much attention to the working class in the workplace. The Panthers, in particular, evolved their thinking in the direction of a focus on the hard-core unemployed (including the criminal element, in part based on a misreading of who the revolutionary element had been in the Algerian national liberation struggle against France) and away from workers who were actually employed.

Increasingly, sections of the political left—particularly what came to be known as the New Left—saw in the *idea* of unions an instrument for transformation. In some cases, particularly in the early 1970s, there was a tendency that developed within the New Left that thought that radical unions or radical quasi-unions could be formed that would be at the center of an anti-capitalist strategy. Organizations such as the League of Revolutionary Black Workers (mentioned earlier), the Health Revolutionary Unity Movement (based in New York and initiated by the radical Puerto Rican organization known as the Young Lords Party), the Telephone Revolutionary Union Movement (early 1970s), and Transfusion (a radical independent union effort in Boston) fit into this category. Consciously or not, this section of the New Left drew its inspiration from the anarcho-syndicalist tradition in which unions are seen as the principal instrument to bring about radical social change and, as such, are mobilized for broad political purposes that may or may not address specific workplace issues.

Yet most of the political left recognized that the ideological diversity of unions, as a form of workers' organization, made it unlikely (short of a *revolutionary* situation of profound social instability) that a labor union could serve as the principal instrument of radical change. Nevertheless, much of the left saw evidence that unions, as one of the few institutions in U.S. society that bring together workers across racial, ethnic, and gender lines, have a potential role in bringing about change and challenging capitalism. With that in mind, a cross section of the left made work in the union movement more central to their respective strategies. This included a wide range of organizations including but not limited to Michael Harrington's Democratic Socialist Organizing Committee (DSOC), the New American Movement (NAM), various organizations out of the Marxist-Leninist tradition, but also formations such as ACORN, which, in the early 1980s, began its own union organizing (known as the United Labor Unions).

The dominant framework in the 1970s and early 1980s for left work in the unions was focused on the notion of evicting the so-called misleaders. Specifically, the focus was on removing the existing, relatively conservative leadership of the union movement and replacing it with leaders who were, instead of being collaborationists with capitalists, partisans of pro-working-class struggle. This approach coincided with a period of rank-and-file union reform efforts that had been under way since the 1960s, with movements in the United Mine Workers and the International Brotherhood of the Teamsters being among the most noteworthy.

The relative optimism among many rank-and-file worker activists, certainly in evidence in the 1970s, reflected both the vivacity of social forces in the United States, and indeed the world, that were advancing progressive change, but also an oversimplification of the institutional and social forces that stood in the way of thoroughgoing transformation. An assumption that removing the so-called misleaders was virtually all that needed to be done in order to transform labor unions into true vehicles for positive change ignored, again as Gapa-sin and I have noted, the relative bases that these "misleaders" had within the unions themselves.

By the 1980s, the approach toward unions by many on the politi-cal left had shifted in important respects. First, the broader political/economic picture had changed dramatically. The mid-1970s had re-sulted in the worst recession since the Great Depression. This was followed by several years of economic stagnation, leading to yet an-other recession in 1980–82 (the so-called Reagan/Volcker reces-sion) during which the phenomenon of so-called deindustrialization became very pronounced with factory closings across the country. This was accompanied by a change in the political climate with the rise of Ronald Reagan and the adoption of an approach toward the economy which came to be known—internationally and eventually in the United States—as "neoliberalism." This approach emphasized the elimination of all obstacles to the accumulation of profits, and those obstacles included, but were not limited to, labor unions. This *offensive* threw progressive social movements onto the defensive, and one can argue that they have been on the defensive ever since. "Rea-ganism" challenged the narratives that came out of the New Deal and later the 1960s, where the suggestion was that government could play a role in protecting the populace from the ravages of capitalism. Rea-ganism offered an alternative narrative that was summarized in the famous film *Wall Street* where the major character (played by Michael Douglas) argues that *greed is good*.

Within the segment of the left that took organizing the working class seriously, particularly in the workplace, dual unionist strategies had, for all intents and purposes, been dropped. An increasingly dis-organized political left adopted more gradualist approaches toward transforming the union movement. In fact, the approaches tended to be increasingly individual (if not individualist) as leftists worked from the inside, often under very deep cover, to bring about different approaches on the part of organized labor toward issues of the day. In some cases, such individuals played instrumental roles in various reform initiatives, but more often than not, individual leftists and groups of individual leftists had their efforts harnessed by progressive

non-left reformers—such as the leaders of Miners for Democracy—
to bring about very partial change. In few cases, by the mid- to late
1980s, did the left within labor have an independent and credible
voice and banner around which it could unite significant numbers of
workers in projecting an alternative left project within labor.

By the 1990s the declining force of the official labor union movement had become so evident that even the mainstream leaders had
to pay attention. The 1994 midterm congressional success by the
Gingrich Republicans signaled to many in organized labor that a different approach was necessary if organized labor was not to face obliv-
ion. This situation provided the basis for the reform effort that, led
by John Sweeney from the Service Employees International Union,
gained control of the AFL-CIO in October 1995.

Ironically, many left leaders and their constituents went from
thinking that the mainstream leaders needed to all be evicted to
placing a significant degree of its emphasis on its ability to influence
many of those same leaders. Many of the more pragmatist-oriented
of the mainstream leaders, such as the SEIU's John Sweeney or the
Teamsters' Ron Carey, were, under the circumstances of the evident
crisis in organized labor, prepared to seek allies from within the political left. They did so insofar as the left remained both relatively invisible as well as nonthreatening. In that context, many leftists as well
as other progressives placed much attention on the theme of organizing the unorganized workforce as the key to labor's revitalization.
Evidence of this could be found in left/progressive journals such as
Labor Research Review and *Labor Notes*, but also in the theories and
strategies that were being elaborated in unions such as the SEIU, the
Communications Workers of America, and the American Federation
of State, County and Municipal Employees. At few points did many
progressive and left labor activists grapple with the necessary changes
that needed to be introduced within the unions (with the exception of
formal democracy) and within the consciousness of the rank-and-file
workers in order to result in a qualitatively different approach to labor unionism. Examples of this in the mainstream union movement
could be seen in the limitations on worker education, as well as the

focus on organizational technique in bringing about change rather than the need for a more comprehensive cultural change.

Thus, by the mid-1990s a paradox was unfolding. Many younger progressives and leftists who came to activism and consciousness through Union Summer, anti–World Trade Organization protests, family wages for campus worker campaigns, and student worker and teaching assistant unions started to see in mainstream organized labor a vehicle for significant social change. The rhetoric of the movement had shifted and there was a new openness to coalitions with other liberal and progressive forces. The emphasis on organizing the unorganized worker such as through the SEIU's Justice for Janitors campaign or the United Farm Workers' efforts—supported heavily by the AFL-CIO—to organize strawberry workers seemed to signify mainstream labor's interest in militant struggle, and a particular interest in workers who had been traditionally ignored.

Despite important reforms, however, mainstream organized labor did not actually catch fire. On top of this, many of the younger progressive and left labor activists who had looked to organized labor as the vehicle for social justice over time became increasingly disheartened as they witnessed institutional changes advance at glacial speed and the institutions themselves, beyond rhetoric, prove less than enthusiastic—or at best inconsistent—about sincerely challenging neoliberal globalization.

The reform effort initiated by the Sweeney-led coalition of unions in 1995 stalled, evidence of which became clear by the late 1990s. Organized labor became increasingly unable to muster the vision and the forces to address the expanding crisis facing not only itself but, more importantly, that facing the working class. Among other things, the bulk of AFL-CIO-affiliated unions continued a profound dependence on the Democratic Party. This meant that during the Clinton era (1993–2001) there was a near universal refusal to criticize the administration for anything of substance. There was an aborted effort to develop a labor-based narrative on the economic crisis (the effort was known as "Common Sense Economics") and only limited efforts to build sustained alliances with progressive social movements.

While globalization was publicly challenged, insofar as the Clinton administration advanced neoliberal globalization (including the military side of globalization), there was both silence and inconsistency in criticism. And, as noted earlier, while there were real changes from earlier AFL-CIO administrations, and pre-1995 administrations among many of the affiliated unions, there was virtually no change in the role of the individual rank-and-file union member vis-à-vis their relationship to the union. Heavy reliance on staff replaced the need to build membership control of the unions and member ownership of the project of badly needed union renewal.

While mainstream labor has remained an effective player in the electoral realm, in 2008, at the time of the financial crash, the associated subprime mortgage debacle, and full evidence of deepening economic crisis, the official union movement played out a "deer in the headlights" scenario, nearly paralyzed in the face of the dramatic attacks on working people.

The labor movement generally and unions in particular have been a source of inspiration in U.S. history when they have been the voice from the "outside." In other words, when unions have been seen, to borrow from A. Philip Randolph, to be the instruments of and advocates for the *dispossessed* they create an aura around themselves that generates a culture and practice of mass struggle. In cases such as the period of the growth of the Congress of Industrial Organizations (CIO) in the 1930s and 1940s, but also that of the dramatic growth in public sector unionism in the 1960s and early 1970s, being perceived as a voice and advocate from the outside lent itself to unions constructing alliances—sometimes longer-term, sometimes shorter-term—with other progressive social forces and movements that spoke to the needs and concerns of the dispossessed. When organized labor has played the "insider" game, it has tended toward increasing isolation, except and insofar as others have sought out the financial coffers of mainstream labor to support their endeavors, for better and for worse.

In this regard, the focal point for the revitalization of labor, a revitalization essential in order to build a broader progressive coalition for change, cannot be seen in the context of tactics. New and better approaches to organizing the unorganized, as important as they may be, run the risk of providing new wine to old bottles unless accompanied by qualitative changes in areas such as organizational culture, the role of the rank-and-file member, strategic alliances with other social forces, global worker solidarity, welcoming previously excluded and/or marginalized groups, and a level of militancy in the face of the economic juggernaut.

There are countless examples of how this renewal can be pressed forward. In the middle of this Great Recession, for instance, organizing the unemployed should be a strategic priority. Individual unions are not going to be able to carry this out, for the most part, but central labor councils can. By pooling the resources of unions at the local level, central labor councils could establish councils of the unemployed to organize around the need for new jobs, indeed, green jobs. While the AFL-CIO-sponsored organization known as Working America is doing some work among the unemployed, that is very different than a full-blown campaign to reach the unemployed. At a point when right-wing populists are attempting to appeal to disgruntled white workers—employed and unemployed—the AFL-CIO and the split-off federation known as Change to Win need to be paying attention to tapping the anger and the desire for a new direction.

In the electoral arena, where unions are heavily involved, they must pay attention to developing, along with community-based organizations, alternative electoral projects. The efforts in the 2010 June primaries to challenge Arkansas senator Blanche Lincoln were noteworthy in that organized labor was attempting to make it known that betrayals will not be tolerated. But throwing millions into one campaign is not sustainable. Building independent organizations that can identify, train, and support candidates represents a different scenario. Organized labor's electoral approach needs to focus on building projects on the ground that can begin to articulate a new set of politics.

It is also important to move toward cultural changes. In 2005 the AFL-CIO split when several unions, led by the SEIU, chose to establish a new federation (Change to Win). In the lead-up to the split, as Gapasin and I note, there was not a full-blown debate concerning the most important issues facing rank-and-file union members, not to mention workers who want to join or form unions. To reverse this, the split must be recognized as a failure. It has brought no clarity as to what needs to be done. Reunification is necessary, but a reunification that engages rank-and-file workers in a discussion regarding the future of organized labor. Yet there seems to be little interest in such a broad-based dialogue within organized labor, even among some of the more progressive-minded leaders. Again and again there is over-reliance on leader-to-leader discussions rather than embracing and including the members in discussions about the future of organized labor. Should this shift and discussions take place, we might be looking at a dramatically different union movement.

Labor unions, in a word, must understand that they can be part of an equation that leads toward the renaissance of a labor movement. "Can" is the operative word because it is premised on the willingness of both the leaders and members of existing unions to recognize that as far as contemporary—neoliberal global—capitalism is concerned, labor is certainly now and will forever be considered an obstacle to be overcome. In that sense this is a fight for our lives and a fight to determine whether there will be a union movement in the United States as we plunge further into the twenty-first century.

ECO-KEYNESIANISM, GREEN JOBS, AND LABOR'S NEED TO EMBRACE CLIMATE JUSTICE

Andrew Ross

How should labor respond to the climate crisis? In the past, institutional concerns about joblessness have often put labor on the wrong side of environmentalist issues, not least because trade unions were so well established in the dirtiest energy industries. There are still reasons to worry that any transition to a clean energy economy will be seized upon as a corporate opportunity to usher in union-free work sectors. But the time of reckoning with climate change is fast approaching, and, with it, the momentous opportunity for labor to make common cause with advocates of climate justice. Doing so should allow the U.S. labor movement to expand and deepen its newfound commitment to international organizing, while holding fast to more traditional demands that the post-fossil transition must safeguard hard-earned rights of workers to bargaining power and sustainable livelihoods. Many obstacles lie in the path, however. It is by no means easy for labor advocates in the North to identify with a climate justice movement dominated by the concerns of peasant farmers and rainforest communities in the South. In addition, there is no guarantee that the much-vaunted campaign to create green jobs will deliver a solid fraction of its potential in the absence of a concerted legislative program of binding emissions reductions. Yet the failure of labor to fully embrace the respective spirit of either of these initiatives would be a death blow to any hopes of reclaiming its rightful role in the vanguard of progressive causes.

One of the win-win prospects to emerge from the wave of hope that swept the Obama administration to power was the promise of creating a new generation of sustainable livelihoods as part of the shift to a post-fossil economy. All of the ingredients were in place. The pressing threat of global warming had taken up residence in the public mind. The bailout of the financial industry established an appetite for government intervention that included warm federal support for sunrise industries producing clean electrons. Swayed by evidence of the long-term profitability of green capitalism, corporate and political elites looked to assuage the national shame at being left behind in the global competition for clean energy. Last but not least, green jobs were held up as the solution to rebuilding a national workforce hollowed out by offshore outsourcing, destabilized by the rise of temping, and knocked to the ground by the recession.

By the spring of 2008, there was talk of a new speculative bubble in clean energy—some were even calling it the "Good Bubble." Hot money, alienated from the collapsed real estate markets, poured into venture funds for backing alternative technology start-ups, and it was reported that Heidi Fleiss (the erstwhile Hollywood madam) had dropped her plans to open a bordello for female clients in Nevada because she had decided to invest instead in renewable energy. When asked why, she echoed the famous words of bank robber Willie Sutton. "Because that's where the money is." Beginning with the American Recovery and Reinvestment Act (ARRA) stimulus package in the spring of 2009, which allocated $60 billion to clean energy, the Obama administration rolled out a series of federal subsidies and incentives to support a broad range of green initiatives. With federal funding came the requirement that the green jobs would have to be well paid. Wherever this precondition was implemented, it was a welcome upgrade from wage scales in the existing solar and wind sectors, which lagged far behind the average paycheck in the mature energy industries.

Naturally, most of the labor movement swung into line behind what looked like a savvy industrial policy, and commentators were not slow to conclude that the long-hoped-for alliance between labor and greens had finally seen the light of day with the formation of new groups and initiatives like the Blue-Green Alliance, the Apollo Alliance, and Emerald Cities. These coalitions were hardly starting from scratch. The points of division between the labor and the

environmental movements had always been magnified out of all proportion by jobs blackmail on the part of employers, and, besides, there
was a busy history of earnest efforts to unite on a range of issues and
campaigns. Notable among the early initiatives were Environmentalists for Full Employment (formed in 1975), the Labor Committee for
Safe Energy and Full Employment (in 1980), and the OSHA/Environ-
mental Network (in 1981). Even so, the new alliances were infused
with an acute sense of ripe timing, and they carried over into support
for the International Trade Union Confederation's (ITUC) efforts to
intervene in the UN climate summits in Copenhagen, Cancún, and
Durban.

Yet only eighteen months after the stimulus funding was passed,
pressure from the oil, gas, and coal lobbies had succeeded in rendering the term "climate change" all but persona non grata on Capitol
Hill, and the nuclear option had been brought back from its shal-
low grave, pitched as the GOP's preferred clean (if not renewable) energy source. Even after the catastrophic meltdowns at the Fukushima
Daiichi power plant in the wake of Japan's March 2011 earthquake,
the Obama administration held firm, in principle at least, to its commitment to relaunch the U.S. nuclear program. By then, its resolve to
push through climate change legislation had wilted, and its fallback
efforts to use the EPA as a carbon regulator were everywhere on the
defensive. Where does the promise of green jobs stand today, as the
bloom fades on the moment of eco-Keynesianism and the dictate for
a new politics of austerity begins to kick in?

Trade unionists could ill afford to relegate on their list of priorities
any new industrial policy, and least of all one that finally put them on
the progressive side of the carbon equation, so the commitment of
many unions to sustainability initiatives has been substantial. Even
so, the efforts to embrace clean energy initiatives must be undertaken
in a more fully internationalist spirit than has already been the case.
Take the response of the United States to the dramatic lead forged
by Chinese industry in the manufacture of clean technologies like
solar panels and wind turbines. In September 2010, the United Steel
Workers (USW) filed a comprehensive trade case to the U.S. trade
representative against allegedly illegal policies and practices designed

to unfairly advance China's domination of the clean tech sector. The Obama administration dutifully brought the case before the WTO. In many ways, the complaint was a reprise of several other cases brought to bear jointly by the U.S. government and the American labor movement against China over the last decade, many of them tinged with an air of Sinophobia. In an election season during a recession, China-bashing was guaranteed to be high on the agenda, and there was no better reminder of the longevity of labor's tradition of viewing the Chinese as "the indispensable enemy," to cite Alexander Saxton's memorable description of the situation of the Chinese workers in nineteenth-century California.

But consider the basis of the USW charge. The Chinese government was being faulted for pouring subsidies into the production of renewable energy technologies for export to countries that need them to meet mandates for greenhouse gas reductions. Yet under WTO rules, it is illegal to subsidize renewable tech for export. However dumb a rule, it was also a somewhat hypocritical charge. Consider that in 2009, China ploughed 0.31 percent of its GDP ($34.6 billion) into clean energy. Not as much as Spain, at 0.74 percent, or the UK, at 0.51 percent, but far more than the United States, at 0.13 percent (or $18.6 billion). None of these funding commitments was adequate, but to point a finger at a country that had responded so quickly and so effectively to the challenge of producing cheap renewables seemed misguided, and especially when China was still being blamed for the dismal failures to reach binding agreements on greenhouse gas reductions at the Copenhagen climate summit in December 2009. The USW, the lead union in the formation of the Blue-Green Alliance, argued for what it called a level playing field. To its credit, it tried to put a domestic spin on the trade complaint, intensifying the drumbeat for more eco-Keynesianism from the Obama administration, which is really the only way, in the short term, of building a viable green manufacturing sector. But castigating the Chinese was tantamount to playing the same old political football with free trade rules (which protect capital and not labor). Instead, we should have been praising the Chinese subsidies, and insisting that the Obama administration outmatch them. But it is always safer to blame the Chinese—one of the most reliable ethnic instincts of American labor.

That is not to say there are no problems with the Chinese sector, which is pursuing the same low-road path with clean tech in the area of labor standards as it has done in other export manufacturing sectors. Yet the need for cheap solar panels is crucial in the race to decarbonize as much of world industry as possible. Reconciling that urgent need with strategies for maintaining and raising labor standards is one of our biggest challenges in an era that has been earmarked for transitioning away from the fossil economy. Taking Beijing to task is not the solution, least of all when Chinese firms are beginning to create clean energy jobs in the United States itself.

In November 2009, Suntech, China's largest solar panel manufacturer, announced plans to build a facility in the metro Phoenix area. It was the first such plant to be built in the United States by a major Chinese clean energy company and, in this regard, was something of a national milestone. Media coverage made comparisons with the first Japanese auto factories in the 1980s, touching off all the usual alarms about the loss of U.S. competitiveness. But the comparison with Toyota and Honda was flawed for many reasons. For one thing, the main losers had been Germany and Spain, since the United States lost its early lead in renewables many years earlier. In addition, there was an appreciable downgrading in the kind of jobs expected of this new wave of Chinese investment. Manufacturing (and design) of Suntech's solar cells would continue to be done in Wuxi, China, where wages are ten times lower than in the United States. The jobs that were coming to Arizona were for assembling panels that would be sold regionally and that are not cost-effective to ship from Asia. The panels would be stamped "Made in the USA," and the firm would take advantage of the 30 percent investment tax credit available to solar firms from ARRA funding, along with Arizona's own incentives for green manufacturing. But only the least-skilled portion of the manufacturing process would occur on American soil.

For the best part of two decades, U.S. corporations have treated China as a cheap assembly platform for export goods. Now, it seems, the favor is about to be returned. Regions of the United States with high solar exposure may well become the new assembly platforms, supplying cheap labor and local government subsidies to Chinese firms that have already benefited from Beijing's formidable state subsidies, central industrial planning, and preferential treatment. Cities such as Phoenix, devastated by joblessness and abandoned by U.S. corporations, may well be lucky to land even those low-skill assembly jobs. The comparisons being made there are with the decisive recruitment of Motorola to the region in the 1950s, an investment that set the pattern for the rise of the Sun Belt, with defense-based high-tech firms seeking out cheap right-to-work locations with friendly business climates and tilting the balance of the national economic investment away from the Frost Belt.

Yet any analogies with that generation of high-tech manufacture are as misleading as the ones that invoked Toyota. Motorola and other technology firms brought a wide range of jobs—high skill as well as low skill—to the Southwest, but beginning in the 1970s these were progressively sent offshore, many of them to China itself. China's own solicitation of foreign investment for the last two decades has been driven by the desire not just for foreign currency earnings but also for technology and knowledge transfer. But no such spinoff rewards will accrue to the United States for landing the new generation of Chinese clean-tech investors. After all, the core technologies for photovoltaic cells and wind turbines were all developed with Department of Defense funding during the Cold War, and the patents were sold for pennies on the dollar to Germans and Japanese after Ronald Reagan brought down the curtain on funding for renewables in the early 1980s.

Yet even if U.S. companies were somehow to become leading players in the renewable energy manufacturing field, what would guarantee their provision of decent American jobs? Tempe, next door to Phoenix, is home to the corporate headquarters of First Solar, one of the world's leading solar producers (in thin film tech), but it has no production facilities in the state, and has only looked stateside when large federal and state incentives were dangled. In the fall of

2009, it inked a deal with California's PG&E for a large 550-megawatt solar farm, in a state that was the first to institute a feed-in tariff, and in January 2010 the firm snagged $5 million in advanced energy manufacturing tax credits from the ARRA to expand its token U.S. manufacturing plant, in Toledo. But it is by no means clear how long these new jobs can be kept in the United States. With the price of solar panels falling so rapidly, U.S. firms that entered the field with government help are already transitioning to Asia. Evergreen, a Massachusetts-based solar start-up, which opened its doors with more than $43 million of state backing in the fall of 2008, began to transfer operations to China only a year later, and, in January 2011, moved its entire production plant to a heavily subsided joint venture with Jiawei Solarchina in Wuhan. Indeed, a survey, conducted by the Apollo Alliance and Good Jobs First, of the ninety recipients of the ARRA's advanced energy manufacturing tax credit showed that twenty-three of them were also investing in manufacturing facilities in low-wage countries like Malaysia and China.

A bigger problem for labor is the fact that most of the clean-tech industry is nonunionized. As long as the government sticks to subsidizing green initiatives, employees and host communities can reasonably expect some degree of employer accountability when it comes to the provision of decent pay and benefits. But the job quality standards attached to the subsidies vary widely, by state, city, and county, and, in right-to-work states, those guarantees are especially precarious. The new clean-tech ventures are going up against the heavily unionized dirty energy sector—utilities, centralized power generation plants, and extractive industries. Concerns about joblessness and the lowering of labor standards have kept unions in these fossil industries on the wrong side of the green aisle for a long time, and they are being swayed by a new round of Chamber of Commerce propaganda that EPA regulation is a "serial job-killer." This mantra about the threat to jobs, repeated ad nauseam by the National Organization of Manufacturers, the oil and coal lobbies, and GOP lawmakers, is consistent with corporate responses to the first wave of environmental legislation in the 1970s. There is no evidence, in the intervening decades,

that environmental protection laws have resulted in the elimination
of an appreciable number of jobs in any sector, least of all when compared to the joblessness from offshore outsourcing.

Indeed, studies have consistently showed that investment,
whether public or private, in decentralized and labor-intensive green
enterprises creates many more jobs than in the highly automated,
capital-intensive, centralized facilities of the mature energy sector.
The most recent such study from Ceres and the Political Economy
Research Institute at the University of Massachusetts shows that the
EPA carbon regulations will create nearly three hundred thousand
new jobs in the first five years after their implementation. Such estimates have helped to combat the employers' myth, recirculated
by some self-interested union officials, that green industrial policy
can only result in job losses. Over time, several far-sighted initiatives
have emerged from the energy unions themselves. Among the more
concrete union proposals to address job loss was OCAW vice president Tony Mazzocchi's idea, in the early 1990s, of a Superfund for
Workers, which would provide four years of retraining at full wages
and benefits to workers displaced by environmentally driven shifts
in production—the costs to be borne by employers in the extractive
or fossil fuel industries. After all, there is no reason why the replacement of dirty with clean energy should be pursued on the backs of
working people or at the expense of labor power.

The spirit of Mazzocchi's proposal can be discerned in labor's
current efforts, at the international level, to press for incorporating
"just transition" language into climate policy agreements. The ITUC
pushed this phrase into initial drafts of the Copenhagen Accord, but
it was dropped from the final wording, only to be included a year later
in the voluntary "shared vision" adopted at the Cancún summit in
December 2010. The Cancún signatories pledged to "promoting a
just transition of the workforce, the creation of decent work and quality jobs in accordance with nationally defined development priorities
and strategies and contributing to building new capacity for both production and service-related jobs in all sectors, promoting economic
growth and sustainable development." Looking to embed the rights of
those displaced or sidelined by the transition to a low-carbon future,

the ITUC also pushed for basic International Labor Organization rights regarding workplace democracy. Regardless of their increasing participation in these international climate forums, the role of labor unions is still viewed as obstructive by many climate activists, who regard their proposals as little more than delaying tactics. For example, the AFL-CIO, having vigorously opposed the Kyoto treaty, is now engaged in the international process, but it still tends to advocate for the most minimal levels of carbon reduction. So, too, there is a significant split in the U.S. labor movement between unions that support science-based and binding reductions and those that back the "voluntary commitments" approach pushed officially by the United States in Copenhagen and Cancún.

Activists who are solely focused on combating climate change want to bring atmospheric carbon levels down by the quickest means available, and some are prepared to shortchange the social justice ideals to which the labor movement broadly subscribes. James Lovelock, the progenitor of the Gaia theory, recently advised that to properly confront the threat of climate change, "it may be necessary to put democracy on hold for a while." This belief, that civil liberties should be suspended until adequate action can be taken, has its advocates, not least among those who favor top-down geo-engineering schemes to manipulate the global climate balance. Presuming that the means will justify the ends lends itself overtly to authoritarian measures of the sort entertained by Lovelock. Any solution is worthy of consideration, one might respond, but not if it subverts democratic pathways. After all, the primary reason for climate inaction has not been a failure of democracy, but rather a failure to throw off the stranglehold of fossil power upon democracy.

A more common response can be heard from those who prize their own civil liberties above those of others. They are more inclined to favor some version of the "lifeboat ethics" popularized by Garrett Hardin in 1974, which held that sharing resources more equitably with the world's poor would capsize any effort at ecological stability. After all, Hardin argued, the lifeboats of rich nations only had so much room, and those already onboard were unlikely to give up their places. The warmed-over social Darwinism preached by Hardin has

found new acolytes in the heady debate about global warming, fuel-
ling a backlash against the notion that rich nations owe a carbon debt
to poor ones, let alone a humanitarian lifeline to swimmers trying to
catch up.

Labor advocates should stand firm against these tendencies, and
look instead to the burgeoning climate justice movement for a clear
alternative to the neo-authoritarian solutions advised by Lovelock and
Hardin. Climate justice challenges the assumption that the advanced
economies, through focusing on some upmarket sector of global production and consumption, can solve the climate problem on their
own. Instead, it insists that no one can be left behind, and that the
green wave must lift all boats or else everyone will sink. Second, climate justice, like the most effective social movements, is driven by an
abolitionist goal—the abolition of an oppressive debt, which imposes
the most negative impacts of climate change on the most vulnerable
and marginal populations. Adding to the claim of right of these populations is the moral standing that flows from their own low-impact
lifestyles, among the least ecologically harmful. Third, and most importantly for labor, climate justice stands at the head of a broad international movement that includes government officials as well as
civil society groups, lawmakers as well as activists, peasants as well as
workers, rebels, and artists.

In recent years, American labor has taken some fledgling steps
in the direction of international organizing, entering into coalitions
with overseas unions that have members in the same industrial sector or in the same nodes of the global chain of production. The new
spirit of internationalism would be enhanced by solidarity with a
movement that includes all kinds of workers, including small peasant
farmers. Yet there were few U.S. labor activists in attendance at the
first people's summit meeting of the movement in May 2009. Held
in a center of indigenous socialism, Bolivia's Cochabamba (notable in
this regard as a counterpoint to the petro-socialist capital of Caracas),
the open deliberations of its democratic process were a striking contrast with the backroom deal making that characterized the Copenhagen and Cancún UN climate summits.

Those who did attend struggled to make connections to a

movement that is largely dominated by indigenous rights and the cause of sufficiency agriculture. Where do urban workers in fully industrialized societies find points of identification in the Cochabamba ethos of "Living Well" (*buen vivir*), or living in harmony with nature? After all, the labor movement in the global North has long been hitched to the consumerist wagon of Living Better, a principle that stands in diametrical opposition to *buen vivir* because it is associated, in the Cochabamba mind, with plunder and unfettered materialist growth. While they may share the same enemies, enriched and empowered by thirty years of neoliberalism, the interests and priorities of urban workers are not necessarily the same as those of dispossessed *campesinos* and rainforest communities.

In the North, the food movement is probably the leading edge of Cochabamba's agrarianist consciousness, and its zeal for local control, healthy provision, food security, and self-organization has been surprisingly contagious. Devastated industrial cities like Detroit and Baltimore are emerging as centers of grassroots urban farming, with the potential to build an alternative economy in the hollowed-out core of the old. For ex-industrial workers, abandoned in the "food deserts" of these inner cities, the opportunity to fashion livelihoods in their own backyards is a profound exercise of social and environmental justice. In more traditional, rural agricultural locations, however, the food movement has had its own labor problems, since food activists routinely ignore the dependence of their idealized small growers on underpaid and marginalized migrant workers who are excluded, in most states, from any workplace protections.

Notwithstanding their agrarianist leanings, climate justice advocates can and should be able to embrace clean energy reindustrialization as a vital part of the alternative economy. Yet even if clean-tech industries were to expand exponentially on a mercurial growth path, the prospects for adequate levels of employment would still be dim. Given the long-term likelihood of mass joblessness and increased precarity, now surely is the time to consider whether the ITUC's demand for a "just transition" ought to go well beyond its current framework for protecting workers at risk of losing jobs or income. Guaranteeing an income, health care, or retraining during a transition may turn out to be a shortsighted strategy. "Just transition" should stand for a vision of sustainable livelihoods with or without a job, whether in the form of a basic income or some other guaranteed green dividend from the ever-growing GDPs of rich nations. The divorce of income from work, long overdue in technologically advanced societies, would be consonant with the spirit and practice of *buen vivir*. Without it, many of us will be facing a world without income or work because the "people formerly known as employers" no longer know how to behave like stewards of livelihoods, and are clearly chasing the goal of maintaining their rate of profit through new models of unpaid labor: rent seeking, productive consumerism (prosumerism), proliferating internships, work-as-welfare, and the cut-price economy of amateurism that now prevails in many sectors of the knowledge and creative industries.

In conclusion, it is fair to say that the campaign for green jobs in the United States has lost some momentum. In the absence of pressure from carbon reduction policies, American companies have invested in renewable energy only when they are lavishly subsidized to do so. In the meantime, other countries, especially China, have moved to dominate clean-tech production. Moreover, the pendulum in national legislatures in Europe and North America has swung quite savagely from the eco-Keynesian moment to what looks like a more prolonged era of public austerity. Austerity is a very bad climate in which to argue for green labor policies because the long-standing public perception of environmentalism is one of liberal elites asking workers to lower their standard of living as a concession to nature. Carbon-conscious labor advocates have worked hard to alter this perception that sustainability does not equate with sacrifice. Most recently, the belief that a system-wide response to climate change would be a job-builder and not a job-killer attracted the support of many unions who had dragged their feet, or voiced opposition, over the years to environmental policy making. With the commitment of the "just transition" to fairly distribute the costs and benefits of low-carbon policies, some of the doubts about the viability of a unified red-green front had begun to recede. There's no doubt that the impact of the new austerity politics will set back the green-labor cause, but there can also be no doubt now about the political potential of synchronizing the movements for social, economic, and environmental justice—a potential that has gotten a big boost from the climate crisis. Indeed, and this may seem like a good place to conclude, if the climate crisis did not exist, it may have been necessary to invent it so that this synchrony could finally occur.

ON ECONOMICS AND LABOR SOLIDARITY

Marcellus Andrews

THE ECONOMIC PRIMACY OF LABOR

I have been teaching, talking, and writing economics for more than three decades, and I never fail to be surprised and, to be honest, alarmed at a basic mistake people make when they think about economics. Most people think economics is about money: who has it and who doesn't, how to get it, keep it, spend it, grow it, and pass it on to your kids. But economics is not about money: economics is about labor, about the lives and prospects of working people. This mistake is dangerous because the illusion that economics is about money causes too many of us to forget that the only way that workers can get ahead in a market economy is through solidarity on the job and especially in politics.

Most working people do not have much money, and therefore worry about getting, keeping, and spending money, because we trade money to get what we need and want in life. We get paid in exchange for the work we do, and our incomes are usually too low and uncertain for us to live in comfort from our labor. A few of us have money coming to us from property—stocks, bonds, real estate, and the like—or from enormous paychecks because the work they do is so valuable to others that they pay them a great deal. The rest of us earn far smaller incomes, because the work we do is not valued very highly, or at least not highly enough to make us feel secure.

The real point of economics is to understand how a society gets its members to work together to provide for what they need, and especially how it distributes this bounty among the people. That means that economics is about labor, not money. Money is a brilliant invention that helps us organize the millions of tasks we perform as workers and business people into a coherent system of production and trade. The real point of economics is to understand how work gets done, who benefits from work, and why this system of work falls into the abyss of recession and depression or explodes in ruinous inflation from time to time.

Workers are, in any society, the most important economic force in the system. About 70 percent of the costs of doing business are labor costs and about 70 percent of all production goes to consumption that sustains the well-being of working people. The upshot of all this is that the deal between workers and employers about wages and working conditions is the most important bargain in the economy—far more important than anything that happens on Wall Street. This bargain is a political bargain masked as a commercial transaction. The single most important question in economics is, at bottom, whether workers are able to thrive under conditions of dignity, security, justice, and equal opportunity or whether they are forced to submit to the relentless pressure of competitive markets, which require men and women to be such flexible, pliant, and, if necessary, disposable implements of their employers that they submit without complaint to the imperatives of the marketplace.

The labor bargain is not just a bargain about the conditions of work and pay within private enterprises and public agencies, but is also a moral bargain about the substantive meaning of economic freedom in a market society. Thirty years of right-wing dominance in practical politics and political culture has narrowed the meaning of the term "economic freedom" to unlimited freedom of contract between individuals while suppressing a more basic idea of economic freedom as access to the material conditions for individuals to develop and exercise their capacities to act on their own behalf. The formal freedom to enter contracts on the basis of self-interest is of little value to men and women without the means to make life-enhancing choices because of ignorance, sickness, or poverty so deep that they cannot refuse work that injures, degrades, or threatens life on pain of penury for themselves or their children. There is no "freedom to choose" without a real freedom to refuse based on the material ability to reject dangerous or destructive offers of work. Labor solidarity is, at its root, a necessary precondition for real economic freedom for the vast majority of people in this country (the United States) and on this planet who lack substantial property by granting people the right to reject work without starving or suffering physical harm or humiliating themselves.

I write these words in 2011, during the third year after a global economic catastrophe so severe that it has shaken and perhaps broken the very foundations of capitalism in the United States. The official unemployment rate is 9 percent, though more accurate measures of unemployment—that include those who have stopped looking for work and those who are working part time—would put the jobless and near jobless rate at close to 17 percent of the American labor force. This catastrophe has been so great that the banking system of the United States not only slipped into insolvency, but could only be sustained by government pumping billions of dollars into the system to buy worthless bits of paper that were once used for insane gambles on the value of houses that effectively turned the market for shelter and homes into a mindless casino. Right now, as I type, the conservative party of the United States—not just the Republicans but the antilabor sector of the Democratic Party—is propping up the banks with public money, workers' money, at the same time that they seek to destroy public sector unions, most notably in Wisconsin and New Jersey, and reduce the size and pay of the federal government's labor force, all on the pretext that the economic crisis brought on by witless buccaneer capitalism can only be solved by the tearing up the American social contract. All this at a time when millions are not just without work, but without homes, savings, or medical care, without any prospect of recovering a decent style of life because economic change after the crisis has permanently destroyed their jobs, rendering many millions of people obsolete. The government of the United States, though the effective owner of the banking system and, at least in theory, the servant of the people who saved the bankers' bacon, is largely captured by and serving the interests of economic elites who have bought the political system—with the blessings of a corrupt Supreme Court permitting capital to use its power in politics without restraint—which means that working people injured by the crisis and ultimately bearing the cost of bailing out the bankers who've destroyed their lives are completely shut out of politics. This crisis, which will be with us for at least a decade, has laid bare the real meaning of economics: an economy is about labor and whether we are citizens of a decent society or fearful serfs doing what we are told by people who believe that they have a right to rule over us by virtue of the wealth we make but that they take.

If we are honest, we know why we are in this mess: we fooled ourselves into believing that an economy is about making money instead of about making a good life for all. Worse, we got so busy beating up on each other—fighting over race, religion, ethnicity, culture wars, and other nonsense—that we gave away our power to use politics to shape the conditions of the wage bargain. Some of us even joined forces with the bankers and corporate parasites who promised to make us secure and to help us live apart from those hated others—of whatever color, ethnicity, or language—if only we'd grant our corporate elites unlimited power in the marketplace, free from regulation or any government supervision, free from taxes, free from any social responsibility. Now the monster we made has turned on us, and is devouring us whole, and we are unable to fight back because we gave up on each other. Basic economics tells us that whenever workers abandon each other for the false promise of a separate peace with capital, we get crushed. We can recover our power in the wage bargain, even in these dismal times, but we must revisit the principles of basic economics in order to review our mistakes, and, perhaps, to relearn what we used to know.

LABOR SOLIDARITY AND THE ECONOMIC VEIL OF IGNORANCE

Labor solidarity is not just about unions—vital though these institutions are. Labor solidarity is about forming a common economic and political culture, a common political economy, aimed at promoting the freedom, dignity, and opportunity of all working people on the deep, realistic fear that the alternative to an enduring federation of workers at every level of economic life—from workplace to the White House—is the world of frightened and angry people who turn over their right to self-government at work and in politics to elites who view wealth as the only legitimate source of authority. Unions are but one part of the political economy of labor, which seeks nothing less than to write a new social contract between workers—as consumers, citizens, and the force that makes the human world—in defense of our dignity, freedom, and prosperity, in full recognition of the fact that the only way to secure our collective well-being is to subordinate capital and markets to the needs of society, not the other way round.

A labor organization or movement that sees its goals as limiting labor market access to certain kinds of favored workers is doomed to long-term failure, and well-earned derision, because it wants to collectivize a portion of the labor market in the name of an identity group rather than seek to enhance the position of workers in general. Of course, a strategy of identity-based supply-side labor collectiviza- tion is self-defeating because it weakens the political conditions un- der which workers can alter the legal and political environment of the labor bargain—unless identity-based labor organizing is accom- panied by an explicit support for suppressing the political and civil rights of presumed racial and other enemies. Even widespread labor xenophobia will fail in a world where capital markets can allocate funds to regions and nations that contain sources of cheaper labor, or where the multiple and partially conflicting identities of workers- as-consumers and workers-as-taxpayers can be cracked open to the political advantage of business.

THE PERILS OF NARROW LABOR SOLIDARITY

Labor solidarity is, from a (sympathetic!) economist's point of view, a tremendous asset for members of a labor collective—whether trade union, labor federation, or, at best, a national labor movement—and can be a boon to all workers, under certain conditions. An effective union that manages to improve the wages, benefits, employment se- curity, and working conditions of its members not only redistributes income from owners to workers, but can also boost the efficiency of work and thereby lower cost if unions play an active and forward- thinking role in the organization and supervision of work. Yet the re- distribution of income and power from capital to labor that inevitably follows on labor solidarity necessarily reduces the rate of return to capital in most cases, thereby encouraging management to find ways to cut costs—by finding cheaper labor within the local economy, moving production operations to regions of the nation or world with lower wages, replacing people with technology, or by using the political clout of capital to hamper prospects for unionization. Narrow labor solidarity—limited to a particular region, or racial, religious, ethnic, or gender identity grouping—will invariably create temporarily privileged labor insiders as well as angry and resentful labor outsiders. In turn, this division of workers will invariably fail because insiders will rightly see outsiders as threats to their privileged position just as outsiders correctly attack protected workers for erecting durable barriers to equal opportunity.

The failure of narrow labor solidarity is a predictable and even welcome aspect of competitive capitalism. Competition requires businesses to seek to either evade or overcome all barriers to managerial flexibility that threaten to boost costs and limit profitability—including the barriers to managerial prerogatives and cost controls associated with unions. Narrow labor solidarity creates the conditions for its own demise by establishing pools of excluded and angry outsiders who are more than willing to oust their privileged racial or ethnic enemies from their good wages and working conditions by offering a much less demanding labor bargain to capital. The deep problem in this context is that narrow labor solidarity is wishful thinking that ignores competitive capitalism's relentless push to keep costs as low as possible in the vain hope that racial or ethnic solidarity can somehow offset the consequences of capital's ruthless pursuit of profit.

WHY NARROWNESS ALWAYS FAILS

The clearest example of the doomed nature of narrow labor solidarity is the slow but certain death of government-sponsored white supremacy in the United States. We should be careful to distinguish white supremacy from ordinary racism, especially irritating forms of petty color-based animosity that makes life unpleasant but that do not matter in any ultimate sense. Ordinary racism in this context is an individual's choice in favor or against interacting with others on the basis of their perceived "race." Decisions about where to live, study, pray, play, or shop; and whom to marry, vote for or against, or trust and revile are all influenced by our ideas of which kinds of people are valuable and which are not. One of the great lessons of economic analysis is that this sort of ordinary racism, while the driving force of racial discrimination in every area of life, will backfire on racist labor organizations and racially phobic working populations.

A moment's reflection shows why this point is correct. If government policy follows the rule of equal treatment before the law, thereby treating each citizen in the same way with regard to every aspect of public life—from law enforcement to public education, health care, and important developmental goods—then modern genetics and common sense tell us that most population groups will be characterized by a roughly equal distribution of intelligence, talent, ambition, energy, honesty, effort, perseverance, and other traits and habits that matter for economic success. Racial discrimination in favor of one group—in the American case, whites—against nonwhites in markets for jobs, credit, housing, education, health care, and other essential goods will certainly create educational, income, wealth, mortality, and morbidity gaps between whites and nonwhites, so long as access to essential developmental goods like schools and health care depends on a person's or family's ability to pay. If the white majority also has overall control of hiring, firing, and promotion policies by virtue of owning most of a nation's capital assets, as well as control over democratic politics by virtue of its numerical majority, then the law of supply and demand along with democratic politics will convert numerical and economic dominance into persistent racial disparities in incomes and well-being across color lines, but only so long as racial solidarity trumps the profit motive.

Though discrimination against nonwhites will push their wages and incomes down, limit access to housing, health care, private education, and credit, and thereby impair their opportunities for development, discrimination also increases the cost of white labor as well as the availability of housing, private education, and credit for whites. However, so long as the distribution of ability, ambition, and effort are roughly the same across color lines, very competent non-white workers will be a very tempting and very cheap source of labor for all capitalists who value money over racial solidarity. Mundane self-interest among white capitalists in highly competitive markets pushes them to seek out the cheapest sources of labor of whatever color, with the consequence that the profit motive argues against any form of racial favoritism in hiring, firing, and promotions. While many, perhaps most, white capitalists may feel special affinity for white workers compared to nonwhite counterparts, the pressure of competition means that business survival requires owners to choose workers on the basis of their cost and competence. Competitive capitalism will gradually destroy all white supremacist capitalists foolish enough to hire incompetent white workers at the same time that it will reward all capitalists that value money over racial solidarity in hiring. In time, the exploitation of nonwhite labor in the interest of profit will gradually push incompetent white workers into joblessness, poverty, and social isolation while incorporating competent nonwhites into the system, albeit as very subordinate participants in an economy that despises them.

The key point here is that racial discrimination in a competitive market society lacking any form of redistribution—no public schools or health insurance or any other familiar government intervention in the economy—but under conditions of equal treatment before the law cannot guarantee all white workers higher incomes and economic well-being than nonwhite workers as long as some capitalists value money over race. A low-income white majority could use its voting and buying clout to wring all sorts of concessions out of business owners, including commitments to discriminate against nonwhite labor on pain of strikes, work slowdowns, and a loss of customers among those whites who demand that business honor racial identity. The history of white supremacy in America includes many episodes where white workers use the power of government to close off economic opportunity for nonwhites in order to guarantee higher incomes and better lives for themselves. But a white supremacist economic regime can only be sustained if white labor is able to impose severe costs on any business that crosses the color line in hiring, promoting, lending, or other ordinary economic activity.

Any multi-class white coalition will quickly crumble if the benefits of crossing the color line are greater than the costs. All sorts of economic events can turn a situation of stable white supremacy based on narrow labor solidarity into one where racial hiring and promotion codes melt down under the combined pressure of competition and the powerful anger of hitherto dominated outsiders. A full-employment economy will blunt the capacity of narrow labor solidarity to close off opportunity for nonwhites because labor shortages make white labor very expensive and limits any economic fallout to white workers associated with hiring racial enemies. Demographic change that reduces the proportion of white workers in the population will necessarily reduce white power in politics and the economy because, again, narrow labor solidarity makes white labor expensive labor relative to nonwhite labor. An increase in the supply of nonwhite labor relative to the white working class will push the wages of nonwhites down relative to whites, thereby increasing the profitability of hiring nonwhites. One especially important force that must break the power of narrow labor solidarity is the growing importance of technical, scientific, and analytical knowledge for high-wage employment, which creates enduring divisions between well and poorly educated members of the white majority. While modestly educated, low-income white workers would naturally seek to protect themselves from competition with their racial enemies by forming a durable coalition with better-educated, high-income white labor and white capitalists, better-off white populations have no economic incentives to join with poor white people. At best, better-off white populations might use the threat of nonwhite economic competition to extract concessions from poor whites over what few forms of redistribution exist in society by demanding lower taxes and less progressive forms of taxation along with a reduction in any regulations that are seen to compromise profitability. Low-income white labor's pursuit of narrow labor solidarity becomes an economic and political trap once this sector of society loses its overwhelming numerical clout in politics and in the labor market for the simple reason that the market is bound to make the least-educated and -skilled, and therefore most vulnerable, white workers expendable in the eyes of capitalists who have every logical reason to seek cheaper and less powerful sources of labor. Discrimination creates the pools of cheap, weak, easily exploitable nonwhite workers who have every reason to cooperate with capitalists to break the dominance of racially phobic white workers. In the end, narrow labor solidarity is no solidarity at all, but instead a road to enduring racial hatred and broad labor weakness.

THE BETTER WAY

Narrow labor solidarity in a market economy must fail because racial or ethnic boundaries between workers will invariably create an abused and resentful "bottom" that is a permanent threat to insiders. The insiders can dominate their racial enemies if they have the numbers in politics, or can form an unholy racial alliance with capital when the "bottom" groups become too numerous or become such a temptation for capital that the labor insiders must make concessions to retain their privileged position in the job market. But it is only a matter of time before labor aristocrats—whether defined by race, religion, region, or level of schooling—lose their special place in society because of the relentless push to cut costs through innovation, relocation, and the discovery of ever cheaper sources of supply, especially labor supply, that is the defining feature of capitalism. Once the former insiders are turned into outsiders, they find themselves in the same position of economic vulnerability as their racial enemies, but unable to form enduring alliances with other despised outsiders who remember the abuse at the hands of their former social betters.

One final example of the futility and stupidity of narrow labor solidarity is the endless and useless debate over affirmative action. Affirmative action—whether considered a form of reverse discrimination, a necessary corrective to continued discrimination by insiders against outsiders, or both—would be unnecessary if American labor would finally abandon race as a focus of solidarity and instead pursue economic and social justice. The fight over the use of government to break through residual attempts by a declining sector of white America to control access to jobs, income, and opportunity is just another round in the endless self-destruction of labor in the name of racial idolatry. Nothing so weakens workers as the delusion of race—which has the same scientific status and value to workers as a belief in witches.

The only way that labor, even narrowly, racially defined labor, can improve its bargaining power in the labor market is if it eliminates "bottom" labor castes by improving the basic well-being of all workers, no matter their color, creed, or ethnicity. Since capitalism pushes firms to seek, and if necessary create, ever cheaper sources of labor, workers can permanently alter the balance of power between themselves and capital if they use political and market power to lift the weakest members of the working majority, thereby eliminating potential competition by turning former enemies into compatriots. Labor is in the best position to bargain with capital when there is no "bottom" for capital to exploit, no pool of trapped and therefore easily abused workers that can be tapped whenever workers with economic power begin to press their demands.

The elimination of the "bottom" within a nation is most easily and effectively pursued by a program of real equal opportunity for education, health, shelter, employment, and other basic human needs via a labor-focused form of redistribution that emphasizes the role of basic equality of capability to work as a primary condition for equal opportunity and individual achievement in society. In turn, the most effective form of redistribution for strengthening the capacity of workers to make better deals in their bargains with capital is one that increases the capacity of all workers to achieve by guaranteeing the capacity as well as the opportunity to work—not just by providing a basic needs safety net in the event that economic misfortune strikes. Safety nets are important components of any comprehensive system of economic protection, but do not necessarily boost each person's capacity or opportunity to work, which must be the goal of any respectable labor movement. While space limitations prevent us from outlining a detailed economic analysis of labor in a mixed economy that combines the best aspects of competitive markets—robust innovation, growth, and flexibility—with a genuinely fair and green progressive regulatory mechanism that can meet human needs at a tolerable fiscal cost, we have already explained why any just and sustainable form of labor solidarity must seek to include all workers within the community under the protections of economic and social justice.

IMMIGRATION AND GLOBAL LABOR SOLIDARITY

The need for American labor to eliminate the "bottom" of the labor market through solidarity instead of exclusion applies not only within U.S. borders but across the world, particularly with regard to issues of immigration. Cool-headed economic analysis tells us that immigration is, among other things, the movement of people from low-income and low-opportunity regions of the world to places of greater opportunity, just as the movement of capital and jobs from low return to high return is driven by the imperatives of profitability. Attempts by workers in the United States to erect durable barriers to undocumented immigration are doomed to failure for the same reason that race-based labor solidarity fails: an effective barrier to illegal immigration will just create a vast economic underclass of vulnerable, easily exploited immigrant workers that will gradually coalesce into an enduring enemy population whose primary relationship with the local, state, and federal governments of the United States is mediated by the station house, the courthouse, and the jailhouse. Undocumented immigration from Latin America to the United States is just a reflection of the fact that the America south of the Rio Grande is so poor compared to the United States. So long as that gap remains, Latin American workers have a powerful incentive to risk life and limb to travel to the United States in search of work. Attempts to deal with illegal immigration by imposing criminal penalties on undocumented immigrants and those who hire them cannot possibly work unless these measures so reduce the gain in earnings from migration that migrants are better off staying home.

Yet basic economics tells us that measures which manage to slow illegal migration will actually boost the wage gap between the United States and Latin America by trapping migrant workers south of the border, thereby increasing unemployment and reducing wages in the region. Further, the level of wages for various categories of unskilled workers will rise on the U.S. side of the border since the expulsion of unskilled immigrant labor generates labor shortages for many enterprises—and therefore leads to increases in the prices of goods and services that are produced by unskilled labor, including every-thing from fruits and vegetables; meat and meat products; domestic and janitorial labor; construction and landscaping; hotel, restaurant, and health care work; and most others sectors requiring backbreak-ing effort. The combined result of anti-immigration measures is likely to be more attempted immigration in response to a larger cross-border wage gap; price inflation in those parts of the economy depen-dent on unskilled labor; more illegal migrants captured, imprisoned, and deported by the government; greater government discrimination against Latinos—not least because of laws that allow the police to de-tain Latino citizens on the basis of nothing more than the suspicion of illegal immigrant status on the basis of race or demeanor—all result-ing in the creation of another racial "bottom" to the labor market. One might be forgiven for thinking that American workers would have learned the futility of using race to defend the economic fortunes of racial and national insiders by the poisoned legacy of white labor soli-darity for ongoing black-white racial strife in the United States.

Labor is the primary force in any economy. Justice for workers re-quires labor solidarity, which in turn means that workers must accept what economic logic tells us: racism, xenophobia, and many other forms of identity politics cripple prospects for a decent society by un-dermining the possibility of a social contract between workers. The logic of the argument is clear. History speaks loudly in this matter. Will we ever learn?

GHOST MARKS AND RISING SPIRITS IN AN INDUSTRIAL LANDSCAPE: COMMUNICATION AND IMAGINATION IN THE REBIRTH OF LABOR

Elizabeth Faue

The political landscape of organized labor has changed significantly in the past hundred years, as labor unions and workers have passed through the tumultuous terrains of mass protest and calmer territories of public support and labor mediation. Since the 1950s, however, the labor movement has experienced a precipitous decline in numbers and influence. Even as public employment increased and public workers unionized in the postwar decades, an increasingly stagnant American economy and growing conservative opposition weakened the labor movement as a public force. This essay seeks to understand how we might challenge the fate of the labor movement in the United States. By reimagining what labor can do and be, and publicizing what labor is and who workers are, the union movement might retake strategic political ground and reverse its decades-long decline.

Political terrain, like its physical counterpart, bears the signs of political journeys and rhetorical battles. It records as outcroppings partisan struggle and also consensus—the incremental actions of voters and citizens, of politicians, policy makers, advocates, and beneficiaries that take shape in government. Beneath the surface, the ghost marks of political choices surface time and again. Seeking answers to the current economic crisis, and faced with labor's political losses, we explore the marks left by the New Deal, probing lost possibilities, examining hidden political agendas, and reawakening historic animosities. For union advocates, the recent assaults on the labor movement heard in congressional debate on the automobile industry and in state legislatures seeking to rein in unionized public employees echo earlier arguments on labor, its political capacities and allegiances, and what constitutes workplace justice.

Recent press coverage of the auto industry's comeback would have us forget that only two years ago a different image of Motown and its favorite industrial sons dominated the news. The economic downturn of 2008 had brought American automobile companies close to bankruptcy. At first in private jets and later in American-made automobiles, the CEOs of GM and Chrysler went to Congress for loans and subsidies that might enable them to survive the roiling economic seas. Only months before, bank officers had arrived with a similar mission. While Wall Street bankers encountered hostility, there was nothing quite like the reception the corporate officers of GM and Chrysler received. Senators from Tennessee and Alabama, nicknamed "the senators from Toyota and Nissan," argued that the American auto industry did not need or deserve public support. Auto-workers in Detroit were the $73-an-hour slackers, whose lax work habits and lack of skill undermined the industry. The UAW was greedy, and American auto companies weren't worth saving. Indeed, as unionized autoworkers in the Rust Belt faced layoffs, contract conces-sions, and permanent unemployment, many Americans, published in the *New York Times*, heard on network news, and quoted in the *Congressional Record*, were in favor of cutting loose the losing proposi-tion of American manufacturing. For workers in the Midwest, such arguments threatened both their livelihood and their understanding that government has a responsibility to bolster a flagging economy and workers cast adrift.

Underlying the debate was the chaotic, competitive, and contra-dictory industrial policy of the United States. Tax subsidies, trade agreements, and hostilities toward unionism and union workers shadowed a public debate centered instead on the ethics of the auto bailout. The precarious fate of the auto industry, one of the remain-ing major private employers in both the Midwest and the South, and the allegiance of the mainstream labor movement to the Democratic Party, gave additional meaning to the auto industry's requests. Sim-ply put, unionized manufacturing jobs competed with Southern economic and conservative political interests. In the end, a federally engineered package benefited the auto companies while failing to preserve the wage standards and level of employment in Midwestern plants. Corporations, not labor, received unprecedented federal support. The UAW, in contrast, made major concessions. It guaranteed companies that they would accept tiered and uneven compensation for workers and agree to further outsourcing of jobs. In the end, the battle over the bailout was less about corporate responsibility than about unionized workers as an at-risk population. Union workers, in the current political environment, have few supporters and ever-diminished clout.

The contemporary labor movement has lost both its public voice and the support it once gained from national media. Despite high unemployment, Congress and state legislatures have resisted extending benefits to the unemployed and refuse to support union wages and benefits for employed workers. The prolonged struggle over and defeat of the Employee Fair Choice Act proved a convincing demonstration of this fading public power. Moreover, there is little sense that the fate of workers, let alone of the declining labor movement, are newsworthy. Information about labor can be gained from specialized online media and the occasional news story of worker unrest in specific locales or nationally. What that has meant is that, facing the worst economic numbers since the Great Depression, workers across class lines are marginalized and ignored at the bargaining table. The labor movement further has lost its ability to shape or even influence the debate over economic policy during a major employment crisis.

The labor movement has not always been as invisible in the media nor as lacking in cultural resources as it is today. Beginning in the late nineteenth century, labor leaders faced an even greater level of political and corporate hostility. After more than a decade of labor conflict, the labor movement faced growing opposition from corporate leaders, community business organizations, and politicians. Seen as illegitimate, rapacious, and violent, labor unions lost traction in the treacherous and uncertain political terrain. Chambers of commerce, citizens' alliances, and civic federations marshaled considerable resources against labor unions and succeeded in stopping labor's growth. After 1903, labor unions repeatedly lost organizing drives,

campaigns for labor legislation, court battles against labor injunctions, and strikes. Mass-circulation newspapers and journals were
biased and selective in their reporting, and the coverage they gave to
strikes, boycotts, and class-based activism portrayed an alien working
class—immigrant in origin, radical in belief, prone to violence, and
criminal in its disregard for property and the law.

By the 1910s, what labor reformers discovered was that "publicity," public demonstrations and displays of who workers were and why
unions were needed, was a central requirement for power in a mass
democratic society. "Truth telling" in the media—about the des-
peration of the working poor and of working women in particular—
brought public opinion to side with workers, who often had little
means to bring strikes to a negotiated end. For labor leaders, it became clear that the public needed fundamentally different stories
than those published in mass media. The labor movement sought,
through its own and mass-circulation newspapers and magazines,
to change its political profile. Its efforts politically and culturally focused on equating honest workingmen with labor and labor with improvement in society. The *American Federationist*, and trade union
journals as a whole, expanded in size and coverage. Union leaders
went on public speaking tours and had their own public relations
campaigns. They were able to elevate their status from troublemakers
to statesmen for the respectable working class. Hiring professional
journalists, editors, and agents, they publicized labor union participation as the model of good citizenship. At the same time, labor leaders
often sought to create a distinction between trade unions and their
radical, often alien, counterparts. This distinction, which played on
fears of immigrants, bolstered organized labor's claim to legitimacy
and political voice.

After the devastating defeats in strikes and political battles during
and after World War I, the labor movement once again had to enter
public debate about workers and their organizations. Throughout the
1920s and early 1930s, union organizers and leaders, and their allies
in government and in the media, began to rebuild movement institutions, especially the labor press. Central to these efforts was the need

for continual publicity in contract negotiations, strikes, and political campaigns. Labor's media strategy revealed the heart of labor unionism not as a limited strategy for the wages of the few but a broader campaign to revitalize civil society by integrating workers and their institutions into American political life. As a break from organized labor's earlier nativist past, arguments about political integration were important for workers still rooted in and identifying with immigrant and ethnic communities. The inclusiveness of social unionism signaled a change in organized labor's position and greater legitimacy for the labor movement as the voice of workers. In its public relations campaign, labor advocates began by creating news services and labor publications that were national in scope and influence, among them the Federated Press. This "laboring" of American culture spoke to the integration not only of skilled tradesmen and industrial workers into the labor movement but also white-collar workers, service workers, and public employees. Today's public employee unionism, which expanded with new legislation in the 1960s and 1970s, had its beginnings in the regeneration of the labor movement during the New Deal.

By the 1940s, the passage of Taft-Hartley, the anticommunist purge of labor unions, and the massive public relations campaign launched against "Big Labor" once again undermined the generally favorable public image and voice of labor. Corporations, business coalitions, and the Republican Party viewed the role of labor within the Democratic Party as unhealthy for the nation. Indeed, the campaign to reform labor relations after the passage of the Wagner Act in 1935 was the result of conservative opposition to the New Deal and to the influence of the labor movement in electoral politics. While unions reached their greatest representation in the 1950s, there were signs of a gradual erosion in the power of labor. National newspapers and news magazines gave unprecedented coverage to the labor movement, but their reports were not all good news. Indeed, there was both ambivalence about the power of organized labor and strategic reporting of labor's troubles—political division, corruption and graft in powerful unions in transportation and construction, and contractual work rules that created unnecessary jobs. Unions, conservatives increasingly argued, acted as a drag on American productivity and economic growth.

Despite the erosion of private sector unionism, the triumph of the New Deal in the 1930s and the resurgence of public education bought the labor movement key allies in government. Pressures to lower adult unemployment redefined school age and education during the Depression, and defense work during World War II underlined the importance of schools in the creation of a skilled labor force. The growth of the school age population during the baby boom further expanded the teaching labor force. Finally, the expansion of government in social services and in oversight dramatically increased the number of public workers. For these reasons, there was growing support for the unionization of public employees and for public employee strikes. The civil rights movement also demanded the expansion of individual rights to all workers. By the 1960s, these developments stirred President Kennedy to issue an executive order permitting collective bargaining among federal employees. State governors and legislatures across the United States, with notable exceptions in the South, passed laws that guaranteed public employees the right to bargain collectively.

As the wave of public sector unionism grew, its strength compensated for declining private sector unions. While manufacturing firms relocated to the South or offshore, and antiunion campaigns undermined private sector unions, the increasing number and political clout of public sector unions made up for lost revenue and influence. This development had a conflicting and paradoxical effect on the labor movement. The labor movement, especially public sector unions, had continued political strength and influence, based on engagement in and contributions to electoral campaigns and political candidates, overwhelmingly from the Democratic Party. That allegiance gave them limited options in terms of political strategy. It also made labor unions vulnerable to charges that they had unwarranted influence in public life. Conservative state legislators recently have argued that public employees manipulate contracts and, basically, set their own salaries and benefits. Conservatives in Congress have proposed budget cuts in discretionary public spending and particularly in public services, an area of unionized public employment. Opponents of labor's political agenda pushed such claims in order to undermine the case for such demands as repealing Taft-Hartley or passing new labor laws.

Today's chief critics and opponents of labor unions have a much smaller target than existed in the 1950s. The labor movement has lost numbers and relative representation in the labor force. The balance of unionized workers are employed in the public sector, and public employees are the chief target of legislation in states from New Jersey, Michigan, Ohio, Indiana, and Wisconsin, among others. State governors have zeroed in on worker health benefits, pensions, and bargaining rights, either directly or as part of plans for emergency financial management and government "reform." Stories about unionized public service employees saturate the print and broadcast media and overshadow the fate of their peers in private industry. As some commentators have quipped, teachers, indeed all public workers, have become the new welfare queens—public enemies, not public employees.

The viability and value of public services is one aspect of the debate. Put simply, contemporary arguments focus on the extent of and support for public services, including fire and police departments, public transportation, public schools, libraries, and parks. More painfully, unfunded promises of good pensions and benefits for public employees, used to bolster compensation in years of budget deficits and tax revolts, are threatening to swamp current government budgets. Teachers and teachers' unions in particular have come under fire, as the stratified tangle that is the American school system has come under attack. There is a continuing and unresolved debate over the role and achievement of public and charter schools, school vouchers and education budgets, proper methods of educational testing, and the conflicting goals of educational reformers. That debate shades our understanding of who "government workers" are and the role they play. Massive layoffs that threatened to exceed one hundred thousand teachers nationwide are no cause for celebration. Indeed, a nation dependent on an educated labor force needs teachers.

Teachers—and teachers' unions—nonetheless became some of the chief targets of the conservative push for retrenchment and privatization. Conservative political organizations and foundations dedicated to private, for-profit education have supported the drastic reduction of school budgets, an increasing reliance on vouchers, and the slow strangulation of public education.

The activism in Wisconsin against Governor Scott Walker's efforts to strip public employees of their bargaining rights and force concessions has become a model for how one might counter the political opponents of labor. What one historian has called "the uprising of the 70,000" brought national media attention to the plight of organized labor in the public sector and in private employment. The Wisconsin crusade—and its less well-covered counterparts in Ohio, Michigan, Indiana, and other states—made public hundreds of "true stories" of workers: teachers, police officers, firefighters, and social workers. It also revealed that unions are not only about individual gain but about democratic rights at the most basic level. Public opinion viewed the tactics of the conservative Wisconsin governor and his Republican-dominated state legislature, which were designed to overturn decades of labor relations practice, as fundamentally unjust. Reaching to political allies in the Democratic Party but also employing their own strategies of mass demonstration, publicity, and organization, public employee unions have, at this writing, fought this retrenchment to a draw.

Social networking also played a major role in organizing opposition to Walker's tactics. Active recall campaigns for the governor and state legislators, a court injunction barring the implementation of an act passed in violation of the open meetings law, and the continued media campaign conducted both by Wisconsin unions and their supporters nationwide have persuaded the majority of those polled that public employees, and not elected officials, are in the right. Similar efforts in other states have challenged budget measures that dismantle bargaining rights, invalidate contracts, disempower locally elected governments, and fly in the face of public opinion. Public employee unions and their private counterparts remain embattled even as they garner increased public support.

It is difficult to know what this battle portends for the future, and yet the lessons of 2011 remind us that the labor movement, its leaders, and its members must work to communicate a different image and role for organized labor. That means necessarily a rethinking of how labor functions in society, how it might increase its resources and recapture the support it had under the New Deal, and how it can use the democratic possibilities of online media and social networks to recharge labor's political batteries. Alliances among workers, unionized and unorganized, have been a central part of the campaign, but they will lose their power without a more integrated vision of how labor's prosperity and clout benefit those who are not union members.

AFL-CIO president Rich Trumka's recent speech before the National Press Club has suggested some ways of reshaping labor's political landscape. Distancing labor from its historic but currently ineffective allegiance with the Democratic Party opens the door for more strategic use for workers' votes and unions' political resources. Reasserting the labor movement's claim to speak for all workers—and realigning labor's political agenda with that claim—is another crucial step. Labor advocates must acknowledge that the struggle for workers' rights and for fair wages and adequate benefits goes beyond labor law reform and labor negotiations. Indeed, the labor movement and the labor force today are diverse in racial, ethnic, gender, educational, and age terms. The social unionism that underwrote the New Deal revolution and the growth of labor's power that resulted was connected to the central ideas of common wealth, shared destiny, and public service. Labor's political agenda must not only publicize labor's needs but ground them in a realistic and compelling analysis of how interests of young and old, unionized and nonunionized, employed, unemployed, and retired citizens must be balanced. It means accepting that in the current economic and political context the battle to retake and reinvent the political terrain is a generational one. It will involve loss, compromise, and continuous engagement. The true stories of labor will not only reflect the ghost marks of the past but build upon the rising signs of the postindustrial resurgence of labor.

Part Five

Beyond Borders

For more than a century, the American labor movement has been bounded by the implications of what it means to be an American citizen and by the geography of the American nation-state. Those boundaries have shifted over time and between different unions. Workers' organizations at times have denied access to women, blacks, and immigrants of all kinds. Even the Knights of Labor, the most inclusive of labor groups in the nineteenth century, embraced Chinese exclusion. While the AFL and the militant CIO embraced the Wagner Act of 1935, they accepted its limitations. Agricultural, laundry, and domestic workers, industries in which blacks were disproportionately concentrated, still have no protections under the federal labor law. And for fifty years after World War II, the mainstream labor movement supported American foreign policy interests over independent and democratic labor movements around the world.

American capital never failed to take advantage of either labor's blindness to the most marginal segments of the working class or labor's blind nationalism. Capital's response to labor's patriotism was often to move high-wage industrial jobs out of American labor's reach.

Since 1995, the AFL-CIO has been moving, at least rhetorically, toward an acknowledgment of the need to organize immigrant workers within the borders of the United States, regardless of citizenship status, and the need to partner with labor movements around the globe. The essays in this section speak to the need for greater, more concentrated efforts in both those regards.

Ruth Milkman starts off by reminding us that the European immigrant origins of militant trade unionism in the beginning of the twentieth century are again reflected among Latino workers in the late twentieth and early twenty-first centuries. Not only are assumptions false that low-wage or undocumented workers are less able to be organized, but indeed their links to tight-knit immigrant communities offer advantages that make them more likely to form unions. Matthew Garcia and Mario Sifuentez nevertheless show that Hispanic-dominated working-class movements are not monolithic. There are deep philosophic tensions and conflicting political and organizing strategies between the more conservative United Farm Workers (UFW) and groups like the Pineros y Campesinos Unidos del Noroeste (PCUN) of Oregon. The UFW, they argue, settled contracts and supported legislation in favor of U.S.-born workers at the expense of Mexican and other Latin American immigrants. They posit that the PCUN, in its embrace of immigrant rights and support for issues like LGBT rights, constructed a model of community organizing and coalition building that is preferable to that of the UFW.

Nelson Lichtenstein explores the questions of how supply-side economics has restructured the global economy and shifted power along the supply chain from producers of goods to distributors of goods like Wal-Mart. The weakness of unions and the lack of regulation at home and abroad has produced, he argues, a universal sweatshop, where production can be shifted easily from one region to another if, for example, a union forms in one country. He finds hope as he draws parallels to the nineteenth-century antislavery societies, which drew on moral suasion to combat the global ills of human bondage, and the rhetoric of human rights activists against global sweatshops. Dorothy Fujita-Rony highlights the links between American imperialism abroad and the plight of immigrant workers in the United States. She argues that a viable working-class movement in the United States needs to understand that the immigrants confront conditions in their countries of origin as well as the United

States that restrict their choices. The American militarization of the Philippines throughout the twentieth century determined everything from which, how many, and when Filipinos could come to the United States to how young girls ended up in a sex industry to service American soldiers and sailors, and how Filipino immigrants came to be regarded in the United States.

Finally, Dana Frank agrees that a movement for immigrant rights at home must be linked to a movement for international solidarity. She offers a pathway to how Americans can partner with indigenous movements for workers' rights without imposing a kind of left form of cultural imperialism on groups around the world. She argues that workers' movements in Honduras, for example, need to be supported, not guided, and that opposing the recent coup there needs to be on the top of labor's agenda. Unions and other groups supporting workers' rights there must come to terms with the AFL-CIO's past history of supporting governments that crushed Communist and other progressive labor movements. She argues for the AFL-CIO to stop accepting federal money and for unions and the left to refocus their efforts and commit real resources to an international solidarity movement.

IMMIGRANT WORKERS AND LABOR'S FUTURE

Ruth Milkman

Labor is in deep, deep trouble. With unionization plummeting to levels not seen since the early 1930s, it is becoming more and more difficult to imagine a scenario in which the U.S. labor movement might rebuild itself. Although recent survey data suggest that most of the nation's unorganized workers would vote to unionize, given the opportunity, the reality on the ground is that determined private sector employers can usually outmaneuver unions on the rare occasions when new organizing efforts do take place. And public sector unions, until recently largely immune from attack, are now under siege as well from cash-strapped state and local governments struggling with massive deficits, urged on by right-wing politicians eager to eliminate a major source of Democratic Party campaign financing.

In this bleak landscape, one of the few remaining sources of hope is the immigrant labor movement. Against all odds, foreign-born workers in the low-wage labor market have shown enormous determination to organize in recent years, and have chalked up many successes. They will be central players if conditions change so that the labor movement is able to rebuild itself to confront the challenges workers face in the twenty-first century.

Immigrant workers have played a leading role in the U.S. labor movement before, although this history has been largely obliterated from public memory. First- and second-generation immigrants from southern and eastern Europe figured prominently among the leaders of the industrial unions that emerged in the 1910s and then exploded in the 1930s and 1940s into the single largest labor upsurge in the nation's history. Those unions not only brought improved working conditions and economic security to millions of workers, but also served as vital engines of Americanization and upward mobility for European-born workers and their children. In this way, labor movement success in the New Deal years brought a generation of previously impoverished "white ethnics" into the mainstream of American society. They came to consider themselves "middle class" in the years of prosperity that followed World War II, as unionization levels peaked and income inequality hit record lows.

That hard-won status was threatened, however, as the achievements of the New Deal era came under assault starting in the 1970s, as deindustrialization and deregulation transformed the U.S. political economy. The unionized share of the labor force declined precipitously, income inequalities widened, and working conditions deteriorated. Minimum wage laws and other legal protections that organized labor and its allies had struggled mightily to establish in the 1930s came to be violated with impunity by more and more employers, especially in the burgeoning low-wage labor market.

Those who toil in the nation's newly degraded jobs today are often—though by no means always—immigrants, who arrived in the United States in growing numbers after 1965, when immigration restrictions imposed in the 1920s were lifted. Unlike their predecessors in the early twentieth century, most of these newcomers hail from Latin America, Africa, and Asia, not Europe. The majority have legal status, but others overstayed visas or crossed the U.S. border without documents, gradually forming a vast unauthorized workforce with no historical precedent.

After some initial hesitation, employers welcomed the new foreign-born workers, whether or not they had documents, seeing in them the striving ambition and industriousness long associated with migrants the world over. That these workers were "willing" to accept newly degraded jobs that many U.S.-born workers shunned further endeared them to employers.

Virtually no one expected the new immigrants to organize. After all, the conventional wisdom went, they were grateful for even the worst U.S. jobs because in their countries of origin pay rates were even lower and conditions often inferior. In addition, since so many immigrants intended to return home after a short stint of wage earning, few observers imagined that they would be willing to sacrifice their earnings to secure long-term organizational gains they would not themselves benefit from. Finally, especially for unauthorized immigrants, the risks inherently involved in labor organizing—not only of being fired but also perhaps of being deported—seemed to make their involvement in such efforts extremely improbable.

However, contrary to the expectations of their employers—and just about everyone else—that they would be docile, pliable workers, and unreceptive to organizing opportunities, low-wage immigrant workers engaged in extensive collective action in the late twentieth century. The same aspirations for economic advancement that motivated their migration itself, frustrated by the many obstacles they encountered after arriving in the United States, have galvanized many immigrants into labor activism. In the 1980s and 1990s, foreign-born factory workers, construction laborers, hotel workers, taxi drivers, service workers, and, most famously, janitors began to mobilize behind demands for higher pay and better working conditions.

The once conventional wisdom that immigrants, and especially the unauthorized, are unlikely candidates for labor organizing was not so much wrong as incomplete. It overlooked several factors that make low-wage immigrants more "organizable" in the workplace than many of their U.S.-born counterparts. First, because new arrivals find jobs through social networks comprised of other immigrants from the same place (and often from the same extended family), many workplaces contain within them an unusual potential for solidarity rooted in those very networks—a relatively rare phenomenon among U.S.-born workers. Further contributing to that potential is the shared racialization and stigmatization that many immigrants experience, which often serves as a unifying force. And while organizing is risky, the risks it involves are relatively modest compared to, for example, crossing the border without papers, or for that matter labor organizing in many of the countries immigrants grew up in. All these factors have facilitated immigrant workers' engagement in organizing in recent decades.

Moreover, the available evidence suggests that many low-wage immigrant workers (unlike most of their U.S.-born counterparts) understand their fate not only as determined by their individual attributes or achievements, but also as bound up with the fate of other members of the immigrant community. That worldview can spur collective action, when the opportunity for it arises. The hostility immigrants routinely experience—whether or not they are undocumented—reinforces this collectivist worldview. And some immigrants have a background of political and/or union activism in their home countries, which also predisposes them to engagement in immigrant labor organizing after they arrive in the United States.

Today, immigrants comprise about 15 percent of the U.S. workforce, or 23 million workers, about a third of whom are unauthorized. Whereas immigrants come from all over Asia, Africa, and Latin America, the unauthorized are predominantly Mexican or Central American. But even the Latino working-class population is highly stratified internally, and this constitutes another critically important driver of immigrant labor activism. That activism often focuses on improving the position of the most disadvantaged migrants, a group that includes the millions of unauthorized Mexican and Central Americans laboring in low-wage, precarious jobs at the very bottom of the U.S. labor market. The fact that other Latino immigrants have been able to secure more stable working-class jobs with better pay and conditions motivates those stuck in the worst jobs to hope that they can do the same. It is precisely this aspiration for upward mobility that informs the new immigrant labor movement.

That movement embraces and enriches traditional trade unionism, but is not limited to that organizational form. It also includes worker centers and other community-based organizations, and a broad immigrant rights movement whose core agenda is to win legal status for the unauthorized. Whereas earlier waves of immigrant labor organizing involved unions and community-based organizations like today's worker centers, the immigrant rights movement has no historical precedent. In the early twentieth century, the number of European immigrants who lacked legal status was minuscule, so there was no need for an immigrants' rights movement per se. In contrast, an estimated 11 million of today's immigrants are undocumented, and lack of legal status presents a key obstacle to economic advancement for them and their families.

Immigrant labor activism today, then, has three distinctive

strands: traditional trade unionism, the worker centers, and the immigrant rights movement itself.

IMMIGRANTS AND LABOR UNIONS

Although U.S. unions have a mixed record in relation to foreign-born workers (often having supported restrictive immigration policies in the past), that has changed dramatically in the twenty-first century. In the year 2000, the AFL-CIO reversed its long-standing support for immigration restriction and embraced a new policy favoring immigrant rights and a path to legalization for the undocumented. While immigrant union organizing and membership remain uneven across industries, occupations, and types of unions, today virtually all U.S. labor unions support immigrant workers' rights.

Survey data show that immigrant workers have more favorable attitudes toward labor unions than do U.S.-born workers. Indeed, those unions that have actively recruited immigrant workers into their ranks in recent years have been welcomed enthusiastically on the ground. Such union efforts to organize and represent low-wage workers have been among the most successful labor movement campaigns in recent years. Although public sympathy is often in short supply for union struggles on behalf of high-wage industrial workers in declining industries like auto or steel, who are often perceived as unfairly advantaged over other U.S. workers, precisely the opposite is true for organizing efforts targeting poorly paid, precarious immigrants—even if they are unauthorized. Campaigns like the Service Employees International Union (SEIU) Justice for Janitors drives have been highly effective in this regard, capturing widespread public support. Although such success stories involve relatively small numbers of workers, they remain important models for unions interested in rebuilding the labor movement.

But replicating such efforts is no easy task. That is partly because, even with a low-wage workforce that is ripe for organizing and capable of winning popular sympathies, union representation drives must overcome daunting challenges. Intense opposition from private sector employers is virtually ubiquitous in the United States, and recently, antiunion animus has emerged in the public sector as well. Given these formidable obstacles, it is not surprising that relatively few unions have actively organized unorganized workers, whether immigrant or native-born. Instead, available resources are typically devoted to servicing the existing membership and to defending past gains, and to lobbying, voter mobilization, and other electoral efforts.

Union density has declined dramatically in the United States over recent decades: in 2010, only 6.9 percent of all workers in the private sector were union members, down from 24.2 percent in 1973. The unionization rate for foreign-born workers still lags behind that for the U.S.-born, but the gap has virtually closed in the private sector, where the vast majority of immigrants are employed.

Like other unionized workers, unionized immigrants typically enjoy higher wages, better working conditions, and more job security than their nonunion counterparts. Indeed, for those immigrant workers who are unionized, there may be no better form of protection from employer abuse. But the option of union membership simply is not available to the vast majority of workers (whether U.S.- or foreign-born), given the winner-take-all exclusive representation system that exists in the United States. In the face of this unmet need, a rich variety of nonunion forms of organizing and advocacy among and on behalf of low-wage workers has taken shape in recent years.

WORKER CENTERS

Whether or not they have the right to vote, immigrants can and do participate in U.S. politics in a variety of other ways. They can protest in the streets, testify at public hearings, and make personal appeals to legislators and other elected officials, as well as to the wider public. All these forms of civic participation are actively promoted by the worker centers that have sprouted up all over the United States since the late 1980s. They are devoted to exposing employer abuses—many of which violate long-standing workplace laws and can easily spark popular outrage—and to mobilizing immigrant workers to demand their rights.

Worker centers sharply diverge from the traditional union model, both structurally and culturally. Yet like unions they are extremely appealing to immigrant workers striving to improve their economic situation. The centers are community-based organizations that target casualized occupations in which conventional unions are difficult to establish—such as day labor or domestic service—or decentralized industries that unions long since abandoned as "unorganizable," like garment manufacturing or restaurants. Some worker centers organize on the basis of ethnic or national identities; others adopt a geographic or neighborhood focus; still others target workers who are excluded from coverage under national labor law, like taxi drivers or street vendors.

The centers are hybrid organizations with multiple functions. Sometimes they organize low-wage workers at the grassroots level to campaign against workplace injustices. Most regularly provide assistance to workers experiencing labor law violations. Some offer social and educational services as well. Many also engage in policy and legislative advocacy to improve labor law enforcement, and seek to expose employer abuses to the public through media outreach as well as direct appeals to consumers.

Worker centers routinely provide basic information—both in written form and through educational workshops—to low-wage immigrant workers about their rights under U.S. labor and immigration law, assistance that is much needed and highly prized by recipients. Many centers also offer direct services to workers, especially by filing legal claims to remedy labor law violations. However, the demand for legal assistance is so vast relative to the modest staff and financial resources available that most worker centers that start out with a service provision mission tend to limit this aspect of their work early in their organizational development. Not only are they fearful that service provision could rapidly absorb their limited resources, but they view it as incompatible with the goal of long-term institutional change—as treating the symptoms rather than the root causes of the problems facing low-wage immigrant workers. Worker centers therefore devote considerable energy to grassroots organizing and education, and to leadership development. They lack the resources to mount large-scale popular mobilizations, although many do encourage participation in mobilizations organized by others.

Although unauthorized immigrants in the contemporary United States are denied other basic civil rights, in principle they are protected by nearly all laws covering wages, hours, and union representation. However, in recent years those laws have been widely violated by employers. Payment below the minimum wage, failure to pay legally mandated overtime premiums, "off the clock" work, outright wage theft, and retaliation against those who complain or attempt to organize their coworkers have become commonplace. U.S.-born workers experience these violations at times, but immigrants, and especially the unauthorized, are particularly vulnerable. Hardworking immigrants abused by employers can often win public sympathy and support, despite the fact that they may lack legal status. Shining a bright light on such workplace violations and seeking justice for the victims is a central aim of the worker centers.

Worker centers often lead campaigns that pressure employers for concessions directly or through legal avenues. Such efforts often succeed in winning settlements from employers, under which individuals or small groups of workers receive back pay or other types of remedial compensation, and which also may include employer promises to refrain from future labor law violations. The centers have also launched many successful public policy organizing campaigns, winning passage of new legislation or regulations that provide concrete benefits for low-wage and immigrant workers—although enforcement often proves difficult. For example, in a breakthrough victory for a coalition effort led by Domestic Workers United, the New York state legislature enacted a Domestic Workers' Bill of Rights in late 2010, granting nannies, housekeepers, and others employed in private households basic legal rights like time-and-a-half pay for overtime work for the first time.

For worker centers, "organizing" has a different meaning than in the union world. Some centers actively recruit "members," but most find it difficult to forge long-term relationships with workers once the immediate need for services has been met. Only rarely do they attempt to establish long-term collective bargaining relation-ships with employers or to build permanent membership-based orga-nizations. Often this reflects practical considerations—for example, if employers are geographically dispersed or constantly shifting (as for day laborers or domestic workers); in other instances it reflects worker center leaders' political disillusion with trade unionism. Low-wage workers often work long hours, commute great distances, and have families to care for, leaving little time for membership activities inside the centers, particularly without the incentive of ongoing rep-resentation of the sort unions can provide. Yet some worker centers have launched unionization drives, and many have alliances with es-tablished unions to whom they refer interested workers.

Just as immigrants are highly responsive to union organizing efforts, worker centers find many willing participants among im-migrants in their target industries. When those involved are un-documented, as is often the case, their participation in worker center campaigns may draw them into active civic participation. Indeed, the centers vitally depend on the willingness of ordinary workers to tell their stories. Those stories—strategically disseminated via the mass media—fuel the symbolic politics that are a signature feature of many worker center campaigns.

THE IMMIGRANT RIGHTS MOVEMENT

The third strand of immigrant labor activism takes the form of a popular social movement, with little resemblance to either unions or worker centers, although both actively support the immigrant rights movement. The broad-based effort to win a path to legalization for the millions of undocumented immigrants in the United States burst into public view in the spring of 2006, as millions of immigrant workers marched in cities across the country to protest the punitive H.R. 4437 legislation that threatened to criminalize their presence in the country. No comparable mobilization has taken place since then, but the immigrant rights movement continues in a variety of other forms. Although it uses the language of human and civil rights, its underlying thrust is to improve the economic opportunities available to immigrants, especially the unauthorized. In that sense the immigrant rights movement is a form of labor activism.

In the past, when enforcement of immigrants' legal eligibility for employment was minimal and jobs were easily secured by the unauthorized, the struggle for legal status was a less pressing concern than it has become in the twenty-first century. The 1986 Immigration Reform and Control Act (IRCA) was intended to resolve the problem of unauthorized migration, but in retrospect friend and foe alike agree that it proved an abject failure. For one thing, the intensification of border enforcement and militarization that followed the IRCA's passage (and was continually reinforced in the years that followed) had the unintended consequence of stimulating dramatic growth in the influx of undocumented immigrants. The unauthorized population had swollen to an estimated 12 million people by the time of the 2006 marches, as the previous pattern of circular migration of individual wage earners was replaced by more permanent migration, not only of workers but also their family members.

The IRCA did provide amnesty to a few million undocumented immigrants. It also (with support from organized labor at the time) institutionalized "employer sanctions" that were intended to penalize those who hired undocumented immigrants. However, this too had some unanticipated consequences. Employers were rarely prosecuted under the IRCA, which merely required them to affirm that the documents immigrants present to them appear genuine. In practice, penalties were borne largely by unauthorized workers themselves who lost their jobs in workplace raids and in many cases were also detained and/or deported. As for the employer, he or she simply replaced them with new recruits—an inconvenience to be sure, but one that came to be seen simply as a "cost of doing business."

Escalating political pressure from advocates of immigration restriction was unable to stop the continuing influx of new migrants, even if it made the journey more arduous and the stigma attached to Latino immigrants increasingly powerful. But restrictionist efforts did make the process of securing and maintaining decent employment increasingly tenuous, so that unauthorized migrants found it more difficult to climb out of the precarious entry-level jobs at the

bottom of the labor market, as their predecessors had done. Their desire for a path to legalization thus became increasingly urgent.

These are the developments that led immigrant rights groups to
begin organizing a grassroots protest movement. Street protests demanding immigrant rights became a regular May Day ritual from
the turn of the twenty-first century on. The choice of May Day, a labor
holiday in Latino immigrants' countries of origin (but one seldom observed in the post–World War II United States), is itself significant in
that immigrant rights and labor justice were inextricably intertwined
in the movement from the outset.

In the political arena, meanwhile, conflict escalated between immigrant rights advocates, on one side, and the equally well-organized
supporters of immigration restriction, on the other. Even with support from elements of the Republican Party and from the Bush administration, repeated efforts to pass comprehensive immigration
reform legislation foundered, intensifying the growing frustration
within immigrant communities. Many households included both individuals with legal status and others who were unauthorized, and
legal immigrants from Mexico and Central America regularly experienced the stigma attached to "illegal aliens" despite their status, so
that support for the immigrant rights movement rapidly spread far
beyond the unauthorized population.

This movement surfaced publicly in the spring of 2006, after the
U.S. House of Representatives passed H.R. 4437 in December 2005.
This legislation would have made living in the United States without
documents a criminal felony (in addition to the civil offense it already
was), and also would have criminalized anyone who assisted unauthorized immigrants in any way. H.R. 4437 was the greatest threat yet
to the working-class immigrant community and rapidly galvanized
the embryonic immigrant rights movement to mount a series of well-
organized protests. In Chicago, Los Angeles, and other cities and
towns across the nation, millions of immigrants and their supporters
took to the streets in a huge outpouring that culminated on May 1,
2006. On a scale that surprised even the organizers themselves,
thanks largely to enormous publicity by the Spanish-language media for the marches, the vast but hitherto invisible Latino immigrant

working class peacefully rallied to protest H.R. 4437. Many carried signs declaring, "We Are Workers, Not Criminals."

H.R. 4437 never became law, and in that sense the 2006 protests were successful, but their larger purpose remains unfulfilled. Immediately after the marches, the Bush administration dramatically stepped up its workplace raids and deportations, which only served to deepen the existing sense of economic threat in immigrant communities. As a result, since 2006 public demonstrations have been few and far between, and relatively modest in size when they do take place, yet the immigrant rights movement remains very much alive. One manifestation of its influence was the overwhelming pro-Democratic political tilt among Latino voters—many of them newly naturalized citizens—in the 2008 election, following a concerted campaign by the same coalition of immigrant rights groups that sponsored the 2006 marches, now encouraging naturalization and voting among those eligible. Indeed, the surge of Latino voting fulfilled the promise of a slogan that had been prominently displayed in the 2006 street demonstrations: "Today We March, Tomorrow We Vote." And if the day that unauthorized immigrants themselves can vote remains a distant prospect, their children and other family members who are U.S. citizens have already shown their potential for political mobilization as voters. They helped elect Barack Obama in 2008 in key battleground states and made a difference in some crucial races in 2010 as well. Alongside this development, undocumented youth, brought to the United States as children in the company of their parents, have surfaced on the front lines of the immigrant rights movement, demanding legal status and the right to work outside the underground economy.

If labor has any future in the United States, immigrants will be its heart and soul. All three strands of immigrant labor activism—service-sector unions, worker centers, and the immigrant rights movement—will be essential building blocks of any future workers' movement. Although there are tensions among the three, they have increasingly cooperated with one another in recent years. All three have found willing and energetic constituencies for their efforts to confront the extreme forms of labor exploitation that mark the new age of unfettered capitalism. All three lift up the voices of those new-comers who—despite sweatshop wages and working conditions, de-spite the unrelenting hostility of anti-immigrant forces, and despite well-founded fear of deportation—still dare to dream the American dream.

A century ago, an earlier generation of immigrants arrived on these shores with similar aspirations, and eventually they and their children helped to rebuild the U.S. labor movement. If an opportu-nity to do that comes again—a big if!—today's immigrants, who have already risked so much on their journeys, are poised to lead the next rebuilding effort. Meanwhile, the rest of us should be doing as much as we can to defend them against abuse and exploitation, and to make it possible for them to achieve their dreams.

THE FOUNDATIONS OF MODERN FARM WORKER UNIONISM: FROM UFW TO PCUN

Matthew Garcia and Mario Sifuentez

On September 15, 1985, in the dining hall of a dilapidated church in Woodburn, Oregon, four hundred farm workers gathered to announce their decision to form a union. The workers chose the symbolic date to commemorate the beginning of their own struggle: "It was on this day in 1819 that the Mexican people demanded their independence. In this same spirit, we will come together to also demand our legitimate right as workers." After ten years of battling the Immigration and Naturalization Service and suffering the exploitation of the reforestation industry in Oregon, workers decided that they had had enough. That day the Pineros y Campesinos Unidos del Noroeste (Treeplanters and Farm Workers Northwest United, or PCUN) was born. Over the course of the past twenty-five years PCUN has grown to over four thousand members and has become a major force in Oregon politics. Their success stands as an object lesson for the future of the American labor movement. Their dedication to building a union on the foundation of immigrant rights for everyone regardless of documentation, collective-bargaining rights, and coalitions with allied organizations has sustained and expanded the union in a time of growing antiunion sentiment. These tactics also mark some significant departures from the way in which the United Farm Workers practiced farmworker unionism during its heyday in the late 1960s and 1970s.

The United Farm Workers (UFW), most famously led by César Chávez, used a combination of strikes and boycotts to bring growers to the bargaining table for the first time in California history in 1970. The signing of contracts marked an important achievement for farmworkers who had been left out of the National Labor Relations Act of 1935 thereby denying them the same collective-bargaining rights as industrial laborers. Most histories of the union focus on the lead-up to this moment, though over the last decade, there has been a significant push by scholars to understand why the UFW did not turn this victory into a nationwide movement or even a sustained presence in California. While the union and its allies like to point to the resistances of the growers and the incursions by the Teamsters as a reason for their shortcomings, more recent studies demonstrate that the UFW suffered important self-inflicted wounds that offer lessons to avoid for those aspiring to bring justice to farmworkers today.

THE SINS OF THE UFW

Although Chávez faltered in many ways after 1970, there is an emerging consensus on three core mistakes: a failure to convert the movement into a bona fide union; an uneven record in organizing workers, especially immigrant workers; and a failure to fully commit to the California Agricultural Labor Relations Act after UFW attorneys had a significant hand in drafting the law in 1975. The failure to convert the energy of a grassroots uprising into institutional reform is not original to the UFW, as many scholars who study social movements know. For example, Frances Fox Piven and Richard Cloward have documented the struggles of the black civil rights movement to convert mass popular will for change into long-lasting political reforms identified with a party to enforce it. In the case of the farmworkers, Chávez and a handful of advisers mobilized people across class, ethnic, and racial lines to get the attention of consumers, growers, and ultimately the established unions such as the UAW, AFL-CIO, and the Teamsters to take farmworker justice seriously. The success of such "social movement unionism" is always contingent upon more powerful unions to help institutionalize reform. The UFW was no different, struggling to assert its autonomy among sponsoring and competing national unions, though Chávez and much of the leadership also struggled internally to shift from the exciting "missionary work" of leading marches and rallies to the imperatives of building a union.

This work included the more mundane duty of running a hiring hall to deploy workers in the fields, a requirement that the union made a mess of after signing contracts. The UFW's imposition of a seniority policy with regards to assignments favored local resident workers over a substantial number who were migratory. These problems led to the first significant defections from the fledgling union between 1970 and 1973, most notably Filipino workers who had grown accustomed to traveling from as far away as Alaska, through the Pacific Northwest, to California for jobs that had formerly been held by Filipino foremen. The disempowerment of the foreman and the disruption of the migratory labor system contributed to the fracturing of what had been seen as a multiethnic union.

The new system of employment also discriminated against highly migratory Mexican workers, including undocumented workers. As David Gutierrez has demonstrated, this prejudice was intentional and stemmed from the accepted position of national unions—including the UFW's sponsor, the AFL-CIO—that undocumented workers could be nothing more than scabs who drove down wages and make organizing national unions more difficult, if not impossible. Chávez embraced the standard industrial union position regarding undocumented immigrants, going so far as to order his field officers to ride along with Immigration and Naturalization Service employees to aid in the capture and deportation of such workers. Records indicate that the UFW's various chapters throughout California continued to report undocumented workers to the INS even after Chávez publicly voiced his begrudging support to undocumented workers. In Fresno County, for instance, the UFW kept meticulous records of the names and numbers of undocumented workers as well as the numerous calls UFW volunteers made to the INS about illegal workers. These reports often voiced frustration at the lack of action taken by the INS to deport undocumented immigrants. This position belied the growing reality of farm work during the period of the union's creation: that undocumented workers constituted a major portion of the employment pool, and that border agents, U.S. economic foreign policy, and agribusiness lobbying had made these workers a permanent presence.

In the 1970s, another Mexican American leader, Bert Corona, argued that organizations like the UFW should recognize the power of organizing all workers regardless of citizenship. Eventually, the student organization known as Centro de Acción Social Autónoma/ Center for Social Autonomous Action (CASA) articulated a "Sin Fronteras" ("Without Borders") policy with regard to relations among Mexicans and Mexican Americans, or Chicanos, and challenged Chávez to drop his anti-immigrant practices. Chávez begrudgingly obliged but he remained committed to a "citizens-first" agenda, never really embracing the idea that organizing the undocumented could strengthen the new farmworkers union. The growers, of course, understood the advantage of having a mostly undocumented *and* unorganized workforce on the cost of labor and became increasingly invested in assigning employment duties to labor contractors who hired a higher percentage of workers without documentation from the mid-1970s to the present.

The UFW could have stemmed this trend through the Agricultural Labor Relations Board (ALRB) created by a revolutionary state law, the Agricultural Labor Relations Act of 1975 (ALRA), though Chávez's distrust and ambivalence toward state regulations compromised this strategy. The UFW's general counsel, Jerry Cohen, invested heavily in the construction of the law, one that, according to then-California governor Edmund "Jerry" Brown, would "extend the rule of law to the agricultural sector and establish the right of secret ballot elections for farmworkers." Cohen preserved the right to the secondary boycott in the legislation, though the net effect of the law made the boycott less important than the state-sponsored electoral and arbitration process that Chávez grew to hate. The union won a majority of the initial elections in 1975 and 1976, though the dependence on the state had its consequences.

When the ALRB ran out of money due to the enormous demand for elections, conservative representatives within the California Assembly forced it to close up prematurely until the new fiscal year, all but killing the momentum the union had established. Annoyed by

the funding crisis, Chávez attempted to resolve the problem by insert-
ing the union into the political system, redirecting boycott workers
to campaign for politicians in California who supported the ALRA
and placing an initiative, Proposition 14, on the 1976 November ballot that would ensure year-round funding for the board and increase
the UFW's access to workers during union elections. The gamble did
not pay off. Though the union's influence helped some politicians, it
did not carry Proposition 14 to victory, which went down to defeat by
a three-to-two margin.

Although the ALRB got its funding back through the regular budgetary cycle, the union never really recovered from the loss of Proposition 14. Looking for a scapegoat for the electoral defeat, Chávez
blamed members of the boycott team for dragging their feet in moving back to California and, worse, accused some of intentionally con-
spiring against the union. Over the next two years, Chávez focused
a greater share of his attention on purging alleged communists and
disloyal members from the union rather than taking advantage of the
gains made by passing the ALRA.

The UFW executive board also struggled, inconclusively, with
the decision of how to staff the union: would they continue with an
all-volunteer staff or move toward paying people and developing a
more professional approach to organizing? Chávez did little to hide
his preference for maintaining the volunteer system, going so far as
to devise a renewed community at the union headquarters, La Paz,
that he hoped would inspire quality people to give their lives to the
UFW. For example, in an interview in October 1977 with the Catholic publication *Sojourner*, Chávez laid out the challenges before the
union, number one of which was to consolidate the gains made by
negotiating contracts where they had won elections. Such a task, he
contended, depended on the stabilization of a long-term staff that
he believed had eluded the union due to a lack of common understanding and commitment among volunteers rather than a lack of
pay. "I am convinced," he told his interviewer, "that we have to do
something to replace what we lost. We had a kind of community."
Chávez wanted to turn back the clock to a time before the ALRA when
volunteers flocked to the movement out of a sense of altruism and

a willingness "to give up some of those individual rights . . . for the good of the group." "We're at a crossroads now as to whether we're a 9-to-5 group or a more disciplined, more religious community," he told his interviewer. "If we choose this community style," he shared, "we will have some kind of religion—either we invent one or we keep what we have, but we cannot be without one."

Most on the executive board were dubious of Chávez's plan, though no one was willing to transition from an all-volunteer staff to paid representatives despite the fact that board members themselves complained of not being able to exist on the $5 per week stipend. Eliseo Medina, one of the most effective organizers and a leading voice on the board, lamented how he could not draw farmworkers to join the staff because of the paltry benefits. "I go out there and talk to a worker," he shared, "and I say: 'You're making $3.40 per hour . . . come and work for *cinco pesos* [*por*] *la causa*."—$5 for the movement. "[They say] '*Ay, chingada*! You're loco, cabrón!' " ("Oh, fuck! You're crazy, asshole.") "We're making farm work so goddamned attractive." Medina alleged that the workers had no interest in sacrificing their emerging "middle class" existence for the poverty associated with union work. Jerry Cohen, who was not a member of the executive board but attended all meetings as the union's general counsel, was the only one who took a strong position, stating in one board meeting: "I want to take a clear position and my position is that we're going to have to pay people." Eventually, some board members came over to his side and the union hired a limited number of paid representatives, though Chávez's near-complete control of the union allowed him to snuff out the experiment and maintain an all-volunteer staff.

In the end, Chávez and the union struggled to make sense of a world in which the ALRA, not the public or the union, became the arbiters of farmworker justice. The boycott, for all its value in drawing growers to the bargaining table and gaining public sympathy, had taken a back seat to the elections after the passage of the ALRA in 1975. "[The law] changed everything," Chávez often lamented, an acknowledgment that he missed the missionary work of building and sustaining a movement that counted among its goals more than just earning collective-bargaining rights for farmworkers. Chris Hartmire, who headed the new Community Life Department in the union and had a front row seat to the changes in his friend, later reflected, "I think the Agricultural Labor Relations Act threw César off course." He saw Chávez as a master tactician in what he called "a guerilla movement," of which the secondary boycott served as the ultimate weapon. "But now," Hartmire remembered, "the law and lawyers, and the government, which he never much trusted . . . threw him off his natural course." That "natural course" for Chávez—leading marches, fasting, holding rallies, and generally pressuring the state from outside its strictures—became less effective and perhaps even counterproductive in a world where lawyers, state bureaucrats, and union professionals dictated the terms of justice.

The history of the UFW during the late 1970s provides important lessons for farmworker justice organizations elsewhere. Given the dominance of the UFW in California, experimentation with new forms of organizing necessarily took place outside of the Golden State. These organizations included the Texas Farm Workers Union, the Coalition of Immokalee Workers in Florida, the Farm Labor Organizing Committee located mostly in the Midwest and Southeast, and PCUN. The recentness of their emergences has limited scholarly treatments of these organizations, though new paradigms in farmworker organizing are now emerging from what we know of their successes. Many leaders within these organizations got their start as volunteers and/or allies of the UFW and have used that experience in charting their organizations' strategies. In the interest of brevity and focus, we will now turn to a brief history of the organization we know best: Pineros y Campesinos Unidos del Noroeste, or PCUN.

A NEW MODEL OF ORGANIZING: PINEROS Y CAMPESINOS UNIDOS DEL NOROESTE

Like the UFW, PCUN also utilized strikes and boycotts to force Oregon growers to the collective-bargaining table, but at the same time avoided many of the mistakes of its predecessor organization. PCUN paid its staff, organized undocumented workers, created a democratic union structure, and established an organizing base before organizing. For instance, PCUN did not engage in the "missionary work" until seven years after its founding. Its leaders believed that they needed to establish a financial base before effective striking could take place and spent most of the early years fighting deportations, adjusting the status of some of its membership after the Immigration Reform and Control Act (IRCA), and challenging Oregon's anti-picketing law. The combination of casework, fund-raising, and foundation money ensured that PCUN staff members were paid, and it was never realistically thought of as a volunteer organization. But perhaps what sets PCUN apart from the UFW is its commitment to coalition building and "social movement unionism."

By the 1990s, PCUN believed that farmworker organizing could only be successful by forming alliances with lesbian, gay, transgender, bisexual, and queer (LGTBQ) organizations, progressive religious communities, student movements, and solidarity networks. By building coalitions with social justice movements around the region, PCUN has successfully fended off attacks from anti-immigrant organizations, conservative lawmakers, and agribusiness. At the same moment that the UFW became increasingly insular and ineffective, PCUN built coalitions that defeated anti-immigrant legislation, anti-gay legislation, and anti-worker legislation in Oregon, all the while maintaining its effectiveness as a bargaining agent for its members.

PCUN's vision was due largely to an ex-UFW member, Cipriano Ferrel. Born in Delano, California, in 1949, Ferrel labored in the table grape harvest with his parents and ten siblings, counting César Chávez as an inspiration during his formative years. After a brief stint as an organizer and Chávez's bodyguard, Ferrel moved to Oregon to enroll in the University of Oregon but became involved with local activists based out of Colegio César Chávez, a four-year college dedicated to the education of Chicano/as. The college served as a hub for local radical activists and played an instrumental role in the development of PCUN's ideology.

While at Colegio César Chávez, Ferrel met Ramon Ramírez, a young man with a formidable physical presence from East Los Angeles. Ramírez had worked as part of the antiwar National Chicano Moratorium Committee and belonged to Bert Corona's Centro de

Acción Social Autónoma (CASA). PCUN's early foundation in the immigrant rights movement put the union at odds with many of the mainstream Mexican American organizations. Since War World II, the League of United Latin American Citizens (LULAC) had supported deportation efforts by the INS, such as Operation Wetback, and the implementation of fines for employers who knowingly hired undocumented workers. Similarly the National Agricultural Workers Union (NAWU) and the UFW often supported stricter enforcement of immigration laws and thought of undocumented workers as strikebreakers.

Despite their public support of the UFW, Ferrel and PCUN adopted a very different strategy. Instead PCUN embarked on an organizing campaign that focused on the exploitation of undocumented reforestation workers. Borrowing a tactic from the UFW, organizers conducted a survey of reforestation workers in the early 1980s concerning their working conditions and their needs. PCUN discovered that out of Oregon and Washington's estimated population of fifteen thousand reforestation workers, nearly twelve thousand of them were Mexicans. Most were severely underpaid, paid late, or not paid at all. Others received cash payments with no record of deduction and were often threatened with deportation if they complained. One-third of workers had some type of work-related injury and nearly half reported unusual illnesses (i.e., any sickness more severe than the flu or the common cold). The survey confirmed the horror stories they had heard from workers and their families, and convinced the leadership of PCUN to concentrate on addressing their needs.

The findings inspired PCUN to address the dire situation by combating the wave of immigration raids in the forests conducted by the INS. Raids in and of themselves were a destructive and disruptive force in the lives of immigrant workers and their families, but adding the isolation of the wilderness made them even more frightening. Being caught by the INS meant deportation, though escaping them was potentially life-threatening. Workers who managed to evade the INS faced hypothermia, starvation, dehydration, and death. Finding a way back to a main road or a town bordered on the impossible.

Regardless of the difficulty, PCUN embarked on organizing the unorganizable. PCUN did not ignore the vulnerability of its members or abandon them; it instead adopted a philosophy that encouraged coalition building in order to provide support for undocumented workers. Ferrel often reiterated that farmworkers and undocumented workers in particular could not win a strike on their own, and PCUN sought to include various organizations and groups into its fold that would come to the aid of striking workers.

One of the more surprising coalition partners that PCUN sought out were gay and lesbian rights organizations in Portland, specifically Basic Rights Oregon (BRO). Given the tradition of the farmworkers movement and its connection to the Catholic Church and religious iconography, especially that of César Chávez and the UFW, reaching out to the gay and lesbian community seemed counterintuitive. Despite the perceived homophobia that existed in the farmworker community, PCUN's commitment was to fairness and equality, not just to farmworkers. Even within its own leadership the alliance proved divisive, Ramírez recalled: "Cipriano saw the growth of an anti-gay alliance and it had overtones of racism and anti-immigrant rhetoric. Even though his position at the time was very homophobic . . . he was able to overcome that." Ferrel did not let his own homophobia hamper the efforts of the union to build partnerships with other progressive organizations.

The force that brought BRO and PCUN together was the Oregon Citizens Alliance (OCA), a conservative Christian political activist organization founded in 1986 by Lou Mabon. In the late 1980s and early 1990s, the OCA placed numerous initiatives on the state ballot ranging from parental notification for teen abortion and elimination of protections for gay and lesbian government employees to including language in the state's constitution that equated homosexuality with pedophilia.

In 1992, the opportunity to build that alliance came when organizers of "For Love and Justice: A Walk Against Hate" approached PCUN about helping with the event. The walk, a 150-mile, two-week walk, from Eugene to Portland, was aimed to counter an effort by the Oregon Citizens Alliance to place an anti–gay rights initiative on the ballot later that year. The walkers needed hosts along the route and

PCUN's union hall seemed an obvious place to stop. Ramírez stated: "In most places church leaders would give them a place to stay, hand them the keys and leave. Not us! We got farmworkers waving the *Huelga* [strike] flags and we met them outside of town and marched together to the union! It was an emotional moment!"

Normally marchers would rest, eat, and sleep at their stops, but PCUN organizers saw it as a chance build coalitions. Ramírez recalled: "We had some hard conversations that night. We challenged them to get more involved in our movement and we promised to help them defeat Measure 9." Measure 9 would have amended Oregon's constitution to include the phrase "the state recognizes homosexuality, pedophilia, sadism and masochism as abnormal, wrong, unnatural and perverse." The measure failed. PCUN saw this as an opportunity to educate the gay and lesbian community about its struggles and as an opportunity to educate its membership about homophobia. The relationship was further solidified when BRO aided PCUN in stopping anti-immigrant initiatives put on the ballot by the OCA.

Throughout the 1990s, Oregonians for Immigration Reform (OFIR), an offshoot of the OCA, placed numerous anti-immigrant initiatives on the ballot, including a reincarnation of the Proposition 187 initiative in California. The 1994 initiative in California sought to establish a statewide citizenship screening system that would prohibit undocumented immigrants from using social services, such as emergency medical care and public education. The ballot initiative passed but key parts of the legislation were later deemed unconstitutional. At first CAUSA (a sister organization of PCUN) board members wanted to travel to California for training to defeat the bill. But Ramírez had a different idea: "California lost man! They did not have a winning strategy. I was against going down there. We had the gay and lesbian community right here. They have already fought measures here and won." Ramírez convinced the board to work with BRO, and the strategy paid off. CAUSA launched a thirty-five-city tour of Oregon and met with gay and lesbian community members in each city. The grassroots efforts of immigrant, gay, and lesbian communities proved effective; the initiative failed to garner sufficient signatures. Since that time, OFIR failed in every attempt to place an initiative on the ballot. That victory notwithstanding, PCUN maintained its focus on organizing, while the union's sister organization committed most of its efforts to legislative fights.

In the 1990s, PCUN won a lawsuit to declare an anti-picketing law unconstitutional, built a financial base, built wide-ranging coalitions, and embarked on a massive organizing campaign. It launched strikes, organized boycotts, negotiated on behalf of wildcat strikers, documented wage theft, and began organizing campaigns with members in new industries such as nursery work and mushroom plants. Today it stands on a similar ledge that the UFW stood on in 1977 after the passage of the ALRA. PCUN has exerted enough pressure on the Oregon legislature to make the passing of a collective-bargaining law a reality. However, given the effect it had on the UFW, it is unclear how PCUN would deal with the responsibilities of a legal team, and the necessary shift in current resources should the implementation of a collective-bargaining law take place.

PCUN continues to expand and take on the issues of police brutality, substandard education for the ethnic Mexican community, voter registration drives, and farmworker housing. The union has built itself as part of a movement, and not the movement itself. It now works in conjunction with other sister organizations known as CAPACES (Abilities). CAPACES acts as an umbrella organization for the Farmworker Housing Development Corporation; Voz Hispana, a Latino voter education project; Mujeres Luchadoras Progresistas (MLP), which promotes economic and leadership development for farmworker women; Latinos Unidos Siempre (LUS), a Latino youth leadership project; Mano a Mano, a provider of social services; and the Salem-Keizer Coalition for Equality, which empowers Latino families to take an active role in their children's education and in advocating for equity in the public education system. PCUN has succeeded in helping to create and maintain a progressive movement in Oregon.

In March of 2007, with the aid of the Prometheus Radio Project, PCUN launched Radio Movimiento, a twenty-four-hour low power FM station. The radio station has trilingual radio programming including cultural shows, organizing shows, and music. The current development of the CAPACES Leadership Institute (CLI) will formalize the on-the-job training organizers previously received. The union's membership holds steady at just over five thousand dues-paying members and is a leading example of what organizing in the immigrant community can look like. Through the work of the leadership institute, PCUN sees the need to renew, defend, and expand the movement's successes thus far by implementing leadership development programs. The institute's goal to "build the leadership capacity and political consciousness needed to sustain and expand that movement and to propel a host of related struggles, such as immigrants' rights" is indicative of the strength and the vision of social movement unionism in practice.

PCUN is succeeding where the UFW failed largely due to its ability to adapt to the changing population of farmworkers, building a union out of the needs of a mostly undocumented workforce. Unlike Chávez, Ferrel and Ramírez embraced the challenge of organizing workers without regard for documents. This had as much to do with what both men learned as allies and observers of Chávez as it did with their admiration of Bert Corona, who instilled in them a "Sin Fronteras" philosophy when it came to relations among co-ethnics. To be fair to Chávez, Ferrel and Ramírez have not been encumbered by their dependence on national labor federations like the AFL-CIO, who in an earlier period strongly encouraged the UFW to embrace a "citizens only" approach to building the union. The growth of the undocumented populations in the fields combined with the reduced influence of national labor unions have made it not only possible, but necessary, for organizations like PCUN to go it alone and devise new approaches to labor organizing since the steep decline of the UFW. This strategy has included the formation and maintenance of important coalitions with non-labor-oriented movements such as LGTBQ organizations that have broadened the appeal of PCUN and gained it important allies in its times of need.

How PCUN will manage its relationship to the state and avoid the mistakes that the UFW made during the late 1970s remains to be seen. PCUN's success has earned it the respect of lawmakers, the loyalty of rank-and-file workers, and the sympathy of the public, though it has yet to result in a law equivalent to the ALRA. If it does, PCUN will have to manage the demands of a system that often places a greater emphasis on a skilled staff with specialized knowledge in organizing workers, litigating legal cases, and maneuvering through state bureaucracies. The lesson of the UFW suggests that PCUN must be ready to make some hard decisions if it ends up going that route. So far, its history demonstrates its capacity to adapt to the changing environment of pursuing farm labor justice in America.

SUPPLY-CHAIN TOURIST: OR HOW WAL-MART HAS TRANSFORMED THE CONTEMPORARY LABOR QUESTION

Nelson Lichtenstein

I'm not much of a tourist, but I'm proud to think that I have visited what are, arguably, the three most important nodes of capitalist production during the last hundred years. When I toured the huge Ford production complex at River Rouge, during the winter of 1978, "Detroit," as both organizational metaphor and industrial city, was already well past its prime. But the world of classical Fordism still cast an impressive shadow across the economic landscape and the social imagination. The Rouge then employed some thirty thousand workers in a highly integrated complex of seventeen buildings that sucked in iron ore, silica, and coal at one end and transformed them into steel, glass, axles, fenders, and engine blocks, before assembling all those parts into a set of cars and pickups that were the visible marker of U.S. manufacturing prowess and working-class well-being. You could almost touch it: the giant parking lots, the smokestacks belching hot white vapor from the giant Rouge power plant, the modernist glass-and-steel Ford World Headquarters a couple of miles away, and the suburban swath of single-family, working-class houses that stretched for miles from Dearborn to Ypsilanti. Visit the Detroit Institute of the Arts and you can find the still stunning set of Diego Rivera murals that captured this Fordist world in all its romance and brutality.

Twenty-seven years later I flew into Bentonville, Arkansas, to tour a second node of the capitalist world. It is easy to get there because there are so many direct flights, from Denver, Chicago, LaGuardia, and Los Angeles, to this once remote Arkansas town. It is still not very big. Between Fayetteville and the Missouri line, there are hardly more than two hundred thousand people. But it is now one of the fastest-growing metropolitan regions in the country. In Bentonville, where Wal-Mart maintains its world headquarters in an unimpressive, low-slung building hard by the original company warehouse, the parking lots are full, the streets crowded, and new construction everywhere.

Most important, Bentonville is now home to at least five hundred, and perhaps a thousand, branch offices of the largest Wal-Mart "vendors" who have planted their corporate flag in northwest Arkansas in the hopes that they can maintain or increase their sales to the world's largest buyer of consumer products. Procter & Gamble, which in 1987 may well have been the first company to put an office near Wal-Mart's headquarters, now has a staff of nearly two hundred in Fayetteville; likewise Sanyo, Levi Strauss, Nestle, Johnson & Johnson, Eastman Kodak, Mattel, and Kraft Foods maintain large offices in what the locals sometimes call "Vendorville." Walt Disney's large retail business has its headquarters, not in Los Angeles, but in nearby Rogers, Arkansas. These Wal-Mart suppliers are a *Who's Who* of American and international business, staffed by ambitious young executives who have come to see a posting to once-remote Bentonville as the crucial step that can make or break a corporate career. If they can meet Wal-Mart's exacting price and performance standards, their products will be sucked into the huge stream of commodities that flow through the world's largest and most efficient supply chain. For any manufacturer, it is the brass ring of American salesmanship, which explains why all those sophisticates from New York, Hong Kong, and Los Angeles are eating so many surprisingly good meals in northwest Arkansas.

The final stop on my recent tour of the capitalist world was Guangdong Province in coastal South China. With more than 40 million migrant workers, thousands of factories, and new cities like Shenzhen, which has mushroomed to more than 7 million people in just a quarter century, Guangdong lays an arguable claim to being the contemporary "workshop of the world," following in the footsteps of nineteenth-century Manchester and early-twentieth-century Detroit. This was my thought when we taxied across Dongguan, a gritty, smoggy, sprawling landscape located on the north side of the Pearl

River between Guangzhou (the old Canton) and skyscraper-etched Shenzhen. We drove for more than an hour late one Sunday afternoon, along broad but heavily trafficked streets, continuously bordered by bustling stores, welding shops, warehouses, small manufacturers, and the occasional large factory complex. This is what Michigan Avenue or West Grand Boulevard must have felt like in 1925 or even 1950, before recession and deindustrialization had shuttered the shops, denuded the factories, and silenced the sidewalks.

Because of Shenzhen's proximity to Hong Kong and Macao, as well as its remoteness from the capital, the Chinese government in Beijing chose Shenzhen as a special economic zone in 1979. A few years later, the entire Pearl River Delta became a virtual free market, with low corporate taxes, few environmental or urban planning regulations, and, most importantly, the free movement of capital and profits in and out of the region. The results were spectacular. Gross domestic product in the Pearl River region leaped from $8 billion in 1980 to $351 billion in 2006. Shenzhen's population rose twentyfold. Guangdong province itself, which covers most of the Pearl River Delta, produces a third of China's total exports and 10 percent of all that finds its way to Wal-Mart's U.S. shelves.

Although Wal-Mart owns no factories outright, its presence is unmistakable. Its world buying headquarters is in Shenzhen, and it has already put several big stores in the province, with more to come. Wal-Mart is feared and respected by everyone involved with any aspect of the export trade, which is why the executives at the Yantian International Container Terminal in Shenzhen, now the fourth-largest port in the world, gives Wal-Mart-bound cargoes top priority. "Wal-Mart is king," a port official told us. Indeed, when we visited there, two of its top executives were on their way to Bentonville. On the same trip, managers at the huge Nike–Yue Yuen factory complex in Dongguan bragged that they could fill an order from the States in just two months. Modern highways and bridges speed cargo to the container port, where ships are loaded in half the time it takes California longshoremen to accomplish the same task.

The Rouge, Bentonville, Guangdong: the past and present of capitalist production, global trade, and management technique. And a new configuration for a "labor question" which once again vexes all those who work within or comment upon the global pathways that move so much of the world's commerce from one continent to another. Indeed, these regimes of production and distribution, from the Rouge to Guangdong, pretty well mark the arc traveled by my own historical and political imagination. I was part of the New Left generation that "industrialized" around about 1970, following in the footsteps of David Montgomery, Stan Weir, and Archie Green, who were part of the college-educated generation that spent a decade or more on the shop floor during and after World War II. I never actually got my hands dirty in this fashion, but for nearly two decades my intellect and my inspiration were shaped by Rust Belt factories, mills, and mines and the women and men who made them hum or, better yet, brought them to a silent halt during a work stoppage.

My interest in studying the auto industry and its workers in the 1970s arose out of the same motivation that propelled a goodly number of comrades and colleagues to actually get a job at the Rouge, Chevy Gear and Axle, or Chrysler's storied Jefferson Avenue assembly plant. These were the companies, the production facilities, and the workers who occupied the "commanding heights" of the American economy. As the management theorist Peter Drucker put it in 1946, when near continuous warfare between shop militants in the auto factories and their management adversaries seemed the fulcrum for an even larger set of class politics, "The automobile industry stands for modern industry all over the globe. It is to the twentieth century what the Lancashire cotton mills were to the nineteenth century: the industry of industries." The production of motor vehicles then held a cultural and ideological importance that made an understanding of this economic sector central to figuring out the way twentieth-century society worked. Henry Ford had once celebrated the machinery of mass production as the "new Messiah," a viewpoint with which the Soviets could find much in common. So if Engels had studied the condition of the working class in Manchester to seek a revolutionary solution to the labor question of his day, my generation would have a similar motivation for its investigation of the social politics of Detroit and the world historic industry with which it was near synonymous.

Of course, the American automobile industry, which had seemed so solid and stolid during the middle decades of the twentieth century, was already beginning to crumble, putting into question the model of corporate governance and working-class organization that went with it. That was too bad, because both academic mandarins as well as left-wing labor historians found a certain tidy logic to the market-making, price-setting supremacy of General Motors, U.S. Steel, and General Electric. They were all vertically integrated manufacturing firms that truly occupied the commanding heights of the U.S. economy, and whose organizational template was being reproduced throughout the world. Harvard's Alfred Chandler argued that the visible hand of management had replaced the unpredictable anarchy of the free market when it came to actually running these giant bureaucracies; likewise Peter Drucker had greatly irritated top executives at General Motors when he described their company as an essentially political organization, not unlike that of a state planning bureaucracy, when he published *The Concept of the Corporation* in 1946.

All this greatly pleased left-wing labor historians of my generation. If the market was indeed a myth, and if a business elite set prices, cartelized markets, determined wage levels, and influenced government regulatory policy, then a politically sophisticated countermobilization, working-class at its core—but also including a popular front of consumers, liberal intellectuals, and partisans of the newly proletarianized immigrants and African Americans—might well shift American politics to the left. The unions were obviously central to this project, and a farsighted labor leadership essential. C. Wright Mills captured the hopes and fears of this labor metaphysic in his 1948 study of the union leadership, *The New Men of Power.*

> To have an American labor movement capable of carrying out the program of the left, making allies among the middle class, and moving upstream against the main drift, there must be a rank and file of vigorous workers, a brace of labor intellectuals, and a set of politically alert labor leaders. There must be the power and there must be the intellect. Yet neither the intellectuals nor the workers at large are in a position to take up

an organizational key to the matter; and neither intellectuals nor rank and file are now running labor unions in the United States.

It would not be an exaggeration to say that the entire first half of my academic career has been at attempt to figure out why the unions failed to do what Mills and his generation had once hoped they might accomplish.

One reason for that failure is that the structure of American capitalism has been transformed during the last third of a century, and with it the agenda of a good slice of the academic left. The rise of Wal-Mart embodies this transformation, but today it is by no means a unique business enterprise. Rather, it symbolizes the power, at home and abroad, of a set of corporations whose structure and outlook differ quite radically from the mid-century manufacturing titans which once seemed so potent and permanent. Today, more people are employed in the retail sector of the economy than in all of manufacturing and construction combined. Wal-Mart, with 2.1 million employees worldwide, is by far the largest private sector company on earth, and in terms of the proportion of U.S. gross national product that it commands, it rivals that of General Motors and U.S. Steel in their respective heydays. But Wal-Mart owns no factories either in the United States or East Asia; it does not even own or operate the container ships or the 4-million-square-foot San Bernardino distribution center that is so crucial to the transshipment of the billions of dollars in consumer products that leaves Hong Kong and Shenzhen each month, destined for sale on a million Wal-Mart shelves in more than four thousand North American discount stores. Wal-Mart is not General Motors: there are no unions, most employees are women, and the company manufacturers nothing. But just as GM once set the pattern for wages, working conditions, pensions, and health benefits for a huge slice of the American economy, so too do Wal-Mart and its retail rivals to construct the employment template today. With the possible exception of the big Wall Street banks, these retailers are by far the most influential enterprises in American business today.

All this caught us by surprise, and by "us" I don't just mean labor

historians. For decades, neither economists nor politicians gave retailing the respect it deserved. Shopping was what we did once all
the heavy lifting had been sweated out of us: after the steel had been
poured, the automobiles assembled, the skyscrapers built, and the
crops harvested.

But the new and innovative set of great retailers that emerged by
the 1990s were not just huge employers with an enormous stream
of revenue; their connections with a global manufacturing network
were practically incestuous. They might not own the Asian or Central
American factories from which they sourced all those big-box con-
sumables, but their "vendors" were linked to them by a "supply chain"
that evoked the iron shackles subordinating slave to master.

Wal-Mart and the other retailers are global companies, but globalization is hardly a new phenomenon. Ford had begun to sell cars
abroad as early as 1913, and after 1919 it was truly a worldwide corporation with rubber plantations in Brazil, dealerships in Great Britain,
and assembly plants in Australia and South Africa. Early in the twentieth century, U.S. world trade, as a percentage of GNP, was double
the proportional size it would achieve in the 1950s and 1960s and not
all that lower than it is today. But there is a huge difference between
the globalization of Ford and that of Wal-Mart. In the Fordist era, that
Dearborn-headquartered manufacturing enterprise turned the central gear of a supply chain that extended all the way from Brazilian
rubber plantations and the Minnesota Iron Range to your neighborhood auto dealer. The manufacturing enterprise—above all that vast
assortment of buildings, machinery, and men that constituted the
great River Rouge complex—stood at the center of Ford's purchasing/
production/distribution nexus. Indeed, for roughly a century, from
1880 until 1980, during the heyday of domestic, oligopolistic mass
production, U.S. manufacturers reigned supreme, often "administer-
ing" prices in order to achieve healthy profits and cartel-like control of
markets. Even the manufacturers of food items and light consumer
goods, such as Hartz Mountain, Gillette, 3M, Hershey, Kraft, and
Coca-Cola, conducted themselves in an imperious manner when
they stocked the shelves of the regional grocery and drug chains that
sold their wares.

Today, however, the retailers stand at the apex of the world's supply chains: they use their enormous buying power and highly sophisticated telecommunication links to dominate all aspects of the production/distribution/sales nexus. At least one-half of all global trade revolves around and is driven by the supply chains that have their nerve centers in places like Bentonville: Atlanta (Home Depot); Minneapolis (Target); Troy, Michigan (Kmart); Paris (Carrefour); Stockholm (Ikea); and Issaquah, Washington (Costco). Using a wide variety of new information technologies, these retailers collect point-of-sale (POS) data and relay them electronically through their supply chain to initiate replenishment orders almost instantaneously. Thus when Wal-Mart sells a tube of toothpaste in Memphis, that information passes straight through the P&G headquarters office in Cincinnati, flashing directly to the toothpaste factory in Mexico, which adjusts its production schedule accordingly.

Wal-Mart is therefore not simply a huge retailer, but increasingly a manufacturing giant in all but name. The retailer tracks consumer behavior with meticulous care and then transmits consumer preferences down the supply chain. Replenishment is put in motion almost immediately, with the supplier required to make more frequent deliveries of smaller lots. This is "just-in-time" for retailers, or "lean retailing." To make it all work, the supply firms and the discount retailers have to be functionally linked, even if they retain a separate legal and administrative existence. The giant retailers of our day, Wal-Mart first among them, "pull" production out of their far-flung network of vendors. The manufacturers no longer "push" it onto the retailer or the consumer. Or, to extend the metaphor, the nearly continuous stream of container ships which move between Shenzhen and the Long Beach/Los Angeles port complex are "pulled" across the Pacific, not "pushed" by the Chinese manufacturers, who stuff their product into nearly half a million forty-foot containers each year. Moreover, "pull" production requires speed, predictability, and accuracy in the delivery of goods. "Supply chain management"—that is the new business school buzz phrase—is the "science" of getting this to happen in the most efficient and cost-effective way.

All this has made life increasingly difficult for workers both at home and abroad. The rise of a system of global supply chains, with their multilayered set of factories, vendors, and transport links, has created a world system in which legal ownership of the forces of production have been divorced from operational control. This shift has generated a system in which accountability for labor conditions is legally diffused and knowledge of the actual producers is far from transparent. In effect, we are building a universal sweatshop in which the same unregulated competitive pressures have been unleashed that once made life so miserable in London's East End or on the Lower East Side of Manhattan. The globally dispersed system of production that exists today means that if workers fight for their rights in one factory, the manufacturer might well shift its production to another, "friendlier" one—often in another country. Just as tenement sweatshops opened and closed in rapid succession a century ago, so too are contemporary factories readily moved around the globe—even from China, which has reportedly lost manufacturing to other Asian countries (such as Vietnam) as a result of rising wages and the implementation of a new contract labor law.

Globalization is too sweeping a word to describe this new regime or the new labor question it has engendered. I prefer the historically resonant term "merchant capitalism." The retail-dominated supply chains that now organize such a large proportion of international trade herald the return to prominence and power of a particular organizational form in the history of world capitalism which we once thought long past. Merchant capitalism was and is a form of market exchange, primarily in commodities, in which traders, shippers, merchants, and financiers play key roles over and above the commodity producers and manufacturing enterprises of our time. The last time such a system reigned supreme came in the century before the American Civil War, when the sale and distribution of cotton, tobacco, sugar, and wheat was controlled by the great trading companies and financial institutions of New York, Liverpool, and London. Like the global retailers of our time, they favored free trade, a weak regulatory state, transnational production, and cheap, if not unfree, labor. They were often partisans of the Southern cause, not unlike contemporary retailers who find that authoritarian regimes in Asia,

Central America, and parts of Africa are most hospitable to the kind of sweated labor that lies at the base of their giant supply chains.

And it is an economic structure whose global reach, political agenda, and labor relations bulwark the conservative, neoliberal turn that has shifted politics and economic policy to the right throughout those North Atlantic nation-states which once seemed so firmly on the road to social democratic regulation of the market. Contemporary merchant capitalists, like their antebellum ancestors, favor a weak state and an unregulated market, thus limiting the capacity of any polity to regulate and structure labor and employment standards. Needless to say, this thinning of state capacity is not what Karl Marx had in mind when he predicted the withering away of the state.

Nevertheless, the decline of the regulatory state and the manufacturing-based trade unions that once sustained it is having a large impact on the way scholars and activists conceive of the modern labor question and its remedies, making some of the ideas and movements that came to the fore in the nineteenth century relevant once again. Although the socialist idea is certainly in eclipse, the definition, measurement, and advocacy of human rights now constitutes a pervasive way in which we define the extent to which individuals hold and exercise citizenship, both civic and industrial. Indeed it was in precisely such circumstances that the world's first human rights NGO, the British Anti-Slavery Society, came to play an outsized role in curbing the excesses that flowed from the merchant capital regime. And like today's NGOs, it deployed the weapons of the weak: investigation, exposure, moral suasion, and boycott. Similar groups, on both sides of the Atlantic, including the Congo Reform Association, the Consumer's League, and the NAACP, would later utilize many of these same approaches in their efforts to resolve that bundle of social pathologies that constituted the labor question of their era.

Today, many nongovernmental organizations exist which monitor, expose, berate, and measure the working conditions and environmental standards that exist in the factories from which Wal-Mart and other retailers source their products. Human Rights Watch, the Fair Labor Association, the Workers Rights Consortium, and numerous Hong Kong–based groups keep the pressure on Wal-Mart, Nike,

Disney, and Target. In response, Wal-Mart and all the other retailers have developed their own sometimes quite elaborate codes of social responsibility. The effectiveness of these internal monitoring arrangements is subject to considerable debate. In general, they have some impact at the margins, but make no fundamental transformations in the way Wal-Mart goes about purchasing its goods or in the way its contractors go about producing them.

It is revealing, of course, that so much international attention now attaches to the development and implementation of these codes of conduct. In the heyday of American Fordism, most critiques of the social impact of industrial capitalism were directed toward the key manufacturing enterprises, largely by trade unions and the government, but sometimes by organized consumers as well. It is a tribute to and indication of the shift in the structure of world capitalism that we now direct our concern toward the brands and retailers that today stand at the apex of their global supply chains. That is because the essence of the twenty-first-century labor question, as well as its resolution, no longer resides at the point of production in a struggle between workers and the owners of the factories in which they labor. Instead, the site of value production in the contemporary world is found at every link along a set of global supply chains, in which the manufacturer and the warehouse operator, the ports and the shipping companies, the retailers and their branded vendors jockey for power and profit. To tame this system we'll need ideas and institutions, social movements and new legal structures that are truly global in their ambition and effectiveness.

But at this point in the early twenty-first century, no set of voluntary organizations, worker alliances, governmental organizations, or rival economic institutions has generated either the will or the wherewithal to stand athwart these retail-driven supply chains. And that is why Wal-Mart and its clones occupy so much terrain along the heights of our world economy and why, for this historian as well as so many other scholars, these companies have become such a source of fascination and disdain, not unlike that once commanded by the great automobile enterprises headquartered in or near Detroit.

FORGETTING AND REMEMBERING: WORKERS, THE U.S. EMPIRE, AND THE POST-9/11 ERA

Dorothy Fujita-Rony

THE UNITED STATES, THE PACIFIC, AND IMPERIALISM

As a culture, we tend to focus on the journeys and choices of individuals rather than on how U.S. policy in the global arena fundamentally structures resources and opportunities. Success and failure then become individual stories, where people "pull themselves up by their bootstraps," "find their American Dream," and redeem the hard work and sacrifices that they and others have given to make this migration possible. One of the difficulties is that this narrative framework often leaves immigrants and their descendants in a quandary—to take a critical stance about U.S. foreign policy and immigration is to "betray" the sacrifices of immigrants and refugees (especially one's parents and other family members) whose journeys to the United States were so difficult.

By undertaking an alternate telling which brings militarism to the forefront, we can see this history in a different perspective. In the wake of 9/11, one of the lessons that we need to learn as a country is the importance of addressing U.S. military actions overseas, not only for our own knowledge and well-being, but also because these military actions radically shape how others see the United States and its residents. Most histories of the United States emphasize the nation as independent from other countries, effectively downplaying the United States' complex colonial and postcolonial history. The fact that Americans so often think of Asia and the Pacific Islands as leisure destinations hides the violence done to these communities and peoples through U.S. postcolonialism and militarism.

The United States emerged on the world stage in the twentieth century by achieving power over the former imperial giant Spain, and taking over its possessions, which included the Philippines, Guam, Puerto Rico, and Cuba. Hawai'i was another site where the United States would assume colonial rule. At the end of World War II, when the United States emerged as the only major power relatively un-scathed by wartime combat, the country was poised to take on new battles in the Cold War era. U.S. dominance in the Pacific would con-tinue through the rest of the twentieth century, as it regularly inter-vened and took control of the affairs of different countries, including Korea, Indonesia, Cambodia, and Vietnam.

This militarism would have an impact on numerous postcolonial and transnational workers, an experience which is deeply embed-ded in the histories of many communities, such as that shown in the novel *Talking to the Moon* by Noël Alumit. *Talking to the Moon* centers around the lives of a Los Angeles Filipina/o American family shortly after the father, Jory Lalaban, is shot while delivering mail. How-ever, in keeping with the military history of Filipina/o Americans, it also arcs backward to the Philippines to show the impact of the U.S. occupation and World War II. In the context of teaching the novel, I asked my literature class about their memories and knowledge of the real-life slaying of postal carrier Joseph Ileto, whose death in 1999 by a white supremacist shocked the Southern California Filipina/o American community as well as the rest of the country. Most of them would have been young children in 1999, but as a significant event in the Southern California community that made national headlines, knowledge could easily have been passed on to them about this hor-rific crime. Yet when I asked my class in 2009 if they knew who Joseph Ileto was, no one raised their hands, with the exception of one student who later told me that she had learned Ileto's story through another Asian American studies class. Another student had heard about the shootings at the North Valley Jewish Community Center, but had not realized that Joseph Ileto was the only one killed in the shooter's rampage. A third student remarked that he passed by the Joseph Ileto Post Office in Chino Hills on the way to campus, but did not know for whom the post office was named. Joseph Ileto was one of the "lucky ones," who had traveled to the postcolonial metropole of Los Angeles. And, at the same time, he, like many other workers of color, was targeted because of his skin color and his occupation.

Ileto's story contains elements of the postcolonial and trans-national story of American militarism, economic dominance, sup-port for repressive foreign governments, immigration to the United States, and work. If a viable working-class movement is to emerge, that story needs to be understood. This is the history that I recounted for the class. On August 10, 1999, Buford O. Furrow Jr. went to Granada Hills, California, and entered the lobby of the North Val-ley Jewish Community Center, where around 250 children were at play. Bearing a semiautomatic weapon, he fired more than seventy shots, wounding a receptionist, a teenaged counselor, and three young boys. After leaving the scene, Furrow went a few miles away to Chatsworth, where he encountered United States Postal Service mail carrier Joseph Ileto delivering mail. Furrow asked Ileto to mail a let-ter, and then shot Ileto nine times with a handgun. Furrow later said that he killed Ileto because he thought he was Latino or Asian, and also because Ileto was a federal worker. Ileto died from multiple shots to his chest and one in the back of his head. In January 2001, Furrow pled guilty to all sixteen felony counts, including a murder charge for shooting Ileto, and was sentenced to two consecutive life terms and 110 more years without parole. He was ordered to pay $690,294.11 to compensate the victims' families and insurance companies.

After the slaying, Filipina/o American organizations held rallies in San Francisco, Seattle, Chicago, Dallas, Washington, D.C., and New York. Asian American community groups along with the Asian Pacific American Labor Alliance, unions, and religious and civil rights organizations held events remembering Ileto. The Ileto family decided to make public appearances in honor of Joseph, including many that were arranged by the Asian Pacific American Legal Center of Southern California. They have spoken out at colleges, marches, and the 1999 AFL-CIO national convention.

While Furrow clearly was an individual on the fringes, his mur-derous actions represent both widespread anti-immigrant animosity and the impact of U.S. imperial and postcolonial actions around the world. The United States has a connected relationship to militarized sites in many different countries. Hence, work for many postcolonials in the United States is an extension of the transnational labor environment between the United States and its formerly colonized spaces. When we grieve for Ileto and remember his life, we must also think about how his slaying by a white supremacist signifies the gross inequities of U.S. dominance around the world, and the situation of postcolonial workers in the United States and elsewhere in the U.S. diaspora.

A POSTCOLONIAL LIFE

The colonization of Joseph Ileto's birth country, the Philippines, is part of a long history of U.S. conquest and occupation in which the United States fought against indigenous peoples in the continental United States and against Mexico, whose former lands became much of the U.S. Southwest. The United States continued to spread north to Alaska, west to the Philippines, and south to Puerto Rico in its quest for power. During the American occupation of the Philippines in 1898, as the United States fought a long war against Philippine resistance, astounding numbers of Filipina/os paid with their lives for the privilege of American rule. War, accompanied by hunger, sickness, and pestilence, killed hundreds of thousands of people, with estimates ranging from two hundred thousand for the entire nation to six hundred thousand for the province of Luzon alone, where Manila is located.

As with most relationships between the colonizer and the colonized, the United States profited immensely from its rule over the Philippines through economic exports, production, and labor migration. Decades later, the Philippines also was a pivotal site for U.S. war efforts in the Pacific during the Cold War era. Although the Philippines gained putative independence from the United States in 1946, agreements and legislation that favored the United States continued American dominance over the Philippines. As example, the 1947 Military Bases Agreement gave the United States control over facilities in the Philippines for ninety-nine years. The Philippines was barred from giving base rights to other countries, and there was no restriction on how the United States used its bases or the weapons it deployed—in effect making the Philippines, a sovereign nation, a target on behalf of U.S. interests.

The United States poured massive military resources into the Philippines in the second half of the twentieth century, first in the continuing campaign to contain the Huk movement, and then to support Ferdinand Marcos, who came into power in 1965. Clark Air Base, which measured 130,000 acres (roughly two hundred square miles), and Subic Bay Naval Base, which used to contain the city of Olongapo until it was returned to the Philippines, were pivotal installations for the United States. Olongapo became famous as a site where sailors, marines, and soldiers could have "R & R," a euphemism for the excesses of the sex industry which sprang up around military sites and typically employed young women from the provinces who had little recourse to other work because of the declining economy. These representations of Filipinas would be carried around to other U.S. military installations and back to the United States, profoundly shaping images of Filipina women in the United States and elsewhere. The images are part of a discourse that continues to help circumscribe the labor and work conditions available to Filipinas.

In many ways, Ileto's career was characteristic of immigrants in Southern California. Born in the Philippines, Joseph "Jojo" Ileto grew up in Legazpi City with his grandparents, who were both dentists. At age fourteen, during his second year at St. Gregory the Great Seminary, he migrated to Los Angeles from the Philippines to join his parents, two sisters, and two brothers. Typical of many from other countries, Ileto's family household was transnational, so he stayed with his grandparents in the Philippines before traveling to the United States. With the advent of the 1965–68 American immigration reform laws, thousands of Filipinos were leaving for better economic realities in the continental United States and Hawai'i.

The fact that Ileto's grandparents were professionals, and the family still was divided across the Pacific, is an indication of the difficult times during the Marcos era. Migration emerged as a viable option even for the professional middle class. In the mid-1970s, when Ileto migrated, the Philippine economy had worsened considerably, especially under the Marcos regime and the martial law he imposed. The regime was heavily supported by U.S. economic and military investments. By 1975, for example, the average monthly earnings of agricultural workers had dropped 25 percent in three years, while workers in commerce saw their earnings fall by over 40 percent. In Manila and surrounding areas, the wages for both skilled and unskilled fell by almost 30 percent. Thousands journeyed to the United States for better futures, especially for the sake of the next generation.

Enrolling in the U.S. public school system, Ileto attended Schurr High School in Montebello, and East Los Angeles College where he studied engineering. He found work testing electrical equipment at AVX Filters Corp. in Sun Valley. Whereas Filipina/os entering the labor market fifty years before probably would have found work in the California agricultural fields, employment in the electronics industry represented entry-level work for new immigrants. Reflecting his transnational obligations, every year Ileto would send presents to his younger cousins in the Philippines, part of the vital transnational flow of money and remittances that connects the United States to its postcolonial sites. Like many, Ileto worked two jobs to generate more income, which is why he took on the post office work as his second job. This also reflects a common path for postcolonial workers who often have familiarity with the U.S. educational and government systems prior to migration to the United States.

Proud of the work he did, and eager to contribute to his family and community, Ileto lived in Monterey Park with his mother (his father died in May 1999), his sisters Raquel and Carmina, and his younger brother. With family responsibilities on both sides of the Pacific, Ileto delayed setting up his own individual household and was still a primary contributor for his mother and siblings. As the *Los Angeles Times* reported: "Joseph was the family's Mr. Fix-It. He drove his mother around, changed the oil in his sister's car and let Raquel practice hair-cutting on him. He was a master chess player. He loved orchids and jokes. He proudly wore post office t-shirts on his day off." According to his brother Ismael, Joseph would help the garbage collectors when they came to do their job, even though he did not have to

do so—an example of Ileto's concern for others and his working-class
consciousness.

MILITARISM AND THE U.S. GLOBAL CONTEXT

The United States' presence in the Philippines can be read as part of a
systemic plan of dominance in Asia and the Pacific. Obtaining bases
in the Pacific Islands was a vital part of the American strategy in the
region. The Pacific Islands possessed a key resource—geographic location that was vital to U.S. military aims. After World War II, Micro-
nesia was turned into a "strategic" trust territory, as deemed by the
United Nations, with seven administrative districts. As an example
of the extreme imbalance in power and disregard of these islands,
Kwajalein Atoll was used as a ballistic-missile test site, and the atolls
of Enewetak and Bikini of the Marshall Islands were employed for
nuclear testing after World War II and up to 1956. In the 1950s, the
U.S. Navy oversaw most of the Northern Mariana Islands in Micro-
nesia, with its largest island Saipan being used by the Central Intelligence Agency for the training of Nationalist Chinese soldiers. Guam
became an important naval installation as well as a significant air
base during the Vietnam War. Through the 1950 Guam Organic Act
that was passed by the U.S. Congress, Guam became an unincor-
porated territory of the United States, with its people gaining U.S.
citizenship and the U.S. president appointing its governor. Samo-
ans, on the other hand, became U.S. nationals but not citizens when
Samoa was partitioned in 1899 into American Samoa, overseen by
the United States, and Western Samoa, administered by Germany.
American Samoa also was used as militarized space during World
War II, including as a training base for U.S. Marines, to expand the
fitafita (the Samoan marine guard), and to implement infrastructure
developments. Like the other Pacific Islands, Hawai'i too was a key
military installation for the United States well before the bombing of
Pearl Harbor in World War II. Hawai'i emerged as the most militarized state for its size, with key installations like the U.S. Army's Fort
Shafter, Hickam Air Force Base, and the Pearl Harbor Naval Station.

The U.S. military had extensive control over the land. On the sacred island of Kaho'olawe, for example, the U.S. Navy mounted live fire training and detonated five hundred tons of TNT, which had a blast similar in intensity to a nuclear explosion.

Tracing U.S. militarism leads us to a political and economic project that would result in the passage of thousands and thousands to the United States, like Joseph Ileto's family. Initial militarization would lead to U.S. development of these areas, maintaining the militarized space for the United States. In this expanded realm, U.S. militarism had immediate power over workers. Some directly joined the U.S. military, while other people's lives were affected by their association with the navy, either as family members or by being support personnel in other industries.

Sometimes, these effects are far-reaching and indirect. U.S. militarism promotes representations of postcolonial workers that have an impact on how people are perceived in the United States. For example, Susana Remerata Blackwell and two friends, Phoebe Dizon and Veronica Laureta, were shot by Blackwell's estranged husband, Timothy Blackwell, in Seattle in 1995. Susana Remerata Blackwell had arrived from the Philippines in the United States through the "mail-order bride industry," a reflection of global class, gender, and racial inequities where young women from abroad migrate to the United States for marriage, considered a viable route given their economic and social choices. All too often, these women find themselves legally bound to their new husbands in vulnerable and abusive situations in unfamiliar countries. In this case, Susana Remarata Blackwell lost her life, along with Dizon and Laureta, who were supporting her.

And the rise in militarism and its results are likely to continue. Many of us come from families and communities that have been directly affected by the post-9/11 security era. After 9/11, for example, the United States developed renewed interest in Southeast Asia, especially because of its considerable Muslim population, and Southeast Asia was called "the Second Front in the War on Terror." Indonesia, the fourth-largest country in the world, is also the nation with the largest Muslim population. As a result, U.S. military interests in the

post-9/11 era has affected not only many people of color who are serving in the military, but also community members who reside in the
United States. They face new scrutiny, especially in relation to countries overseas. One reason I teach Southeast Asian American studies
is because of the commitment I feel to educating younger generations
about the United States' military ambitions in Southeast Asia, to better equip them for their lives ahead.

For example, in the 2006 film *Sentenced Home*, Cambodian
American men who were refugees to the United States following the
war are profiled. As young men, they committed crimes and served
their time, and then were targeted later on for deportation as security
risks in the wake of 9/11. One person, Kim Ho Ma, arrived in the
United States in the early 1980s. As a teenager, Ma was arrested and,
after his sentence, was placed in INS detention for three more years.
In *Reno v. Ma*, Ma successfully argued in the U.S. Supreme Court
that the INS could not keep detaining him, and that he should be
released until he was deported. In 2002, the United States agreed to a
repatriation agreement with Cambodia, and Kim was deported. The
bitter irony is that he was deported as an adult to a country he had fled
as a child, without the language and employment skills he needs to
survive by himself in the Cambodian economy. Another interviewee,
Loeun Lun, who was married with two daughters, also was deported
and permanently separated from his family. His wife, Sarom, visits
him every year. In a reverse of the family reunification aims of the
1965 Immigration Act, this legislation resulted in separated families.

Joseph Ileto's case and others remind us to consider U.S. colonial and
postcolonial history very carefully. My essay has focused primarily on
U.S. interests in the Pacific, but similar cases could be made for U.S.
involvement in Latin America, the Middle East, and other parts of
the world. In the post-9/11 era, U.S. militarism has become an even
more regular feature of our lives, and one that has both direct and indirect effects on the lives of workers here. Their stories are testament
not only to the dramatic impact on migration brought by U.S. policy

overseas, but also to the fact that migration to the United States, "the land of opportunity," can flow both ways.

U.S. military history should be of paramount concern to everyone in the nation, including those concerned with working-class people and their communities. Rather than focusing on notions of multiculturalism which tend to stress how groups contribute and become part of the nation-state, we need to redirect our gaze to see how the United States is an active participant in world affairs. Using the knowledge we gain through family and community histories, we can reassess national and global narratives about how we understand U.S. history. By doing so, we can more fully understand the role of the United States in the world today, as well as the implications for Asian Americans, Pacific Islanders, and other communities. As so-called beneficiaries of the United States by our residence in this nation, this might place us in a contradictory position in relation to communities overseas. At the same time, only by understanding these contradictions can we better address the lives of postcolonial workers.

These issues underscore the paramount importance of immigrant workers' rights movements, and the continued need to address the role of U.S. postcolonial and transnational militarism across borders. By closely analyzing the complex and connected path of U.S. militarism, we can better understand the economic movement of U.S. companies overseas, the political interventions of the United States in other countries, and the migration of international workers, whether through the sex trafficking industry or as agricultural labor.

Ileto was killed in 1999. We remember his story now not only because he was a good man and a hard worker, but also because he was targeted for his race and labor. Joseph Ileto's story is important to know in this post-9/11 era, because if anything things have become worse for working-class immigrants, especially with the national economic downturn. In the post-9/11 context, with the rise in racism and racial profiling, and the questioning of who is an "American," many feel even more vulnerable, particularly with the casual acceptance of racism and the targeting of so-called foreigners. We need to continue to build coalitions and resources, and to pay special attention to people particularly at risk in the wake of U.S. military interests overseas—this encompasses many of our communities. One of the reasons we must remember Ileto's life is so that others do not have to pay the same price that he did for working in the United States.

BANANAS, ELEPHANTS, AND A COUP:
LEARNING INTERNATIONAL
SOLIDARITY THE HARD WAY

Dana Frank

"Workers of the World, Unite!" has been around since the mid-nineteenth century, but how, exactly, to do that uniting turns out to be thorny, and it's not necessarily clear to many in the labor movement that we should be focusing on international solidarity in the first place. We still face the challenge, moreover, of practicing internationalism while embedded in the imperial center of U.S. military and economic domination, which can make the actual work of solidarity treacherous.

While still thinking like a historian, I'm choosing, here, to talk about some of the lessons I've learned while working on the front of international solidarity in the past ten years—in Dorothy Allison's phrase, "two or three things I know for sure." Much to my astonishment, I have developed a Honduran-centric point of view in the process—which means, in part, that the recent military coup of June 28, 2009, dramatically affected the way I think we should practice international labor solidarity. Working with Hondurans, I've learned to reconceptualize the basic project of international solidarity not as "foreign aid" but as a learning process, as a partnership with social movements taking on global capitalism and other structures of inequality.

BANANAS

I was first pulled into international work with banana workers in 2000, when I received one of those proverbial phone calls that changes your life. It was from Stephen Coats, the director of the

U.S. Labor Education in the Americas Project (USLEAP), a Chicago-based independent nonprofit that has been doing solidarity work with the Latin American labor movement since the mid-1980s. He invited me to Guatemala to meet with delegates from the Coalition of Latin American Banana Unions (COLSIBA, Coordinadora Latino-americana de Sindicatos Bananeros), which was interested in developing a union label for the U.S. market and needed an "expert." Because I was almost the only "expert" on the union label, and had written about the politics of labor and trade, I was suddenly, on two weeks' notice, in the absurd and spectacularly humbling position of advising a piece of the Latin American labor movement—about which I knew nothing.

The union label plan eventually fell apart after four years. But the project pulled me into regular work with COLSIBA. Eventually I started researching women's projects within the banana unions, especially in Honduras, where the women's work began in the 1980s, and I continued to work closely with USLEAP, COLSIBA, and the Coalition of Honduran Banana and Agroindustrial Unions (COSIBAH, Coordinadora de Sindicatos Bananeros y Agroindustriales de Honduras) throughout the 2000s. In more recent years I have been researching and writing a book about the AFL-CIO's Cold War intervention in the Honduran labor movement.

My very first day working with the banana unions, I was immediately slammed by the language issue. I'd had two years of college Spanish, but it took years and years of additional hard work to improve it in order to work effectively with the banana unions, none of whose leaders speak English. At a basic level, any work we do internationally demands a much higher level of second- and third-language competence than most of us who aren't immigrants or organizing immigrants have mastered. We have to factor this very seriously into what we imagine "labor activism" to be.

Right off I also experienced a basic paradigm shift that I think is essential for the U.S. labor movement. I was suddenly in Central America, looking north, rather than gazing south from the United States. It's natural, of course, to view the world outward from one's home. But in order to do the most basic work of solidarity, we have to be able to view economic and political relationships from the outside in as well.

Working through my U.S.-centric point of view, I had to admit I'd assumed the central and most important axis of solidarity was between the U.S. and Latin America, ignoring two equally important if not more fundamental axes. The first is between Europe and Latin America. I was astonished by the number of representatives and euros from Denmark, Germany, Ireland, Norway, and France swirling about the Latin America labor world. These allies and funds were much more important and effective than any U.S. labor support I could identify, and I could trace their impact by the regularity with which my banana union colleagues flew off to Paris or Rome.

Even more important were the South-South alliances I watched develop. The banana unions of Latin America are unique in that they have their own independent, functioning network among nine countries in their region, which is not a subset of an international body such as the International Confederation of Free Trade Unions (ICFTU) or the International Union of Food Workers (IUF), although it works closely with the latter. COLSIBA has also established horizontal links with banana workers in Ghana, the Ivory Coast, the Caribbean, and the Philippines. When we start conceptualizing U.S. labor solidarity with the rest of the world, we have to place ourselves respectfully within a great web of evolving horizontal networks such as these, and, especially, not imagine ourselves as somehow naturally the more important player.

Even at the U.S. end, I had an enormous amount of learning to do about where, exactly, international solidarity work was happening. When I began, I had a rough outline of international work by U.S. trade unions because of research I had done on labor and trade politics. But in Latin America, ironically, I learned quickly about the U.S.-based independent nonprofits and solidarity groups that blossomed in the late 1990s, especially in support work for the maquiladora sector—not just USLEAP, but STITCH, United Students Against Sweatshops, ENLACE, the Workers' Rights Consortium, and many others. These nonprofit organizations often work closely with individual U.S. unions and the AFL-CIO, but have dramatically opened up our imagination of what international solidarity can look like and who can do it. They bring an enormous creativity and dedication to their work and have pioneered all sorts of new approaches, such as protesting against college clothing providers and pressuring transnational corporations to take responsibility for their suppliers. They also provide direct support for a range of organizing campaigns in Mexico, Central America, and Colombia.

But the most important thing I learned, and the biggest point I want to stress here, is that international solidarity, especially between the United States and poor countries, is not a question of a smarter, more experienced Us "helping" an undeveloped, ignorant Them. Quite the opposite. Just take the example of Honduras. Despite being the second-poorest country in the hemisphere, in 2009 Honduras had a union density rate not that much lower than that of the United States. Its unionized banana workers not only enjoy paid vacations, health care, and a lump-sum retirement payout, but regularly participate in union-run education programs—*on company time*—where they learn about union governance, collective bargaining, employers' strategies such as flexible labor systems, and how to run their own nightly radio show. In the biggest union of Chiquita workers, SITRATERCO (Sindicato de Trabajadores de la Tela Railroad Company), all union officials are actual banana workers and have four-year term limits, after which they usually return to their original jobs cutting or packing fruit. Most remarkably, women banana unionists run workshops for women on self-esteem, leadership development, and sexuality, while men and women both participate in—and present—workshops on sex/gender systems and the sexual division of labor within the family. No union in the entire United States comes anywhere near this package of rank-and-file empowerment. I do not want to over-romanticize the banana unions. They have plenty of warts, just like our own organizations. But they can also be spectacularly imaginative, democratic, and, yes, feminist.

It's easy to slip into conceptualizing international solidarity as charity, in which We "generously" help Them out because things are so bad down there and They are so ignorant. We have to tear this attitude out by the roots. Yes, we're rich here, and dripping with privileges. But that doesn't mean we're better and get to tell them what to do. In the late 1990s, after John Sweeney assumed the presidency of the AFL-CIO, a new generation of union activists turned to Latin America, eager to throw off the federation's Cold War cloaks and daggers and do good work abroad. At times, though, that could mean instructing Latin American unionists with decades of experience how to do U.S.-style house visits in cookie-cutter fashion. Other projects involved encouraging long-split labor federations to merge or fostering internal democracy within the Latin American labor movement. The ironies are enormous: shouldn't we be fostering internal democracy at home, first? And sometimes splits are a good thing, if they allow more militant unions to break free. (And of course we were getting ready for our own split.) The point is that U.S. unions should not be telling Latin Americans what to do on these fronts—or telling them what to do in general. It can slide over into a modernized, left form of cultural imperialism. Certainly there are gray areas—such as my own role helping develop the banana union label. But I do think there are some questions from which we need to stay hands off.

In Honduras with the banana unions, then, I was privileged to learn deference. And learning deference is difficult, especially when one's allies are also by turns sexist, undemocratic, egotistic, or you name it, just like labor activists in the United States. If we're going to build true international solidarity, not charity, we have to be able to work as a team of equals within global networks of multiple horizontal partnerships, in many languages most of us don't yet speak.

ELEPHANTS

In order to practice international solidarity, we also have to deal with the elephant looming in the corner, the AFL-CIO's long right-wing history of anticommunist intervention in Latin America, Africa, and Asia. Between World War II and the mid-1990s, the AFL-CIO spent hundreds of millions of dollars in federal, corporate, and union funds manipulating labor movements abroad, in tight cooperation with the State Department and CIA. In Honduras alone the federation, in part through the infamous American Institute for Free

Labor Development (AIFLD), founded and largely controlled the two huge banana worker unions at United Fruit and Standard Fruit (now Chiquita and Dole), trained thousands of union officers in anti-communism and U.S.-style trade unionism, built subsidized housing projects as bribes for members of its captive unions, and worked with the Honduran government to militarily repress any alternatives within the labor movement or criticisms of U.S. economic exploitation of the country. The legacy of this massive intervention haunts the Honduran labor landscape today—not just its capacious union halls with plaques celebrating CIA agents or USAID, but a persistent difficulty involving union members in electoral action, a tradition of collaborationist relations with many private sector employers, and a country that remains under the thumb of U.S. economic and military domination. The AFL-CIO's history also means that throughout the developing world, many trade unionists are understandably still suspicious of any undertaking in their countries by the U.S. labor movement.

In 1997, two years after he came into office, AFL-CIO president John Sweeney finally dismantled AIFLD and its parallel organizations in Africa and Asia, and reorganized the federation's international work into the new American Center for International Labor Solidarity (ACILS, known as the Solidarity Center). With a staff of over one hundred, the Solidarity Center today does an enormous amount of impressive solidarity work abroad. In Honduras, for example, it funds a grassroots maquiladora organizing project in Choloma, supports organizing by private sector port workers, and funds four organizers for COSIBAH, including a long-term project trying to unionize melon and okra pickers. None of these projects has the slightest hint of the federation's former anticommunism; the unions involved represent some of the most creative and militant organizing work in the country.

But U.S. unionists are almost completely unaware of what the AFL-CIO is doing today in Honduras, other parts of Latin America, and beyond—just as they were unaware during the Cold War—because the federation still remains cloaked in an earlier culture of secrecy. The Solidarity Center's annual reports are full of inspiring projects but don't detail country-by-country expenditures. Equally important, they don't specify exact sources of federal monies—the biggest problem. For all the impressive progressive transformation of AFL-CIO international work in the past fifteen years, it is still funded at least 90 percent by the U.S. government through the State Department (through USAID) and the National Endowment for Democracy (NED). This is a direct legacy of the Cold War, when the AFL-CIO served as a happy servant of the State Department.

Let me say quite clearly: the AFL-CIO's acceptance of State Department and NED monies is wrong and should be terminated as soon as possible. It not only sets barriers to the kind of work the AFL-CIO can do—for example, the NED will not want to fund overt support for left-oriented social movements in which most unions abroad are involved—but places the federation in alliance with the very forces that are repressing working people abroad. As a "labor partner" celebrated by the NED, the Solidarity Center helps legitimize the otherwise nefarious clandestine activities of the NED in the developing world. Moreover, the Solidarity Center's acceptance of NED and State Department funds, when combined with its lack of transparency, means that we are dependent on unreliable rumor mills to try to figure out what the AFL-CIO is actually doing or not, such as its possible role in the Venezuelan coup of 2002.

That said, we have another elephant to wrestle. Who, instead, is going to pay for all the solidarity work we need to do? In 2008, the AFL-CIO's own contribution to the Solidarity Center was merely $600,000—in contrast to $28,475,408 from the State Department and the NED. Unfortunately, many critics of the AFL-CIO's ties with the federal government don't want to take on this enormous, concomitant challenge. Not taking it on, though, further reinforces the arguments of those who want to keep accepting the funds.

Most U.S. unions today are still testing the waters of international solidarity, somewhat reluctantly and for quite divergent reasons. In the manufacturing sector, where capital's global strategies have been most obviously destructive, only recently are the unions moving beyond nationalism to explore cross-border approaches (with the great exception of the United Electrical Workers, which figured out transnational solidarity decades ago). In the public sector, most unions don't feel international work is part of their basic purpose. The building trades have been protected by local markets, but the enormous role of immigrants in construction has begun to transform the ways in which they position themselves. Most recently awakened to the need for international strategies are unions of private sector service workers, which are suddenly discovering that service employment can swiftly fly halfway across the world while employers morph into dangerous transnational octopuses. The commitment of the U.S. labor movement to international solidarity, in other words, is still precarious and tentative in the face of smart, slick, highly developed strategies by almost every sector of capital. Even fields that seemed immune to globalization, such as teaching, are now facing vicious, globally coordinated assaults. If we don't have a much deeper, broader, and extremely well-funded commitment to international solidarity on the part of the U.S. labor movement, we're dead meat.

If we are to fund international solidarity ourselves, through per capita taxes or other approaches, we'll need a massive campaign of education at the grassroots. As David Bacon has argued, "What [is] missing is education at the base," so that union members understand the global economy, their place in it, and the need for international solidarity. "That education would help workers understand the political and economic objectives of war and intervention," as well as the causes of immigration in economic displacement and the objectives of U.S. trade policy. We can certainly encourage more worker-to-worker delegations both to and from other countries, an easy and effective form of education that can have a powerful political impact on U.S. labor activists.

. . . AND A COUP

Let's imagine, for now, that the U.S. labor movement and its allies decided to massively fund international solidarity that is respectful, horizontal, and militant. What should we actually do, ideally? That's the final, and ultimately the hardest, question, and I return, once again, to Honduras to answer it, while pulling back to the big picture.

The first key, I think, is to stay tightly focused, in order to get maximum impact from our time, energy, and funds. Preparing to write this article, I called up Katie Quan, a former organizer and manager of the Pacific Northwest District Council of the International Ladies' Garment Workers' Union, and since 1998 a central figure at UC Berkeley's Labor Center, working on international labor issues, especially in Asia. I asked her what she'd do if she had $10 million for international solidarity work. "I'd pick a transnational corporation, an economic sector, and a geographical region," she said. For the first, she gave as an example the global campaign to organize Wal-Mart, embracing workers in Brazil, Mexico, Germany, and the United States. For an economic sector, she proposed hospital workers. Hospital work is still tied to a specific location, she noted, but it's becoming increasingly global as employers import nurses from other countries, promote medical tourism, and send X-rays out to be read by technicians on the other side of the globe. For the region, she'd pick China, the enormity of which drives manufacturing-sector wages and working conditions, and hence any organizing strategies throughout the world.

We can see all these approaches in practice today. In February 2006, Kate Bronfenbrenner of Cornell University organized a conference in New York City to which workers from all over the world were invited to meet and strategize with unionists who worked for the same firms halfway across the world, including workers for Exxon Mobil, Alcoa, Sanofi-Aventis, Kraft, Starwood, and Wal-Mart. Many sectoral alliances are facilitated through Global Union Federations (formerly known as International Trade Secretariats), such as the International Textile, Garment, and Leather Workers' Federation (ITGLWF), the International Union of Food Workers (IUF), and the International Transport Workers' Federation (ITF). On another front, the Service Employees International Union (SEIU) has recently launched a coordinated, multinational campaign against building security corporations based in Europe that exploit U.S. security guards. It has also begun to work with unionized bank workers in Chile, Brazil, Uruguay, England, and Germany to organize Grupo Santander, the world's eighth-largest bank, which last year took over Sovereign Bank.

Solidarity with China looms as an enormous challenge to the U.S. labor movement, which remains fixated on a comically outdated stereotype of "Red China," and has been reluctant to work with the state-controlled All China Federation of Trade Unions. Rank-and-file workers, meanwhile, have often reacted with a knee-jerk impulse to boycott all Chinese products. Katie Quan and Kent Wong, the director of the UCLA Labor Center, by contrast, are establishing innovative ties with Chinese labor activists through labor education programs and horizontal city-to-city relationships between the Los Angeles County Federation of Labor and the Shanghai Trade Union Council.

Trade politics provide another key sphere for focused leverage. Stephen Coats of USLEAP in Chicago, who pioneered the successful solidarity campaign with Phillips Van Heusen workers in Guatemala during the 1990s, stresses the importance of continuing to contest new trade agreements that strip away previous labor-rights trade clauses, while using extant agreements to challenge both free trade and the repression of labor activists in Latin America. Trade campaigns, in turn, can merge effectively with educational programs and solidarity delegations. The strongest work on this front has been regarding Colombia. Activists in Massachusetts and other regions have highlighted ongoing assassinations of trade unionists while challenging the proposed U.S.-Colombia Free Trade Agreement.

But the politics of both trade and Colombia underscore that if we are to take international solidarity seriously we have to take responsibility for the repressive role of our own government abroad, both military and economic—and that's my second key to what we need to do. We can organize focused, strategic union-to-union campaigns until we're blue in the face, but they'll all be wiped out if the United States government backs a repressive regime that swoops in and assassinates workers the minute they talk union.

This lesson was brutally brought home for me on June 28, 2009, when a military coup overthrew the democratically elected president of Honduras, Manuel "Mel" Zelaya. In response, a broad resistance movement immediately rose up in protest, with the labor movement at its center. But individual trade unionists have paid a severe price: at least nine trade unionists active in the resistance have been killed since the coup, among over 150 activists and journalists. In one day, when the coup hit, my solidarity work switched from support for collective bargaining and women's projects to trying to stop my friends and allies from being illegally detained, raped in custody, beaten, or killed. Every morning for over six months I tried to figure out how best I could efficiently get power over my own government. Suddenly I was cranking out op-eds, pleading with congressional aides, and learning fast about the Washington, D.C., world of think tanks and pressure groups interested in Latin American solidarity.

The U.S. State Department backed the coup regime quite clearly—despite politely slapping its hands in public—through ongoing military and other aid, and, more recently, enormous economic pressure on other Latin American nations to recognize the ongoing coup government. Its policies in Honduras are part of a broad, hemisphere-wide counterattack against poor people's political advances in Latin America during the past fifteen years. Currently, the Honduran government is proposing a major overhaul of the country's labor code that would shift full-time, permanent jobs into temporary ones, make it almost impossible to organize a union, and allow companies to pay their workers 30 percent of their wages in company scrip.

We need much more powerful pressure networks in the United States if we're going to stop this kind of ongoing military and economic intervention. The AFL-CIO's International Department— distinct, organizationally, from the Solidarity Center—denounced the coup the day it happened; protested the fraudulent November 27, 2009, election; and lobbied Congress against recognition of the coup government. But the department is down to two employees as of this writing, and they only answer to pressure from the federation's affiliates. Only a handful of individuals within the AFL-CIO have protested the Obama administration's Honduran policies—Bill Camp, executive secretary of the Sacramento, California, Central Labor Council, and the presidents of a few international unions—while nonprofits and grassroots groups such as the Center for Economic and Political Research (CEPR), the Quixote Center, and Chicago's La Voz de los de Abajo have played a much more important role.

I circle back round here, again, to education at the base within the United States. We can't realistically mount pressure campaigns on Congress and the White House without mass pressure from below, district by district, and the will to organize it. We have a shining example of such organizing in U.S. Labor Against the War, which since 2003 has organized horizontally against the war in Iraq and garnered endorsements not just from international unions but also central labor councils, retired union members' organizations, state labor federations, over one hundred union locals, and affiliates like the Asian Pacific American Labor Alliance.

Third, and finally, working with the Honduran resistance has reinforced what I'd already learned studying U.S. labor history: we need to conceptualize the labor movement, both at home and abroad, as a broad social movement interwoven with other movements for social justice. The Honduran resistance is now famous because it unites—through the Frente Nacional de Resistencia Popular (FNRP)—the labor movement, women's movement, GLBT movement, movements of campesinos, indigenous people, and African-descent peoples, militant teachers' organizations, human rights advocates, and members of the Liberal Party loyal to President Zelaya—in a true coalition that is working very hard trying to figure out how to democratically and nonviolently refound its nation from below. They're actually building the grassroots mass social movement that so many of us have dreamed of in the United States. If we conceptualize solidarity with the Honduran labor movement as solidarity with the much-broader FNRP, the pieces of how to do international work start to fall into place. It's not up to U.S. trade unionists alone to stop the coup: we can work with our own social movement allies at home who are also supporting the resistance, such as the gay rights movement, Latino groups, and faith-based communities. We'll have to come up with our own money, because the State Department and NED, backers of the coup, aren't going to fund resistance to it; nor are they going to fund social movement–style projects affiliated with the left rather than narrowly defined organizing campaigns.

Social movement unionism helps the pieces fall into place at home, too. On May 1, 2006, immigrants and their allies, overwhelmingly working-class Latino/as, mounted the biggest demonstrations in United States history, in every nook and cranny of the country. These rank-and-file working people are already on the move. They already understand that capitalism is a global system that uproots families, destroys communities, and has no respect for borders. In most cases they already know two, sometimes three languages. They bring all sorts of creative organizing traditions from their home countries, which they are using to revitalize the labor movement in the United States. On another front, Honduran, Salvadoran, and Nicaraguan immigrants have been essential to the U.S. solidarity movement against the Honduran coup. If we're looking for international solidarity, in other words, we don't have to look any farther than our own backyard. That means putting immigrants' rights at the top of labor's agenda, fighting racism at home, and listening carefully to what immigrants have to teach about how to organize and how to build transnational alliances.

I'm optimistic about the future of U.S. labor and international solidarity. The global monster of corporate capitalism is whipping its tail about right and left, whacking us, too, in the face, waking us up, while our sisters and brothers from other parts of the world, already long acquainted with it, help us imagine what real solidarity might look—and what alternatives we can envision. International solidarity is, in the end, a learning process, and the U.S. labor movement is still emerging from fifty years of imperial anticommunism abroad, trying to figure out what to do instead. We've got a lot of listening to do, a lot of languages to learn, and a brutal, dangerous government to account for. But that learning process is part of what makes international work so exciting, and gives me hope, because it's rather thrilling to be part of a movement that does, indeed, span the globe, and in which we can make the deepest of human connections—while imagining and constructing quite different ways of organizing our economies and our basic relationships with each other.

AFTERWORD

Labor Rising?

Frances Fox Piven

What are the prospects for the empowerment of working people in the United States? Directly or indirectly, most of the essays in this volume are preoccupied with this question. Inevitably, the question directs our attention to labor unions, to their rise in the twentieth century and their subsequent decline. There was after all a time when most people on the left believed that the growth of the union movement was the key to working-class power both in the workplace and in politics. True, unions themselves might be flawed, by a tradition of business unionism, by narrow-minded or corrupt leaders, by internal oligarchy, by racism and sexism, and so on. But these problems could be struggled with and overcome. The main faith was in the power of the working class, and in unions as the vehicle for that power. I think the history of the past seventy years requires us to assess that conviction anew.

Mass unions as we know them largely date from the tumultuous events of the Great Depression when a wave of strikes and sit-downs forced the titans of industry to finally concede the right to a union contract to millions of workers in the mines and the mass production industries. Then, with the onset of World War II, the federal government acted to ensure the growth of membership in the unions. For three decades after World War II, there appeared to be a kind of tacit social compact between big business and the unions. There were strikes and disputes, but nothing like the class warfare of the 1930s, and nothing like the one-sided assault on the unions that was to come later. After all, during these years American corporations were unchallenged in the world economy, and profit levels were high.

Business seemed willing to accommodate wage increases pegged to productivity increases, as well as the expansion of the social safety net that unions supported, at least for the unionized workforce. Of course, many people, including the vast numbers in the secondary labor market and most women and minority workers, were excluded from the deal. Nevertheless, there is no denying that life did get much better for many American workers, and unionism was a large part of the reason.

As the essays in this volume show, the golden era did not last. By the 1970s, the revival of Japanese and West German industries put competitive pressure on the prices and profits of U.S. corporations, and this at a time when American business was also bearing the costs and irritations at home of higher wages, increased government regulation, and an expanded safety net. Business responded by launching a campaign to roll back unions and wages, as well as the regulations that protected workers and the unions—including labor relations and workplace safety regulations, the minimum wage, and safety-net programs. In other words, business declared class war, invoking the big argument that the hyper-competition of a globalized economy required that everything be on the table, not only the recent gains of the 1960s and early 1970s, but the protective legislation of the New Deal and ultimately even collective bargaining itself. Shared sacrifice they sometimes called it, but in fact business profits quickly recovered and, in any case, even the most profitable companies, and companies such as defense manufacturers that were not exposed to global competition, readily joined the campaign.

Labor leaders grown accustomed to the regular dealings of the postwar compact with business were unprepared for the new aggressive stance of American corporations. Business unpacked the arsenal of union-busting strategies that had lain dormant since the early New Deal period, including union-busting consultants, except that now the consultants were more likely to be lawyers and public relations experts than the spies and goons of the Pinkerton era.[1] Baffled and defensive unions turned to the National Labor Relations Board, and unfair labor practices charges against employers skyrocketed by 750 percent between 1957 and 1980.[2] But the back-pay awards that sometimes resulted were trivial costs to employers compared to the far larger stakes in the campaign. A unionized workplace meant higher wages and benefits and a degree of union control over the workplace. As the employer campaign succeeded in rolling back union membership, worker earnings and benefits began to fall, and the enforcement of workplace regulations grew lax. Even unions that held on caved in to the concessions that employers demanded, hoping to protect their membership and their organizations in the new hostile environment.

The United States has always lagged behind other industrial countries in union strength, but now the gap was widening. Canada is often considered the country most similar to the United States, and in 1960 the two countries had similar unionization levels: 30.4 percent in the United States compared to 32.3 percent in Canada. Membership levels remained stable in Canada and in 2005 were still 32 percent, while they plummeted to 12 percent in the United States.[3]

By the 1980s the corporate agenda had expanded to include restructuring the tax system to favor the top tax brackets; dismantling business and environmental regulations; slashing the safety net; and privatizing government or, in another language, opening the public sector to profiteering. In the decades after World War II, big unions had been the institutional stalwarts in political battles to initiate, defend, and expand such initiatives. But as the unions lost ground in the workplace, the limited social democracy created during the 1930s and expanded in the 1960s and early 1970s came under fire. Corporate tax rates fell and loopholes expanded, the income tax became less progressive, environmental regulations were weakened, financial regulations were eliminated or loosened, safety net programs were rolled back, and bigger chunks of the public sector were turned over to for-profit businesses.

Not surprisingly, the United States is now the most unequal established democracy in the world. While this is not solely due to union contraction and union political defeats, both play an important role.[4] As union strength ebbed, wages stagnated, and the safety net weakened, executive pay exploded and taxes on the affluent fell. Economic inequality spiraled out of sight. The top tenth of American earners did better in 2007 than in any year since 1917, while the top 1 percent did far better, capturing almost three-quarters of the overall growth in income between 2002 and 2007.[5] Meanwhile, although Americans were working longer hours than workers in other rich countries[6] and living costs were increasing, earnings for the vast majority stagnated, lagging far behind increases in productivity. Ironically, the economic downturn that began in 2007, precipitated by wild financial excesses and insufficient demand, led to further losses of labor to capital as unemployment rose but economic productivity improved, meaning that output was being sustained with fewer workers.[7] Meanwhile, changes in tax policy that favored the very top strata reinforced these trends, while the protective regulations and benefit programs of an already limited welfare state were chipped away. Instead, prisons expanded, and the levels of incarceration, especially of poor minority men, rose to the highest in the world.

Why the impasse in what we once thought or hoped would be a steady march to a more egalitarian and democratic society? The explanation is a commonplace, quick to spring to the lips of intellectuals and pundits alike. The key fact of our historical moment is said to be the globalization of national economies which, together with "post-Fordist" domestic economic restructuring, has had shattering consequences for the economic well-being of the working class and especially for the power of the working class. I think such truth as there is in this explanation has to do more with the weakness of the inherited repertoire of labor strategies under new conditions than with the more fundamental question of potential labor power. (Whether right or wrong, the economic globalization and restructuring explanation itself has become a political force, helping to create the institutional realities it purportedly merely describes.)

There is no question that globalization and the new lean economy has had large consequences for the *market* power of workers. As has so often been said, globalization means that, in labor market terms, American workers must compete against workers everywhere, whether because capital can move to take advantage of lower labor costs, or because goods made by lower-paid workers cross the border, or because lower-paid workers themselves cross the border. The specter of

worldwide labor-market competition was certainly a powerful ideological weapon against workers and their unions. Add to that the huge
expansion of the domestic workforce as a result of the large-scale
movement of women into the labor market, combined with immigration and the steady proliferation of "lean production" labor-saving
arrangements. So, with labor supply increasing steadily, the price of
labor had to fall—or so the argument goes.

Except that markets are not natural phenomena; labor markets,
like other markets, are neither free nor unregulated; and labor power
does not consist simply or even mainly of market power. After all, the
craft unions of the AFL owed much of their success precisely to their
ability to control the supply of skilled labor, particularly in the construction trades, where the unions established something like monopoly control over labor supply. And industrial unions sometimes
followed suit, exerting themselves to create extra-market arrangements to limit labor supply. On the other side, employers work to expand labor supply by encouraging immigration; by securing "right
to work" legislation, which effectively creates union-free regions; or
by slashing safety-net programs, as with the much-heralded welfare-
reform legislation of 1996, which did indeed push many women into
the low-wage labor market.

Moreover, the great victories of industrial workers were won when
labor's *market* power was extremely weak. The climactic period shaping the modern labor movement in the United States was the Great
Depression, when hardship and electoral instability combined to give
rise to a massive strike movement that shut down or threatened to
shut down the ports and huge rubber, electrical, steel, and auto industries, and spread even to the movie houses and merchants of Main
Street America. Franklin Delano Roosevelt had not gained office as
a champion of labor rights, and he had withheld his support from a
bill championed by the New York senator Robert Wagner that would
throw government support behind union organization and collective
bargaining. The strike movement and the economic repercussions
it foretold forced FDR's hand. The National Labor Relations Act was
passed, FDR signed it, and shortly afterward the Supreme Court accepted it.

Unionization and the panoply of legal rights and contracts on which it depended meant the institutionalization of the strike power in legal and contractual arrangements that regulated and curbed its exercise. The mass production industries were brought to the bargaining table by the disruption of production. What they wanted and got from unions was an intermediary capable of disciplining the strike power and ensuring uninterrupted production. That was why the big auto companies finally agreed to come to the bargaining table. History—and not only American history—suggests that the great labor victories in the past were not mainly expressions of labor's market power but rather the result of labor's disruptive strike power, exercised not when labor's market leverage was great but when the use of the strike power was buttressed and protected by a measure of working-class electoral power. In other words, big unions, especially the mass production unions, were created to tame the disruptive threat of a mass strike movement. And this is the great conundrum of contemporary unions. Unions owe their existence to the disruptive power of the strike. And they owe their continuing existence to their role in limiting disruptive strikes.

Unions have certainly tried to resist the corporate campaign that began in the 1970s. They have invested enormously in electoral campaigns in the hope of electing pro-labor Democrats who would create a legal environment friendlier to union expansion, or who they hoped would support regulatory enforcement of labor rights, or who would defend and expand the safety net. But despite a few successes scored during the Obama administration—a more labor-friendly National Labor Relations Board and health care legislation, for example—the overall score is disappointing. The unions have also tried to broaden their base, largely with a view to shoring up their electoral efforts. Union policies toward immigrants are much friendlier, and the unions have tried to cultivate a variety of community alliances.

The unions have also tried to become more of a social movement, at first largely by sponsoring rallies in state capitals or Washington, D.C. More recently, as the corporate campaign turned aggressively on public sector workers, the social movement turn has escalated, first in the conflicts in Wisconsin, Ohio, and Indiana over collective bargaining rights for public sector unions, and now with forthright displays of union support for Occupy Wall Street.

But what about labor's classical weapon, the strike? It seems often to be assumed that labor's labor market weakness also makes the strike a weak or dangerous tactic. In one sense, it does, because striking workers can more easily be replaced. But aspects of globalization and the lean production methods with which it is associated may actually increase the disruptive leverage of strikes for the simple reason that globalization means increased specialization and integration in complex and far-reaching systems of cooperation and interdependence.

Thus, it is true that globalization enormously expands investor opportunities for exit from relations with any particular group of working people. With the click of a mouse, capital can move to low-wage and low-cost parts of the world. This is the familiar argument that globalization expands the reserve army of labor and weakens the market leverage of workers everywhere. But the very arrangements that make exit easier also create new and fragile interdependencies.[8] Outsourcing is two-sided. On the one hand, it loosens the dependence of employers on domestic workers. On the other hand, it binds them to many other workers in far-flung and extended chains of production. And these chains in turn depend on complex systems of electronic communication and transportation that are themselves acutely vulnerable to disruption.

The old idea that logistical workers located at the key nodes in industrial systems of production had great potential labor power has in a sense been writ large.[9] Many workers, those who run the far-flung transportation systems or the Internet, or are lodged at all the points in vastly extended chains of production, as well as the workers in "just in time" systems of production that the Internet has facilitated, may have potential logistical power, and even more forceful logistical power because they are capable of causing such widespread disruption. South African dockworkers recently reminded us of the boldness that logistical power sometimes encourages when they refused to unload a ship from Israel carrying weapons for Zimbabwean president Robert Mugabe.[10]

The irony is that unions themselves are not in a good position to explore and exploit the possibilities created by a strike power writ large. This is not simply a failure of leadership courage or imagination. The unions are risk-averse for good reason. They have a lot to lose if they defy the multiple legal constraints that limit or prohibit the strike power. When Local 100 of the Transport Workers in New York City walked out during the Christmas shopping season in 2005, they were breaking the New York state law against public sector strikes. The courts responded by jailing their leadership and heaping huge fines on the union, as well as canceling the union's income stream from the dues checkoff.

The outcome might be different today. The full force of labor's strike power probably can only be realized at explosive moments when the narrow calculus of gains and losses is suspended by the urgency of mass anger and hope. Maybe the events in Wisconsin and the rise of Occupy are signals that we are at such a moment today. And remember, the great strikes of the 1930s were kicked off by angry and defiant rank-and-file workers. In the bitter winter of 1936, few rubber workers were members of the United Rubber Workers, whose officials were uneasy with rank-and-file initiatives. But union or not, some ten to fifteen thousand workers walked out in January 1936 to man an eleven-mile-long picket line. Shortly afterwards, sit-down strikes by autoworkers in defiance of court orders paralyzed GM and Chrysler. The CIO leadership saw the possibilities and had the courage to seize them.

So there may well be a future for labor in the United States. We should hope so, for all of us.

NOTES

1. In a study of the union representation elections conducted in 1986, 1987, and 1994, Kate Bronfenbrenner and Tom Juravich report that 87 percent of employers hired outside consultants to manage their campaigns to defeat the bid for union representation. The campaigns that ensued included numerous mandatory antiunion meetings on

company time, and many one-on-one meetings of supervisors with workers. Kate Bronfenbrenner and Tom Juravich, "It Takes More than House Calls: Organizing to Win with a Comprehensive Union-Building Strategy," in Kate Bronfenbrenner et al., *Organizing to Win: New Research on Union Strategies* (Ithaca, NY: ILR Press, 1998).

2. See Paul Weiler, "Promises to Keep: Securing Workers' Rights to Self-Organization Under the NLRA," *Harvard Law Review* 96 (1983): 1769–827.

3. See Jacob Hacker and Paul Pierson, "Winner-Take-All Politics: Public Policy, Political Organization, and the Precipitous Rise of Top Incomes in the United States," *Politics and Society* 38, no. 2 (June 2010): 152–204.

4. See Bruce Western and Jake Rosenfeld, "Union Decline Accounts for Much of the Rise in Wage Inequality," unpublished paper available from the American Sociological Association, Washington, DC, July 21, 2011.

5. Emmanuel Saez, "Striking It Richer: The Evolution of Top Incomes in the United States," *Pathways Magazine*, Stanford Center for the Study of Poverty and Inequality, Winter 2008. Saez defines income as the sum of wages and salaries, pensions, profits from businesses, capital income, and realized capital gains before individual income taxes.

6. Jared Bernstein and Karen Kornbluh, "Running Faster to Stay in the Same Place: The Growth of Family Work Hours and Incomes," New American Foundation Research Paper, Washington DC, June 2005.

7. See John Authers, "The Short Views," *Financial Times*, August 13, 2009.

8. This is what Beverly J. Silver means when she says that "the same processes that undermine marketplace bargaining power often enhance workplace bargaining power." See *Forces of Labor: Workers' Movements and Globalization Since 1870* (New York: Cambridge University Press, 2003), 119.

9. For examples from the industrial era, see Silver, *Forces of Labor*, 6, 19, 42.

10. Associated Press, "South African Dock Workers Won't Unload Israeli Goods," *New York Times*, February 4, 2009.

ABOUT THE CONTRIBUTORS

Marcellus Andrews is a professor of economics at Barnard College and the author of *The Political Economy of Hope and Fear*. His essays have appeared in *The Nation*, and he is a regular commentator for the NPR show *Marketplace*.

Eileen Boris is Hull Professor and chair of the Department of Feminist Studies and the director of the Center of Women and Social Justice at the University of California, Santa Barbara. Among her books are *Caring for America: Home Health Workers in the Shadow of the Welfare State*, co-authored with Jennifer Klein, and *Intimate Labors: Cultures, Technologies, and the Politics of Care*, co-edited with Rhacel Parreñas. She is on the board of directors of CAUSE, the Coastal Alliance United for a Sustainable Economy.

David Brody is a professor emeritus of history at the University of California, Davis, and the author, most recently, of *Labor Embattled: History, Power, Rights*. He was active in the recent AFL-CIO campaign for labor law reform, although the strategic idea he advances (that labor's bill should have included the repeal of the Taft-Hartley employer speech provision) did not occur to him until afterward (not that it would have been accepted anyway).

Michelle Chen is a contributing editor at *In These Times*. She has also contributed to *Colorlines*, Alternet, *Ms.*, *The Nation*, and *Newsday* and reported from China, Egypt, Palestine, and her native New York. When not observing current events, she studies history at the City University of New York Graduate Center.

Jefferson Cowie teaches labor and working-class history at Cornell University. He is the author of *Capital Moves: RCA's Seventy-Year Quest for Cheap Labor* and, most recently, *Stayin' Alive: The 1970s and the Last Days of the Working Class*, which received the Francis Parkman Prize for the best book in American history and the Merle Curti Prize for the best book in social and intellectual history.

Elizabeth Faue is a professor of history at Wayne State University. Her most recent book is *Writing the Wrongs: Eva Valesh and the Rise of Labor Journalism*. She is at work on a history of the American labor movement and a study of gender and the transformation of the American workplace since World War II.

Leon Fink is UIC Distinguished Professor of History at the University of Illinois, Chicago. He is the founding editor of *Labor: Studies in Working-Class History of the Americas* and the author of numerous books, including *Workingmen's Democracy: The Knights of Labor and American Politics; The Maya of Morgantown: Work and Community in the Nuevo New South*; and, most recently, *Sweatshops at Sea: Merchant Seamen in the World's First Globalized Industry, from 1812 to the Present.*

Bill Fletcher Jr. is a longtime racial justice, labor, and international activist and writer. He is a senior scholar with the Institute for Policy Studies; a visiting scholar with the City University of New York Graduate Center; the immediate past president of TransAfrica Forum; and the co-author, most recently, of *Solidarity Divided.*

Dana Frank is a professor of history at the University of California, Santa Cruz. Her books include *Bananeras: Women Transforming the Banana Unions of Latin America; Buy American: The Untold Story of Economic Nationalism; Purchasing Power: Consumer Organizing, Gender, and the Seattle Labor Movement, 1919–1929; Local Girl Makes History: Exploring Northern California's Kitsch Monuments*; and, with Robin D.G. Kelley and Howard Zinn, *Three Strikes: Miners, Musicians, Salesgirls, and the Fighting Spirit of Labor's Last Century.* She is currently writing a book about the AFL-CIO's Cold War in Honduras,

1954–79, and writing and speaking about post-coup Honduras in a range of popular media, including NPR and *The Nation*.

Dorothy Fujita-Rony is an associate professor in the Department of Asian American Studies at the University of California, Irvine. She is the author of *American Workers, Colonial Power: Philippine Seattle and the Transpacific West* and is completing another book project on Filipina/o American farmworkers in California.

Matthew Garcia is a professor of history and transborder studies and the director of the Comparative Border Studies Program at Arizona State University. He is the author of *A World of Its Own: Race, Labor and Citrus in the Making of Greater Los Angeles, 1900–1970*, which was named co-winner for the best book in oral history by the Oral History Association in 2003. The University of California Press will publish his new book, *A Moveable Feast: César Chávez and the United Farm Workers' Boycott*, in 2012.

Richard A. Greenwald is a professor of history and sociology and dean at St. Joseph's College, New York. He is the author of *The Triangle Fire, the Protocols of Peace and Industrial Democracy in Progressive Era New York* (2005); co-editor of *Sweatshop USA: The American Sweatshop in Historical and Global Perspective* (2003); and editor of *Exploring America's Past: Essays in Social and Cultural History* (1996). His next book is *The Death of 9-to-5: Permanent Freelancers, Empty Offices and the New Way America Works* (forthcoming, Bloomsbury Press).

Andrew Herod is a professor of geography and adjunct professor of anthropology at the University of Georgia. He is the author of *Geographies of Globalization: A Critical Introduction; Labor Geographies: Workers and the Landscapes of Capitalism*; and, most recently, *Scale*.

Daniel Katz is a professor of history and dean of labor studies at the National Labor College in Silver Spring, Maryland. He is the author of *All Together Different: Yiddish Socialists, Garment Workers, and the Labor Roots of Multiculturalism* (2011). A former union organizer, he was a

founding board member of the Labor and Working-Class History Association. He currently sits on the board of directors of the New York
Labor History Association and Jews for Racial and Economic Justice.

Alice Kessler-Harris is the R. Gordon Hoxie Professor of History at
Columbia University and the president of the Organization of Ameri-
can Historians. She is the author of the seminal books *Out to Work: A
History of Wage-Earning Women in the United States; Gendering Labor
History*; and *In Pursuit of Equity: Women, Men, and the Quest for Eco-
nomic Citizenship in the 20th Century*. Her latest book is *A Difficult
Woman: The Challenging Life and Times of Lillian Hellman*.

Nelson Lichtenstein is the MacArthur Foundation Chair in History
at the University of California, Santa Barbara, where he directs the
Center for the Study of Work, Labor, and Democracy. His most recent
book, edited with Elizabeth Shermer, is *The Right and American Labor: Politics, Ideology, and Imagination*.

Nancy MacLean is author of, most recently, *Freedom Is Not Enough:
The Opening of the American Workplace; Debating the American Con-
servative Movement: 1945 to the Present*, with Donald T. Critchlow; and
*The American Women's Movement, 1945–2000: A Brief History with
Documents*. A former co-chair of the Chicago Center for Working-
Class Studies, she has also served on the board of the Labor and
Working-Class History Association. After many years at Northwest-
ern, she now teaches U.S. history at Duke University.

Ruth Milkman is a professor of sociology at the CUNY Graduate
Center and academic director of CUNY's Joseph S. Murphy Institute
for Worker Education and Labor Studies. Recent books include *L.A.
Story: Immigrant Workers and the Future of the U.S. Labor Movement*
(2006) and the edited volume *Working for Justice: The L.A. Model of
Organizing and Advocacy* (2010).

Bethany Moreton is an assistant professor of history and women's
studies at the University of Georgia. Her book *To Serve God and*

Wal-Mart: The Making of Christian Free Enterprise won the Frederick Jackson Turner Prize and the John Hope Franklin Prize. She is a founding faculty member of Freedom University for undocumented students in Georgia (www.freedomuniversitygeorgia.com).

Kimberley L. Phillips is a professor of history and dean of the School of Humanities and Social Sciences at Brooklyn College, CUNY. She is the author of *Alabama North: African-American Migrants, Community, and Working-Class Activism in Cleveland, 1915–1945* and *War! What Is It Good For?: Black Freedom Struggles and the U.S. Military from World War II to Iraq.*

Frances Fox Piven is Distinguished Professor of Political Science and Sociology at the City University of New York Graduate Center. A lifelong activist, Piven is the author of numerous books, including *Poor People's Movements: Why They Succeed, How They Fail* (with the late Richard Cloward); *Challenging Authority: How Ordinary People Change America*; and *Who's Afraid of Frances Fox Piven: The Essential Writings of the Professor Glenn Beck Loves to Hate.*

Jacob A.C. Remes is an assistant professor and mentor at SUNY Empire State College, where he teaches public affairs and history. His forthcoming book, *Disaster Citizenship: Urban Disasters and the Formation of the North American Progressive State*, explores how workers and their institutions responded to the growth of the state after the Salem, Massachussetts, fire of 1914 and the Halifax, Nova Scotia, explosion of 1917.

Andrew Ross is a professor of social and cultural analysis at NYU and the author of many books, including *Nice Work if You Can Get It: Life and Labor in Precarious Times; Fast Boat to China—Lessons from Shanghai; Low Pay, High Profile: The Global Push for Fair Labor; No-Collar: The Humane Workplace and Its Hidden Costs;* and *The Celebration Chronicles: Life, Liberty, and the Pursuit of Property Value in Disney's New Town.* He has also edited several collections, including *No Sweat: Fashion, Free Trade, and the Rights of Garment Workers;*

Anti-Americanism; and *The University Against Itself: The NYU Strike and the Future of the Academic Workplace.* His most recent book is *Bird on Fire: Lessons from the World's Least Sustainable City.*

Mario Sifuentez is an assistant professor of history at the University of California, Merced, where he has initiated the Central Valley Oral History Project. He recently completed his PhD at Brown University in American civilization. He is currently working on a book titled *By Forests or By Fields: Organizing Immigrant Labor in the Pacific Northwest.*

Shelton Stromquist teaches labor history at the University of Iowa. He is the author of a number of books, including *Reinventing "the People": The Progressive Movement, the Class Problem, and the Origins of Modern Liberalism* (2006) and the forthcoming *Social Democracy and the City: Class Politics and Municipal Reform in Comparative Perspective, 1890–1920.*

Pamela Voekel is an associate professor of history at the University of Georgia and the author of *Alone Before God: The Religious Origins of Modernity in Mexico.* She is a co-founder of the Tepoztlan Institute for the Transnational History of the Americas and a founding faculty member of Freedom University for undocumented students in Georgia (www.freedomuniversitygeorgia.com). She is currently at work on *For God and Liberty: Catholicism and Democracy in the Revolutionary Atlantic World.*